M

985.37 B613m
BINGHAM
MACHU PICCHU, A CITADEL OF
THE INCAS

                      29.95

MACHU PICCHU

A CITADEL OF THE INCAS

"THE MOST INACCESSIBLE CORNER OF THE MOST INACCESSIBLE SECTION OF THE CENTRAL ANDES"

THE REMOTE FASTNESSES THAT PROTECT MACHU PICCHU. THE SHARP PEAK IN THE RIGHT FOREGROUND IS MACHU PICCHU MOUNTAIN, THE LOWER CONICAL ONE AT THE LEFT IS HUAYNA PICCHU. THE INCA CITY LIES ON THE RIDGE BETWEEN THE TWO, ALMOST DIRECTLY UNDER THE LITTLE CLOUD THAT SHOWS AGAINST THE DISTANT MOUNTAIN

MACHU PICCHU

A CITADEL OF THE INCAS

BY

HIRAM BINGHAM

HACKER ART BOOKS, NEW YORK, 1979

MEMOIRS OF THE NATIONAL GEOGRAPHIC SOCIETY

MACHU PICCHU

A CITADEL OF THE INCAS

REPORT OF THE
EXPLORATIONS AND EXCAVATIONS
MADE IN 1911, 1912 AND 1915
UNDER THE AUSPICES OF
YALE UNIVERSITY AND THE
NATIONAL GEOGRAPHIC SOCIETY

Library of Congress Catalogue Card Number 79-83881
International Standard Book Number 0-87817-252-1

Printed in the United States of America

TO

GILBERT GROSVENOR

WITH AFFECTIONATE REGARD AND
GRATEFUL APPRECIATION OF HIS
ENTHUSIASTIC SUPPORT

PREFACE

·····•——◄◈►——•·····

THE story of the discovery of the ruins of Machu Picchu was told in the pages of *Inca Land*.* The present volume is concerned with the exploration and excavation of that remarkable hidden city, and with the results of the studies of the material found there. Our studies leave no doubt that it was built and occupied by the Incas. Since the Incas left no written records, no hieroglyphics and few rock carvings, our knowledge of them must depend in large measure on the writings of their conquerors and on the physical evidence of the works of art and architecture still in existence. As regards Machu Picchu there appear to be no local traditions regarding it and no references in literature which can positively be identified with it. The Incas seem to have succeeded in keeping its location a profound secret. They were aided in this by the lofty mountains, unfriendly glaciers, and precipitous canyons of the surrounding region. If the Spaniards did find it, of which there is at present no evidence, they had no desire to live in such a remote and inaccessible part of the Andes. Consequently its buildings were not altered or destroyed, its burial places were relatively undisturbed, its middens unaffected by articles of European origin. This gave us a unique opportunity to make a comprehensive review of so much of the manners and customs of an important center of Inca culture as can be seen in those objects of pottery and bronze, stone, wood, and bone, as survived the dampness and decay of the rainy subtropics, the ravages of bears, and the zeal of occasional treasure hunters.

For four months we hunted faithfully for every scrap of man's handiwork, every trace of human occupation, every bit of evidence which could throw light upon the past. Our only object was to find all the things which might help to solve the mystery of those ancient builders. We cut down the hardwood forest. We cleared the

* Published by Houghton Mifflin Company in 1922.

ruins of tangled thickets and the vegetable mold which had accumulated through the centuries. We uncovered more than a hundred stairways whose existence had not been suspected. We made tentative excavations in various parts of the city. Wherever these test holes yielded results we continued the excavations until nothing more could be found. We searched every nook and cranny of the ridge and near-by mountains for burial caves. Every potsherd which by its shape or its decoration could tell a story, and hundreds more which were eventually used in restoring long-lost forms, were collected and studied. Nearly all of the pottery forms and designs are shown in the accompanying drawings, which were made by Mr. William Baake. His drawings also give the spirit of the art of Machu Picchu as exemplified in the ornaments and tools as well as in the utensils and problematical objects.

The architecture and the extent of the city are shown in the drawings of Mr. Bumstead, his plan based on the surveys of Messrs. H. L. Tucker, Robert Stephenson, and Paul B. Lanius, and the photographs which were selected from some five hundred taken by the author. Some of the illustrations were first printed in the *National Geographic Magazine* and are here used by courtesy of the editor.

The collection of Machu Picchu material is now in the Peabody Museum of Natural History at Yale University.

Grateful acknowledgment is due to President A. B. Leguia of Peru for official encouragement and indispensable assistance; to W. L. Morkill, Esq., for his active intervention in our behalf; to L. S. Blaisdell, Esq., for unnumbered kindnesses; to Señor Don Mariano Ferro, the owner of the princely estate which includes Machu Picchu, for his courteous coöperation; to Señor Don Cesare Lomellini, who has always shown himself ready to aid us in every possible way; to Dr. George F. Eaton, who supervised the opening of the first fifty-two burial caves, trained the staff for the work of collecting and preserving the material, and has published a scholarly monograph on "The Collection of Osteological Material from Machu Picchu," which has been of great assistance in the preparation of this volume; to Mr. Elwood C. Erdis, who was in charge of the work of excavation and whose zeal as a patient and indefatigable collector knew no limits; to Mr. Kenneth C. Heald, whose courage and persistence in the difficult task of road construction made possible much of our exploration, and who reached the summit of Huayna Picchu in the face of almost insuperable odds; to Dr. Osgood Hardy, for invaluable help in the examination of the material; to Professor Paul Baur of Yale University, who generously aided me in describing the pottery; to Professor C. H. Mathewson, who has published the results of an exhaustive study of the structure of the bronzes; to Mr. O. F. Cook, for his study of the flora of the region; to Mr. Frank M. Chapman, who has described its bird life; to Mr. Edmund Heller and Dr. Thomas Barbour, who studied other aspects of its fauna; to Professor Harry W. Foote, whose collection of its insects has been deposited in the United States National Museum and partly described in various publications; to Edward S. Harkness, Esq., who had a very generous share in the cost of excavating and clearing the ruins; to President Gilbert Grosvenor of the National Geographic Society and to the officers and members of this great association, whose enthusiastic support actually made possible the Peruvian Expeditions of 1912 and 1914-15, and the publication of this book; to Miss Clara Mae LeVene for invaluable editorial assistance in the final preparation of the manuscript; and, finally, to Mr. Carl P. Rollins, Mr. George T. Bailey, and their associates of the Yale University Press, for the care and skill that they have contributed toward the production of the printed volume.

HIRAM BINGHAM.

TABLE OF CONTENTS

LIST OF ILLUSTRATIONS

CHAPTER I

···•——◆——•···

EXPLORATION AND EXCAVATION

MACHU PICCHU, or Great Picchu, is the Quichua name of a sharp peak which rises ten thousand feet above the sea and four thousand feet above the roaring rapids of the Urubamba River near the bridge of San Miguel, two hard days' journey north of Cuzco. Northwest of Machu Picchu is another beautiful peak surrounded by magnificent precipices, called Huayna Picchu, or Lesser Picchu. On the narrow ridge between these two peaks are the ruins of an Inca city whose name has been lost in the shadows of the past. Although magnificent in character and extraordinary in extent, these ruins appear to have been unknown to the Spanish conquerors, no specific mention of them being found in the writings of the sixteenth, seventeenth, or eighteenth centuries.* Efforts to identify them with places famous in Inca history have been only partially successful. It is possible that they represent two ancient sites, Tampu-tocco, the birthplace of the first Inca, and Vilcabamba Viejo, the "University of Idolatry" of the last Incas. My reasons for so thinking have been already given in the pages of *Inca Land,* together with an account of my first visit to Machu Picchu. The importance of the discovery and the necessity for making a thorough study of the site were among the reasons for my third journey to Peru and the organization of the Peruvian Expedition of 1912 under the auspices of Yale University and the National Geographic Society.

It did not take more than a glance at the preliminary map of the ruins, which had been made at my request in 1911 by Messrs. Tucker and Lanius, to convince the most skeptical that Machu Picchu was worthy of the most careful and thorough investigation. The ruins were not known to any members of the Geographical Society of Lima or the Historical Society of Cuzco. They had never been visited by any of the wealthy and educated planters of the lower Urubamba Valley who annually passed over the road

* In Dr. Richard Pietschmann's edition of the travels of Rodriguez de Figueroa (*Bericht des Diego Rodriguez de Figueroa über seine Verhandlungen mit dem Inka Titu Cusi Yupanqui in den Anden von Villcapampa*) there is a passing reference to a road leading to "Sapamarca and Picho." This may be a reference to Machu Picchu. It is the only thing approaching it that we have succeeded in finding anywhere in the early chronicles.

I. VIEW FROM THE TOP OF MACHU PICCHU MOUNTAIN

Showing Huayna Picchu in the center, with the city on the ridge in front of it, and the winding Urubamba almost encircling its base. San Miguel at the left.

which winds through the canyon two thousand feet below them. Raimondi, greatest and most remarkable of Peruvian explorers, who spent a lifetime in crossing and recrossing Peruvian roads and trails and was in this vicinity in 1865, placed Machu Picchu Mountain on his map, yet he was apparently ignorant of the ruins which lay under the forests, above its lower precipices. Even in the very elaborate geographical dictionary of Peru published by Paz Soldan in Lima in 1877 there is no mention of the ruins of Machu Picchu. The only reference to them in literature which I have been able to find is the brief statement made by Charles Wiener that in 1875 he had heard a rumor of there being ruins "at Huaina-Picchu or Matcho-Picchu," places which he was unable to reach. The fact that in 1911 I had been so fortunate as to find here a remarkably well-preserved Inca citadel, built with great care, unknown to Peruvian scholars, and untouched by the hands of Spanish *conquistadores* or modern builders, offered extraordinary possibilities for exploration and excavation. It was therefore determined in 1912 to make a detailed plan of the ruins, together with a topographical map of the vicinity, and also to collect as much anthropological and archaeological material as could be found. The task was not an easy one.

Our first problem was to open a feasible route for the transportation of supplies and specimens. Our food boxes weighed sixty pounds. When filled with potsherds, they would weigh more. They would have to be carried on men's backs. We had learned in 1911 that there were two trails from the Urubamba River to the huts of Richarte and Alvarez, the Quichua Indians whose little clearings were near the ruins. The trail up which I had been guided in 1911 by Melchor Arteaga was on the east side of the ridge, starting at a frail little bridge formed of half a dozen logs lashed together with vines. This bridge was washed away soon after my visit and only one of the logs was left when Messrs. Tucker and Lanius went to Machu Picchu two months later. Besides, as was said in *Inca Land,* for a good part of the distance the climbing was difficult; sometimes we hung on by the tips of our fingers. The path on the other side of the ridge, which began near the iron bridge at San Miguel, was the one used most frequently by Richarte and Alvarez. They had other huts near the bridge, where they were always able to reach the valley road, even in the rainy season when the bridge connecting with the east trail was sure to be washed away. Mr. Tucker had been obliged to use the west trail and had reported that it was a perilous way, winding along the face of a rocky precipice and

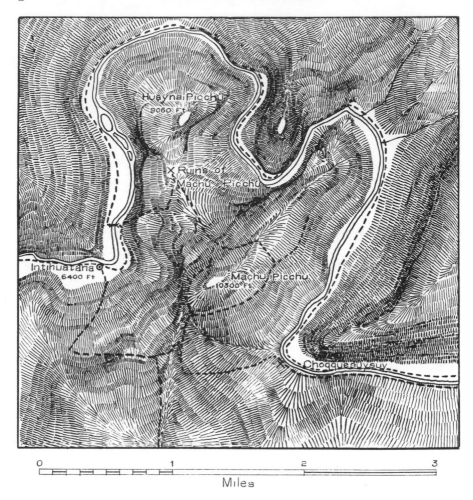

0   1   2   3
Miles

2. MAP OF MACHU PICCHU AND HUAYNA PICCHU
Showing roads and trails.

in two or three places crossing in front of sheer rock cliffs on fragile rustic ladders; in fact, so difficult and so dangerous as to make it impassable for men carrying heavy loads. Although by electing to improve it we could avoid the necessity of building a bridge over the Urubamba, its use would involve an additional climb of five hundred feet for every load that had to be carried up to camp. Moreover, the foot of this trail lay four miles farther down the rapids and also four miles farther from our base at Cuzco. Consequently it was decided to try to build a bridge of our own and construct a new trail on the east side of the ridge.

Fortunately, I was able to intrust this work to Mr. Kenneth C. Heald, one of the assistant topographers of the Expedition, whose Colorado training as a mining engineer and whose determination to surmount all obstacles made him invaluable to our undertaking. Mr. Heald found that the width of the Urubamba River at its narrowest point, the most feasible place for building the new footbridge, was about eighty feet. The roaring rapids, fed by glaciers, impossible to ford even in the dry season, are here divided into four parts by huge bowlders. Between them the first reach was eight feet wide, the next nearly forty, the third about twenty-two, and the last fifteen. For material Mr. Heald had to depend on the tropical forest which grows along the banks of the river. This of itself added another problem, for although there are many kinds of trees in the bottom of the canyon, all the species are infested with parasites and apparently at all ages. Even the young fast-growing trees are covered with moss and lichen, so that it is difficult to determine their character. The quality of the timber also varies greatly: some of the species produce hard, durable wood of great density and fine texture; other, quick-growing species produce wood of inferior quality, soft, brittle, and quick-decaying. Nevertheless Mr. Heald was able to select several fine, straight, hardwood varieties growing close to the east bank of the stream near the spot where he planned to construct his bridge. For tools he had Connecticut axes, machetes, and picks, also a coil of Manila rope. For workmen he had ten dull, unwilling Quichua Indians who had been forced to accompany him by the *gobernador* of a near-by town. This official, it scarcely needs to be said, had received orders from his immediate superior, the prefect of Cuzco, to supply us with the necessary labor. Mr. Heald's only real assistant was one Tomas Cobinas, an excellent *gendarme,* an energetic young *mestizo* who had been furnished by the prefect and who could be counted on to see to it that the Indians kept steadily at work.

The cutting of the logs for the first section of the bridge and the placing of them in position over the eight-foot reach was simple enough. To cross the next forty feet of the icy white rapids proved more difficult. In the absence of derricks or any heavy tackle, the first plan was to lay a log in the stream parallel to the bank above the bridge, fasten the lower end and let the current swing the upper end around until it lodged on the central bowlder. On trying this, however, the timber proved to be of such dense hard wood that it sank immediately and was lost in the rapids. Mr. Heald then very ingeniously contrived a primitive cantilever device with which he again endeavored to cross the torrent. Selecting two long, heavy

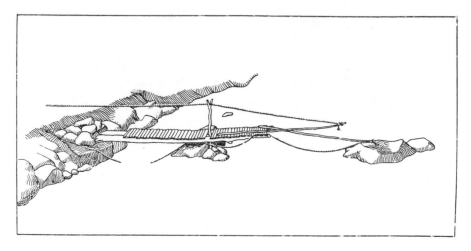

3. METHOD OF BRIDGE-BUILDING

Used by Mr. Heald in crossing the Urubamba River
near Machu Picchu.

logs, he anchored their butts on the bank of the river, laid them parallel
and about four feet apart so that their smaller ends projected some ten feet
beyond the bowlder on which rested the first span of the bridge. The shore
ends were weighted with heavy rocks. Crosspieces destined to form the
floor of the bridge were lashed to the long stringers with *lianas*—sinewy,
rope-like vines common in Amazonian forests. A heavy forked upright,
ten feet high, was wedged into place on the far side of the rock on which
the first span rested and was lashed securely to the stringers. A long, light
log was now pushed out by hand on the completed part and thrust out
over the forty-foot gap, its farther end being supported by a rope which
passed through the fork of the upright. By this means the thirty-foot gap
between the heavy stringers and the large bowlder in midstream was successfully crossed. Three light stringers were put across in this manner and
then a heavy one was tried, part of its weight being borne by the three
light stringers by means of a crossbar fastened to its farther end and part
by means of the rope. Once this problem was solved the rest of the bridge
gave comparatively little trouble. In a short time Mr. Heald had completed an excellent structure which served its purpose admirably until the
beginning of the rainy season and the end of our work at Machu Picchu.

The construction of the new trail up to the ruins was retarded at first
by dense tropical jungle, then by thick bamboo and the steepness of the
slope, and finally by the slowness and extreme caution of the workmen,

4. HEALD'S BRIDGE ACROSS THE URUBAMBA RIVER

who dreaded to take the risk of meeting a snake unexpectedly, this vicinity having a bad reputation for poisonous serpents. Their fears were justified, since during the next ten days eight venomous reptiles were killed, including several specimens of the deadly bush master. Fortunately none of the men was seriously bitten, although later we lost two mules from snake bite.

Mr. Heald had several narrow escapes, but from other causes. On the second day, while reconnoitering the steep slopes above the workmen and out of their sight, he suddenly discovered that they had started a fire in the bamboo scrub. In less than a minute it had gained great headway and was roaring up the mountain side faster than anyone could possibly climb. Retreat by the route he had come was impossible. The flames leaped fifteen and twenty feet into the air. There was nothing to do but make a strenuous effort to get around the raging fire before it should spread sideways. Tearing blindly through the dense thicket, he fell headlong over a small cliff and landed in a mass of bamboo, which fortunately broke the force of his fall and saved his life.

A few days later he had an even more exciting experience. I had asked him to see whether he could get to the top of the needle-like peak called Huayna Picchu and investigate the story that there were magnificent ruins upon its summit. Melchor Arteaga, the Indian who lived at Mandorpampa, who had originally told me about the ruins at Machu Picchu, and whose occupation consisted in selling fodder and pasturage to passing travelers and occasionally providing them with his favorite fire water, had said there were other ruins equally good, though more inaccessible, on Huayna Picchu. He finally admitted that they might be slightly inferior but repeatedly declared that they were of great importance. The needle rises twenty-five hundred feet above the Urubamba River, which surrounds it on three sides. On the south side is the ridge on which the ruins of Machu Picchu are located. On the east side the river has cut a precipice which is nearly sheer from the top of the needle to the bank of the stream. On the north side, below the upper precipices of the needle, are slopes now forest-covered but once cultivated and bearing marks of ancient terraces. The presence of these terraces, some of which had been cultivated recently by Arteaga, made it seem reasonable that there might be important ruins on the slopes of Huayna Picchu which, owing to the density of the great forest which covered the slopes, had hitherto escaped attention. Arteaga, however, insisted that there were beautiful ruins on top of the very peak itself. When Mr. Heald tried to employ him as a guide, he refused to go—possibly having a dim realization of some of the lies he had told. Nothing daunted, Mr. Heald, having found the place where Arteaga had built a rustic bridge to enable him to reach his clearings, started out with four Indians and his trusty *gendarme.* Crossing the river on four shaky poles which resembled the bridge I had used in 1911, he found even the lower slopes to be so vertical that it frequently was necessary to cut steps. He was greatly hindered by the bamboo vines and high coarse grasses which had sprung up in former clearings and also on the higher and steeper slopes, following the fires set in past years by Melchor and other exponents of that primitive system of agriculture known to agronomists as *milpa.* Progress was very slow. Finally the Indians gave out, weary with climbing and cutting their way through the bamboo jungle. Leaving the *gendarme* behind to see that the Indians should continue cutting a trail as fast as strength permitted, Mr. Heald determined to conquer the mountain alone and by a rapid reconnoissance ascertain how much of a path it would be advisable to make. His report is so graphic that I give it in his own words:

I pushed on up the hill, clearing my way with the machete, or down on all fours, following a bear trail (of which there were many), stopping occasionally to open my shirt at the throat and cool off, as it was terribly hot. The brush through which I made my way was in great part *mesquite,* terribly tough and with heavy, strong thorns. If a branch was not cut through at one blow it was pretty sure to come whipping back and drive half a dozen spikes into hands,

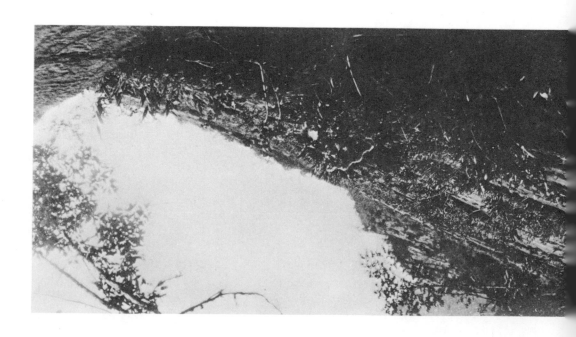

5b. EAST PRECIPICES OF MACHU PICCHU

5a. WEST PRECIPICES OF HUAYNA PICCHU

arms, and body. Luckily I had had enough practice to learn how to strike with a heavy shoulder blow and for the most part made clean strokes, but I didn't get away untouched by any means. Finally, about 3 P.M., I had almost gained the top of the lowest part of the ridge, which runs along like the back-plates of some spined dinosaur. The trees had given way to grass or bare rock, the face of the rock being practically vertical. A cliff some two hundred feet high stood in my way. By going out to the edge of the ridge I thought I could look almost straight down to the river, which looked more like a trout brook than a river at that distance, though its roar in the rapids came up distinctly. I was just climbing out on the top of the lowest "back-plate" when the grass and soil under my feet let go and I dropped. For about twenty feet there was a slope of about seventy degrees and then a jump of about two hundred feet, after which it would be bump and repeat down to the river. As I shot down the sloping surface I reached out and with my right hand grasped a *mesquite* bush that was growing in a crack about five feet above the jump-off. I was going so fast that it jerked my arm up and, as my body was turning, pulled me from my side to my face; also, the jerk broke the ligaments holding the outer ends of clavicle and scapula together. The strength left the arm with the tearing loose of the ligaments, but I had checked enough to give me a chance to get hold of a branch with my left hand. After hanging for a moment or two, so as to look everything over and be sure that I did nothing wrong, I started to work back up. The hardest part was to get my feet on the trunk of the little tree to which I was holding on. The fact that I was wearing moccasins instead of boots helped a great deal here, as they would take hold of the rock. It was distressingly slow work, but after about half an hour I had gotten back to comparatively safe footing. As my right arm was almost useless, I at once made my way down, getting back to camp about 5.30, taking the workmen with me as I went. On this trip I saw no sign of Inca work, except one small ruined wall. . . .

Five days later, although he had had no chance to consult a doctor, Mr. Heald judged that his arm was in sufficiently good shape so that he could continue the work, and he very pluckily made another attempt to reach the top of Huayna Picchu. This likewise ended in failure; but on the following day he returned to the attack, followed his old trail up some seventeen hundred feet and, guided this time by Arteaga, eventually reached the top. His men were obliged to cut steps in the steep slope for a part of the distance until they came to an Inca stairway which led them practically to the summit. The top consisted of a jumbled mass of granite bowlders. Standing on the summit, he wigwagged the result to us in camp at Machu Picchu. There were no houses, though there were several flights of stone steps and three little caves. Probably it was once used as a signal station. And this was what Arteaga had told us was "equally as good" as the ruins of Machu Picchu! Had it not been for Mr. Heald's courage and perseverance in returning to his task while suffering intense pain from his torn ligaments—an accident from which he did not recover entirely for several months—we should not have known the truth. Readers of *Inca Land* will remember that Professor Harry W. Foote and I had often been obliged to add, when discussing reports of "noteworthy and important ruins"—"but he may have been lying."

It is a striking commentary on the very slight acquaintance with the ruins of Machu Picchu possessed by the Indian who lived in their shadow at Mandorpampa that he should have thought the terraces and ancient stone stairway which he had encountered in his clearings on the slopes of Huayna Picchu were no less interesting than those on the slopes of Machu Picchu. In the years he had lived here he had probably not done more than glance at one or two of the ancient buildings. Presumably, to him and his kind, Inca ruins of temples and palaces built by their remote kindred are not in themselves interesting but merely evidence that the latter found the land worth occupying and cultivating.

A day or two after Mr. Heald had completed the new trail from his bridge to the top of the ridge, Dr. Eaton, Mr. Erdis, and I arrived and began our investigations. We were fortunate to have as our chief aide Lieutenant Sotomayor, an officer of the Peruvian *gendarmerie*. His knowledge of the Quichua tongue was of the greatest assistance to us in dealing with the Indians, many of whom spoke no Spanish. A few of our workmen had come with us voluntarily from Cuzco, where they had been employed in the excavations which we had made in that vicinity; apparently they had learned to appreciate the benefits of steady employment at good pay under humane taskmasters. On the other hand, so loath were the Quichua Indians to leave their own villages and undertake profitable employment elsewhere, so often had they been unfairly exploited in the past, that it was impossible to secure enough voluntary labor even though we paid more than the neighboring planters and worked our men shorter hours. We were obliged, therefore, to depend on the chief village officials, the *gobernadores,* who, acting under the orders of the Government, supplied us from time to time with ten or a dozen men for a fortnight. Afterward a few laborers might return voluntarily, but most of them we never saw again.

6. TYPES OF INDIAN WORKMEN EMPLOYED BY
THE EXPEDITION

Shown excavating near the west wall of the Principal Temple, under the direction
of Dr. Eaton (left). Lieutenant Sotomayor at right.

We found it necessary to conform to the ways of the country and provide each workman, the first thing in the morning, with a handful of
dried, green *coca* leaves. This was enough for four quids. The quid of *coca*
leaves, carefully and deliberately made by chewing the leaves one at a
time, usually was allowed to remain in the mouth for two hours. Making
the quid occupied the first ten minutes of the "working day," a ten-minute
recess in the middle of the morning, the first period of the afternoon
"working" time, and a recess about three o'clock. Personally I am of the
opinion that the daily use of *coca* is harmful. It seems to me that it destroys
natural human appetites and desires, and deadens ambition and aspira-
tion. Its use should be strictly regulated by the Government. Until this is
done, however, the employer who fails to provide his Quichua workmen
with the daily ration of *coca* leaves is likely to find it impossible to secure
voluntary laborers and very hard to get willing or cheerful efforts from his
conscripts. We also gave small presents on pay day, Saturday. These consisted of beads, mirrors, or other trinkets which had been carefully selected
from one of Mr. Woolworth's emporiums in New Haven. Mirrors were
particularly in demand and seemed to give the greatest satisfaction. Nevertheless only a few volunteers returned week after week. A small handful

worked regularly, but others would absent themselves for several weeks to attend to the duties of their own little farms and then return for a fortnight of labor with us. The great majority, however, worked only when the *gobernadores* forced them to come. Sometimes we had forty or more; sometimes we had only a dozen.

Our first task was to see whether excavation in the principal structures would lead to the unearthing of any potsherds or artifacts which might throw light on the former inhabitants. Our workmen, who fully believed in the "buried treasure" theory, started with a will. Tests made with a crowbar in the Principal Temple* enclosure resulted in such resounding hollow sounds as to give assurance that there were secret caves beneath the floor of the ancient temple. Amid the granite bowlders under the carefully constructed floor our excavation was carried to a depth of eight or nine feet, but all this back-breaking work ended only in disappointment. Although we penetrated many crevices and holes between the bowlders, there was nothing to be found; not even a bone or a potsherd had been accumulated there in the centuries of its existence. Digging inside the Temple of the Three Windows had similar negative results. Later, we carefully replaced and regraded the floors of the temples.

Digging on the terrace outside and below the three windows, however, resulted in the discovery of an extraordinary quantity of decorated potsherds, most of them from two to four feet under the surface of the ground. It must have been the custom for a very long period of time to throw earthenware out of the windows of this temple. It is extremely doubtful if this building was ever used as a dwelling, since its windows were too large to permit of its being occupied as a habitation by a people unaccustomed to sleeping in the fresh air and anxious to avoid all drafts. Were these pots, then, offerings to the gods? Whether the gods were supposed to be sufficiently blind to be easily pleased with cracked and broken pots, such as Dr. Eaton found were frequently provided for the souls of the departed, I cannot say. It certainly does not seem likely that this great mass of sherds on the terrace under the three ceremonial windows was formed entirely by throwing perfectly good pots out of the windows. Possibly these bushels of sherds represent pottery broken in the course of religious ceremonies or in the drunken orgies which followed.

At the end of a week of hard and continuous labor we had not succeeded in finding anything except these sherds—no whole pots, no pieces

* For the location of this and the other buildings mentioned, see Chapters III and IV.

7b. WIVES OF TWO
OF OUR WORKMEN

Standing in front of one
of the immense granite
blocks in the Temple of the
Three Windows. The one on
the left is wearing a green
skirt and a red waist with blue
stripes; the one on the right,
a blue skirt and a red blouse
with black dots.

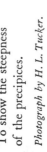

7a. VIEW FROM THE WEST
END OF THE SAN MIGUEL
BRIDGE TOWARD
HUAYNA PICCHU

To show the steepness
of the precipices.

Photograph by H. L. Tucker.

of bronze, not a single ornament or utensil, not even a stray skull or human bone. It began to look as though our efforts to learn any more of the life of the builders of Machu Picchu than could be gained by a study of their architecture and small fragments of earthenware would be a failure. We then began to look for burial caves such as I had first seen at Choqquequirau.* The Indians who lived here, Richarte, Alvarez, and Fuentes, had been instructed by their *patron,* Señor Don Mariano Ferro, the owner of the land, to assist us. They were undoubtedly thoroughly familiar with the whole mountain side and we asked them to hunt for burial caves. They went off for two days but their search yielded no results. Could it be possible there were no graves at all? Remembering the success of the pecuniary rewards which we had offered the *gobernador* of Lucma in 1911† and which had led him to locate for us a number of very interesting ruins, including Ñusta Isppana and Yurak Rumi—the great white rock over the spring—I offered a Peruvian silver dollar to anyone who would report the whereabouts of a cave containing a skull and who would leave the cave exactly as he found it, allowing us to see the skull actually in position. The next day all of our workmen were released from excavations in the city and allowed to follow their own devices. They started out early on a feverish hunt for burial caves. At the end of the day the half-dozen worthies who had followed us from Cuzco came slowly in, one by one, sadder and no wiser, their hopes of the coveted bonus destroyed. They had been tattered and torn by the thickets and jungles and baffled by the precipitous cliffs of Machu Picchu. One of them had split his big toe with a machete while hewing his way through the jungle. The thorny scrub and the ever aggravating bamboo vines had not only torn their clothes to shreds but had cruelly scratched their almost naked bodies. Unfamiliar with the region, they had found nothing. On the other hand, Richarte and his friends were more fortunate. It was not for nothing that they had been cultivating the ancient terraces. Furthermore, they had undoubtedly engaged in treasure hunting between crops. At any rate, they responded nobly to the proposed bonus and came back late in the day with smiling faces and sparkling eyes, none the worse for wear, and cheerfully announced that they had just discovered *eight* burial caves, and desired eight dollars! At the prevailing rate of wages on the sugar plantations this was more than the three of them could earn in a week.

These were the same Indians who had found "nothing" on the two

* Vide *Across South America,* pp. 315-316. † Vide *Inca Land,* pp. 235-246.

8a. URUBAMBA CANYON, LOOKING EAST
FROM THE UPPER TERRACES AT MACHU PICCHU

8b. EAST CITY, HUAYNA PICCHU, AND THE CANYON FROM THE
OUTER WALL. MANY BURIAL CAVES WERE FOUND UNDER THE
FOREST IN LEFT FOREGROUND

preceding days. It was perfectly natural that they should not have been eager to show us the sources of the pottery which from time to time they had sold to passing travelers. Furthermore, a certain amount of bad luck might happen to their crops should they desecrate the bones of the ancient people buried in the vicinity. No possible amount of agricultural good luck, however, could compete with a cash bonus such as we had offered. Consequently they now exerted their utmost efforts and the results far exceeded our expectations. Although the burial caves occurred generally on the steep slopes below the ruins and were frequently in well-nigh inaccessible locations, more or less covered with dense thickets, making the work of finding and excavating them extremely arduous, Richarte and Alvarez were unsparing in their patient, continuous searches and explored the hillside down to the very banks of the river itself. Practically every square rod of the ridge was gone over. The work of the collectors, like that of the road builders, was several times interrupted by poisonous snakes, several of which were killed, preserved in alcohol, and later submitted for study to Dr. Thomas Barbour of Harvard.[*]

More than fifty caves were opened under Dr. Eaton's personal direction and fully as many more were located and explored by his Indian helpers. The caves proved a veritable buried treasure for Richarte and Alvarez. Although the graves did not actually contain objects of gold, they did give forth a quantity of skeletal remains and artifacts which brought prosperity to the cheerful little Indians, who now secured in a week as much silver as they had formerly earned in the course of two months.

In the meantime patient and systematic excavation was being carried on in the city, under the personal direction of Mr. Erdis. With few exceptions the interior of the houses yielded little or no results; but certain localities gave us quantities of valuable material. The most fruitful digging was on the ridge south of the Sacred Plaza between it and the City Gate. Although most of the buildings within the citadel are as compactly located as possible there is quite a little open space between the end of the Sacred Plaza and the stairway which leads from the main part of the citadel to the terrace running to the main gateway. This region is dotted with a considerable number of very large rocks. Possibly it was the quarry from which a large amount of building stone was taken but where blocks too large for the purpose of the stone masons and too difficult to be broken

---

[*] See "Reptiles Collected by Yale Peruvian Expedition of 1912," by Dr. Thomas Barbour, *Proceedings of Academy of Natural Sciences of Philadelphia*, LXV, 505-507, Sept., 1913.

9. SNAKE ROCK

up into desired sizes without the use of blasting materials were left in place. The result of the quarrying left a small area which was not worth terracing; stone quarries naturally do not make good gardens. Between these quarries and the Sacred Plaza are two or three large rocks which have been slightly carved. One of them we called the "Snake Rock" because on top of it a representation of four or five snakes had been incised into the surface. Near it are the very irregular foundations of houses or huts unlike in design anything else in the city, and underneath some of the large bowlders were small caves which at one time might have served as shelters. In the process of his patient digging within the limits of the citadel Mr. Erdis made the discovery that unusual artifacts were likely to be found buried two or three feet underground in the vicinity of these bowlders. In this part of the citadel, on top of the ridge, quite a number of little bronzes, two stone dishes, and some artifacts were found which did not occur in any of the digging in other parts of the citadel nor in the excavations in burial caves on the slopes of the ridge.

For four months Mr. Erdis and his carefully selected Indian assistants excavated and prospected within the walls and on the terraces of Machu Picchu. The zeal of the assistants was kept at high pitch by the sliding scale of bounties and gratuities, and no part of the city was neglected in their efforts to find significant traces of the past. One might have supposed that the pieces of broken pottery would be fairly well distributed among the different houses, or at least among the different quarters of the city, but such was not the case. Digging inside the walls of the houses rarely gave any results, whereas certain fairly well-defined rubbish piles yielded good results. Some quarters of the city had almost nothing, others had an extraordinary amount. The northeast quarter, containing a larger number of dwellings than any other quarter of the city, had very little, sherds of only one hundred and sixty-one pots being found in the excavations here.

The northwest quarter includes the Intihuatana Hill, the Principal Temple, the Sacred Plaza, the Temple of the Three Windows. It contained a surprisingly small amount of material. There was practically nothing on Intihuatana Hill and nothing in the buildings on the plaza, a fact which was most disappointing. It should not be forgotten, however, that this group of buildings adjoins the so-called Snake Rock Cemetery, most prolific of all localities. The southeast quarter of the city was at a considerably lower level than any other and contained rather poorly built houses, so one would not expect to find much there. Yet we did find remains of some seventy-five pots. The southwest quarter of the city, from the City Gate to the Stairway of the Fountains, contains the finest dwellings, the Royal Mausoleum and the real center of the city life, the main thoroughfare, and the water supply. So it was not strange to find this quarter most plentifully supplied with sherds. They represent some 555 pots, of which 58 were found near the City Gate, 53 in the upper terrace group, 28 in the middle terrace group, 108 in a rubbish pile on the north side of the main stairs, and 95 along the stairs and in the fountains. These and other finds will be fully discussed in later chapters.

One of the books which I carried with me to Machu Picchu was a volume by Dr. William H. Holmes of the United States National Museum giving an account of his first visit to the great Maya ruins of southern Mexico. In it he spoke so very appreciatively of the remarkable results achieved by the distinguished English archaeologist, A. P. Maudslay, Esq., in clearing the jungle from some of the most important sites, that I was led to undertake the discouraging task of chopping down the entire hardwood forest which stood on the city terraces and on top of some of the buildings, clearing all the jungle, burning and removing the débris, and even cleaning moss off rocks and ruins. In a word, we made a determined effort to restore the ancient walls to their former appearance. While it would have been folly to have attempted to build roofs for the buildings and restore the thatch, it did seem worth while to learn all we could from the evidence of the stones and to secure photographs which would give

10a. VIEW FROM THE EXPEDITION'S CAMP (UPPER LEFT)
Taken July 21, 1912.

10b. THE SAME VIEW, TAKEN AUGUST 17, 1912
To show progress in clearing.

11. VIEW TAKEN DURING THE PROCESS OF BURNING
AND CLEARING THE JUNGLE

some idea of the beauty of the white granite structures, even though this meant an enormous amount of painstaking labor. During the course of our clearing we found tall trees, two feet thick, perched on the very tips of the gable ends of small, beautifully constructed houses. It was not the least difficult part of our work to cut down and clear away such trees without seriously injuring the old walls. Considering all the pains that we took to preserve the ruins from further spoliation by the forest and to restore them so far as we could to their ancient beauty, it was rather annoying to read, in the decree issued by a new Peruvian Government which came into power during the course of our work, a clause stating that we must not injure the ruins in the slightest particular and must be careful neither to deface nor mutilate them! As a matter of fact, we had had to spend two days in erasing from the beautiful white walls the defacement caused by the great charcoal autographs of Peruvians who had visited the ruins since my first trip. One of these enthusiastic natives had taken the pains to scrawl his name in huge letters thirty-three times on the granite blocks of the principal temples and most attractive buildings. The attitude of the new Government was in painful contrast to that headed by President Leguia, which had given us the greatest possible aid in every way and particularly by furnishing us with the services of so excellent an officer as

Lieutenant Sotomayor. He took personal charge of the gang of Indians who were engaged in cutting down the forest, removing and burning the rubbish, and no one could have been more efficient or persistent. So rapidly did the jungle grow, however, that we had to cut the bushes and bamboo scrub three times in the course of four months. The final cutting, made in ten days by a gang of thirty or forty Indians moving rapidly with sharp machetes, immediately preceded and accompanied the intensive photographic work at the end of the season. With the assistance of Mr. Erdis, I then took five hundred pictures of the ruins.*

* Sets of these pictures are in the possession of the Hispanic Society of America, the National Geographic Society, and Yale University.

CHAPTER II

THE SEARCH FOR INCA ROADS LEADING TO MACHU PICCHU

AFTER the clearing of the citadel was fairly under way, the next object which demanded attention was the location of the ancient highway connecting the citadel with the surrounding country. We were able to locate a paved road running south from the City Gate along the terraces and the back of the ridge toward Machu Picchu Mountain. Due to a rock fall in front of one of the great precipices on the mountain, this road had been destroyed at that point. On the other side of the rock fall we were able to find it again and to follow a carefully made granite stairway to the top of the ridge east of Machu Picchu Mountain. At that point it divided, the left-hand fork leading to impassable cliffs on the south side of the mountain, the right-hand fork following the top of the ridge to the summit, where we found ruins of an Inca house which would

12. SUMMIT OF MACHU PICCHU MOUNTAIN

Showing terraces and primitive ruins, probably of a signal station.
Similar ruins occur on top of Huayna Picchu.

13. SALCANTAY AND THE UPPER AOBAMBA VALLEY

accommodate a dozen soldiers, and a carefully terraced signal station or lookout on the very top of the peak.

We heard from one of the Indians that there were ruins in a region of high mountains and impassable jungles south of Machu Picchu Mountain, but lack of time prevented us from trying to reach those ruins in 1912. It was most tantalizing to think of the possibilities of exploration in a country which in ancient days must have been so closely connected with the hidden city. The mystery of the deep valleys which lie in the quadrant north to northeast of Mount Salcantay had long demanded attention. Separated from Ollantaytambo and Amaybamba by the Grand Canyon of the Urubamba, protected from Cuzco by the gigantic barrier of Salcantay, isolated from Uiticos by deep valleys and inhospitable *punas,* it seems to have been unknown to the Spanish conquerors and unsuspected by their historians. Garcilasso Inca de la Vega, from whom Prescott drew so much of his fascinating *Conquest of Peru,* makes no reference to places which can with any certainty be located in the Machu Picchu quadrant. Cobo and Balboa in their detailed accounts of Inca conquests take the story right around this region. It appears to have been a *terra incognita* until the nineteenth century. Even Raimondi hardly touched it.

In 1914 Ricardo Charaja, a full-blooded Quichua from the town of Santa Rosa who was our most dependable native assistant, located the remains of an old Inca road leading out of the Pampaccahuana Valley in the general direction of Machu Picchu. He pointed it out to Chief Topographer Bumstead. In 1915 rumors reached us of Inca ruins to be found in that direction. It was reported that "there was a large temple built on an island in the center of a lake, a very beautiful place, better than Machu Picchu." It was with mingled feelings of keen curiosity and skepticism that Mr. Osgood Hardy and I undertook in April, 1915, to follow the newly discovered roadway as far as it would carry us. It began at the junction of the Huayllabamba River with the Pampaccahuana, near a small ruin built, like the others, of rough rocks laid in clay. Located on a promontory above the two streams, this ruin probably represented a *tampu,* or resthouse, on the ancient road. Our first camp, on the only level spot we could find, was so near the roaring Huayllabamba that only with the greatest difficulty could we carry on a conversation. During the night the noise subsided considerably; since the Huayllabamba is a snow-fed mountain torrent, it is much larger in the afternoon than in the morning, and during the night everything freezes. We had engaged the services of

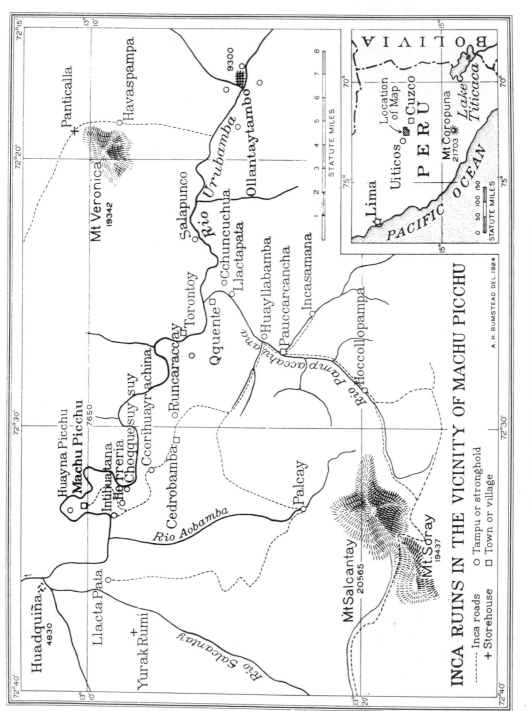

INCA RUINS IN THE VICINITY OF MACHU PICCHU

Inca roads   O Tampu or stronghold
+ Storehouse   □ Town or village

A. H. BUMSTEAD DEL. 1924

14. MAP OF THE VICINITY OF MACHU PICCHU

Inca roads and ruins.

an Indian guide who said he knew all about "the celebrated temple in the middle of a lake in the mountains" but he did not put in an appearance and we had to start without him. He caught up with us later, claiming that he thought we might not start because it was raining that morning. As a matter of fact, his provisions for the journey, consisting of a small quantity of parched corn and *habas* beans, had not been prepared in time. Led by Ricardo Charaja, who greatly enjoyed his ability to act as a guide in a re-

15. OLD TRAIL ALONG THE URUBAMBA RIVER
Photograph by H. L. Tucker.

gion far from his own home, we worked our way through a picturesque primeval forest and emerged in the upper part of a U-shaped valley, on whose grassy slopes we had no difficulty in following the remains of the paved highway constructed by the Incas. It led by easy gradients to a pass at the head of the Huayllabamba Valley and thence descended by a series of sharp zigzags into the Huayruru Valley. Not an Indian hut was to be seen. In fact, the region seemed to be extraordinarily destitute even of animal life. In a wild, unfrequented valley like Huayruru one is very likely to see a few deer, and we hoped to run across an Andean bear; but nothing of the kind appeared and we made our way across the bottom of the valley as best we could, only to find the Inca road disappearing in a maze of bowlders under the remains of a fairly recent landslide. On the other side of the valley we saw two Inca roads winding up the grassy slopes. We decided to take the one to the right, as that appeared more likely to lead

16. AOBAMBA VALLEY, FROM THE OLD INCA TRAIL
Looking toward Arma.

in the direction of Machu Picchu. The left fork probably goes to Palcay, a small Inca ruin which I discovered in 1912.

Halfway up the mountain side, some two thousand feet above the bottom of the valley, we came to an interesting little Inca fortress, the name of which our guide, who had by this time joined us, gave as Runcaraccay. It was apparently a fortified station on the old highway. Circular in shape, Runcaraccay contains the remains of four edifices grouped about a little courtyard which was entered by a narrow passage. In the sides of the passage were bar-holds for the better securing of the gate. The stonework and the arrangement of the niches are typically late Inca. We pitched our camp near the ruins, our half-dozen Indian bearers from Ollantaytambo building themselves a temporary shelter as a protection against the cold rain which fell during the night.

From Runcaraccay we followed the Inca road over a pass out of the Huayruru Valley and into that of one of the affluents of the Aobamba. In most places the road was still in such condition that our mules could follow it with safety, but occasionally the poor animals would get bad falls and had to be entirely unloaded and helped over slippery or precipitous rocks. We had not gone far down into the new valley before we came to another fork in the road. The left branch led by a series of steps up a steep slope to a promontory, where we found the ruins of a compact Inca group, to which our guide gave the name of Cedrobamba. Since this word is half Spanish and half Quichua, meaning "cedar plain," it is obviously not the ancient name. No one seems to have lived in this valley for several centuries, so it is not surprising that the old name has been lost. The ruins of Cedrobamba are in the same style as the others located along the highway, and while too extensive to be merely a fortified resthouse like Runcaraccay, Cedrobamba undoubtedly represents one of the important fortified outposts subsidiary to Machu Picchu. It commands an extensive view on three sides. The promontory is surrounded by steep precipices and is extremely difficult of access except over the paved roadway. It was probably supplied with water by a small ditch brought along the side of the mountain in the manner typical of Inca engineering.

We made a small clearing not far from the ruins and camped here for several days while the Inca roadway was being cleared and made passable for our mules. In several places rustic bridges had to be constructed and a considerable amount of jungle removed before the animals could pass over the ancient trail. In one place we were surprised to find evidences of modern blasting. Our guide said that some years ago a planter of potatoes in the upland region had attempted to utilize this ancient highway in order to get his product to market. The only place where he met serious difficulty was at the point where the roadway ran through a tunnel behind a huge, sloping ledge. The Incas had found it easier to tunnel behind the ledge than to cut the roadway in the face of the sheer cliffs, but the tunnel was not wide enough for loaded mules.

While the road was being made passable for our animals, I went ahead with Ricardo and was delighted to find that as the road progressed it headed more and more in the direction of Machu Picchu. Pushing on in the hopes of soon getting a glimpse of Machu Picchu Mountain, I stumbled on a group of ruins called Ccorihuayrachina, "the place where gold is winnowed." Above the ruins a striking hilltop had been leveled off and surrounded by a retaining wall so as to make it a useful signal station or possibly a primitive fortress. Beneath it we found a huge cave which showed signs of recent occupancy, probably by bears.

The next day, on coming around the bluff in sight of this cave, we were surprised and delighted to see a black Andean bear slowly making his way along the mountain side, feeding on clumps of wild pineapple. This was the first time that any of us had ever seen a Peruvian spectacled bear feeding in the open. Fortunately the wind was in the right direction so he did not notice our presence, and I succeeded in getting the first photo-

17b. OLD INCA
TRAIL

Landslide that caused the
trail to disappear
at this point.

17a. WEST PRECIPICES
OF HUAYNA PICCHU

Showing ancient trail
following a
natural cleavage.

18. WEST PRECIPICES OF HUAYNA PICCHU
Another view of the Inca trail.

graphs recorded of an Andean bear in his native haunts. The bear was slowly working around the ridge in our direction and, in the hopes of getting a better photograph, I slipped back out of sight and climbed the mountain side as fast as my wind would allow me. The elevation was about twelve thousand feet above sea level, and a rapid climb at that altitude is not conducive to being able to hold a camera steady. Unfortunately the bear climbed faster than I did. When he reached the top of the ridge he immediately saw some of our caravan approaching, and all I got was a momentary glimpse of two big ears and a black snout fifty feet away. Before I could get the camera focused even at this small section of Mr. Bear the apparition disappeared. I scrambled to the top of the ridge as fast as possible but our precious visitor was nowhere to be seen. Below the crest of the ridge was a densely wooded hillside which obviously offered him an easy retreat.

The Inca highway led into the ruins of Ccorihuayrachina by a long flight of stone stairs, from the top of which we secured a magnificent view of the Urubamba Valley in the vicinity of Machu Picchu Mountain. The most interesting feature of Ccorihuayrachina is a row of five stone-paved fountains in what is now a swamp, near a huge, slightly carved bowlder. This may have been what the Indians referred to when they spoke of a temple in a lake, but it hardly came up to our expectations. Ccorihuay-rachina may signify "the place where gold is washed." The name may have been given to the locality by reason of the five fountains, where some imaginative Indian thought gold might have been washed. To me it seems likely that this was the residence of one of the most important chiefs who owed allegiance to the rulers of Machu Picchu.

From Ccorihuayrachina the trail led along the crest of the ridge, gen-

19. CCORIHUAYRACHINA

Inca signal station on terraced hilltop. The slope just below
the upper cliffs was the bear's feeding ground.

erally following an easy grade, often the normal contours, and slowly took us toward the great promontory whose most conspicuous point is Machu Picchu Mountain. Here, within rifle shot of the citadel, the ancient trail disappeared; but that did not worry us, for there was no denying the fact that we had reached the immediate neighborhood of Machu Picchu and had done it by following the Inca road which undoubtedly connected the citadel with the Pampaccahuana Valley and the principal Inca towns of the region. In addition to locating the ancient highway, we had also been so fortunate as to discover a number of hitherto unknown ruins which seemed to represent stations at convenient intervals along the road. I had at last achieved my desire of penetrating the unexplored country southeast of Machu Picchu, a region which had tempted me for many years. We had learned a little more of that "something" which, as Kipling says, was "lost behind the ranges."

In order that we might have the satisfaction of actually reaching the citadel of Machu Picchu by the same route used by its former inhabitants, I asked Mr. Clarence Maynard, assistant topographer of the 1915 expedition, to go down the southwest bank of the Urubamba River to Choquesuysuy and thence to the top of the saddle which connects Machu Picchu Mountain with the region we had just been across and from here attempt to find a practical route to the citadel.

Choqquesuysuy lies above the river at a bend where there is a particularly good view. Near a foaming waterfall some Inca chief built a temple whose walls, still standing, serve to tantalize the traveler on the river road. There is no bridge within two days' journey and the intervening rapids are impassable. Every time we had journeyed up and down the river I had longed to get across and see what these ruins contained. They are relatively so near to Machu Picchu that I felt sure they must have belonged to the same people. Accordingly, I was extremely glad when Mr. Maynard reported that he had succeeded in reaching Choqquesuysuy, which we learned later belonged to the late Inca period. Mr. Maynard found that a footpath connected Choqquesuysuy with the saddle at the top of the ridge below Machu Picchu peak. A recent landslide had destroyed the first part of the trail, but he repaired it with difficulty and got his animals safely across the treacherous slope. After a steep climb of about three thousand feet from the banks of the river he camped on a small pampa south of the saddle, and after several hours of hunting, he found signs of the ancient Inca roadway, now almost obliterated. By hard climbing, these fragments of paved road were traced to the saddle.

He found that there were three possible routes which might lead from the saddle to Machu Picchu. One was along the east side of the mountain; the second lay directly up the knifelike ridge and across the top of Machu Picchu peak; the third was along the precipitous west face of the mountain. From the valley below we had often noticed a great fissure which ran across the face of the precipice and seemed as though it might have been used as part of the road between the citadel and the saddle.

At the narrowest point in the saddle was a ruined guardhouse. On the other side of the ruins the trail was again picked up and followed to a point where the side hill merged into a sheer rock wall. Every foot of the way had to be cut through a dense jungle, the footing was extremely

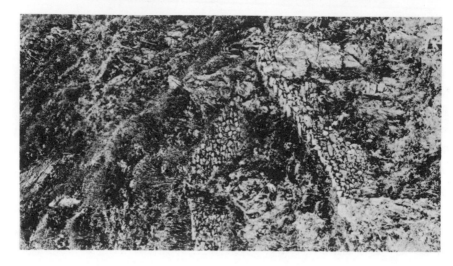

20b. MACHU PICCHU ROAD

Part of the old Inca trail.

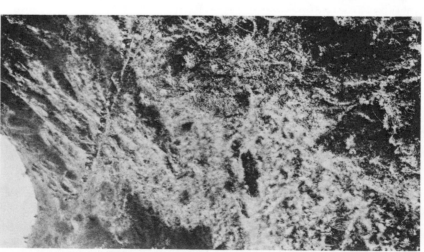

20a. CCORIHUAYRACHINA

Mule caravan on old
Inca trail, coming down
into the ruins.

treacherous, the mountain side exceedingly steep and slippery with recent rains. Here and there fragments of the paved roadway were encountered, although in order to find them it was frequently necessary to
cut over a considerable area. On such occasions the Indian workmen tried
in every way to discourage further search, crying to one another, "There
is no road," "No one can pass here." In the pouring rain they worked half-
heartedly, making no serious efforts to assist in locating the old road.
Finally, at a rock wall all signs of the trail disappeared; yet there was no
indication that it had been carried away by a landslide. Eventually, one of
the workmen uncovered a flight of stone steps covered with decayed
vegetable matter, and leading to a cave, the entrance to which had been
concealed by thick bushes. Here again the Incas had avoided the necessity
of cutting a path across the face of a sheer cliff, by carrying their road back
of it through a natural tunnel. However, when Mr. Maynard attempted
to follow this route he found the passage choked by large rocks, where the
roof had caved in. Since he had no blasting powder, further progress along
the old road seemed at a standstill. He decided that the only possible way
of progressing was by swinging a short, rustic bridge across the face of
the cliff, a plan which seemed rather dangerous and not too feasible. Accordingly, before undertaking it he decided to investigate the other
two possible routes. Dividing the Indians into parties, trails were cut
in various directions, in the hope of running across any other paved
roads which might exist, but several attempts to reach the crest of the
ridge were prevented by impassable precipices. Finally, a way was found
around the precipices and traces of a road were discovered on the crest.
This was followed toward Machu Picchu Mountain until it divided, one
branch continuing toward the peak, the other descending the west face
of the slope toward the great fissure which crosses the western precipices
of the mountain. An attempt was made to follow each route. The upper
one soon disappeared in a maze of cliffs and fallen rocks; the lower one
continued along the west side of the mountain for about a mile and finally
ended at a landslide. This trail was very narrow and exceedingly steep,
crossing rocky precipices and flights of stone steps bordered by a sheer
drop of hundreds of feet. From here it led across a steep slope on which
the road was held in place by well-constructed retaining walls. All of it
was overgrown and every foot of the way had to be cut through a dense
jungle. The stone paving was covered with century-long accumulations
of vegetable mold. Mr. Maynard made an effort to get past the great land-

21. MACHU PICCHU ROAD

Showing old Inca trail south of Machu Picchu Mountain.

slide which intervened between him and the fissure on the western precipice, but this proved to be impossible, the rotten rocks and the steepness of
the slope making any climbing operations excessively dangerous. All three
routes therefore had proved impracticable, and the one hope lay in the
possibility of being able to bridge the cliff in the trail on the eastern slope,
which was the one first investigated.

Sending a man back to camp for a rope, the rest were set to cutting
poles which could be used to span the gap. Projecting from the face of the
cliff about ten feet beyond the end of the trail, and a few feet above it, was
a ledge of rock. Growing out of crevices at the end of this ledge, and also
at the end of the trail, were two small trees. They were rather unsafe foundations, but they formed the only means of further travel along this route.
Poles were laid from tree to tree, and one of the Indians slid across, first
having a rope tied tightly about his body, the other end being held by the
men. Small sticks were lashed at right angles to the poles and where possible were wedged into cracks in the face of the wall. Brush and moss
placed on this support completed the bridge, which was about two and
one-half feet wide.

This was not a bridge over which one could carry a heavy load. In fact,
I found it to be the kind of place where one only breathes easily after it

has been safely negotiated. Beyond the cliff it was fairly easy to locate the Inca road, as it came out of the north end of the cave and penetrated the dense forest which clung to the steep slope. In places the roadway had been carried away by landslides, making progress extremely slow. Heavy rains also interfered with the work. The Indians, who had not constructed an adequate shelter, suffered greatly at night and were very miserable and dejected, repeatedly threatening to quit entirely. It took great determination and courage on Mr. Maynard's part to keep his gang together and

22. PART OF THE OLD INCA TRAIL NEAR CEDROBAMBA

make them persevere in their efforts to reach the citadel. Finally another point was reached where recent landslides and dangerous precipices made further progress absolutely impossible. It was therefore decided to move camp down into the bottom of the canyon to the bridge at San Miguel, climb from there to the ruins of the citadel, and attempt to work the trail back to the neighborhood of the dangerous landslide. This meant a descent of four thousand feet to the hamlet of Intihuatana. The trail, a modern one, over which mules had recently been driven, was too steep to permit of riding in many places. Unfortunately Mr. Maynard's feet had suffered from the rough climbing and the constant rain, so he was tempted to ride in some places where ordinarily he would have preferred to walk. At one point where the trail was bordered by a sheer drop of several hundred feet his mule slipped and fell to his knees. In attempting to rise, he lost his balance and started to go over the edge. Throwing himself out of the saddle, Mr. Maynard landed on his back in the trail. Whereupon the mule, relieved of his burden, by terrific effort scrambled back into the road, on top of the unfortunate topographer, who in his journal laconically remarks: "Landed on my back on a rock. Throwing weight that way evidently righted mule. He floundered around. His hoofs seemed to be all over me, but didn't step on me. Managed to roll out of way. Arrived at camp about eleven thirty."

23. THE ANCIENT ROAD LEADING INTO MACHU PICCHU

The effort to connect the two trails was ultimately successful. By following the road south of the citadel up the stone stairways to the crest of the ridge, Mr. Maynard finally found that he had missed a stairway which led straight up the slopes of the mountain and which avoided the region of landslides that had baffled his attempt to follow the road from the point where he had built the little bridge around the tunnel. Two of the Indians finally found the missing link in the trail and thus completed the opening of one of the old Inca roads which connected the citadel with the saddle back of Machu Picchu peak and thence with the rest of the district. A few days after the work was completed I had the satisfaction of picking up the old road where I had been obliged to leave it some weeks before and entering the citadel by the same road its builders used. I found that it was good enough for llamas and human burden-bearers. Wherever it followed the contour of a steep slope it was banked up and supported by a stone wall. Where it had to climb a steep grade, stone steps were built with care so that the bearers of burdens could be provided with secure footing. The road was brought into the citadel along a terrace over a little bridge which permitted the agricultural laborers to pass readily from upper terraces to lower terraces without climbing across the main causeway. Finally, by a graceful curve, the road was brought to the top of the lower ridge and the citadel gate. Except on some of the steepest stairways, this old Inca road was about four feet wide, thus allowing the human freight carriers to pass without interfering with one another.

Like Mr. Heald, Mr. Maynard is certainly to be congratulated on his success in overcoming not only the tremendous natural difficulties which faced him but also the human handicaps imposed by being obliged to work with discouraged and unwilling Quichua Indians. Without the assistance of men of the type of Heald and Maynard one cannot make much progress in Andean exploration.

CHAPTER III

....•——◆——•....

THE PLAN AND ARRANGEMENT OF THE
CITY AND THE SACRED PLAZA

THE ruins of Machu Picchu are perched on top of a steep ridge in
the most inaccessible corner of the most inaccessible section of
the central Andes. No part of the highlands of Peru has been
better defended by natural bulwarks—a stupendous canyon whose rim is
more than a mile above the river, whose rock is granite, and whose precipices are frequently a thousand feet sheer, presenting difficulties which
daunt the most ambitious modern mountain climber; a canyon so difficult
of access that although it is within fifty miles of Cuzco, the largest city in
the Andes and the center of Peru's most populous highland province, the
ruins remained unknown to her savants until 1911. Here, in a most remote
part of the canyon, on this narrow ridge flanked by tremendous precipices,
a highly civilized people, artistic, inventive, well organized, and capable
of sustained endeavor, at some time in the distant past built themselves a
granite city or citadel. Since they had no iron or steel tools—only stone
hammers and little bronze crowbars—its construction must have cost generations if not centuries of effort. To prevent their enemies from reaching
their shrines, temples, and houses, they relied, first, on the rapids of the
Urubamba, which are dangerous even in the dry season and absolutely
impassable during at least half of the year. On three sides this was their
outer line of defense. On the fourth side the massif of Machu Picchu
Mountain is accessible from the plateau only by a narrow razor-like ridge
less than forty feet across and flanked by precipices. Here they constructed
a strong little fort—a veritable Thermopylae.

As a second line of defense they had the precipices of Huayna Picchu
and those which flanked the ridge between Huayna Picchu and Machu
Picchu. It is true that the lower slopes of Huayna Picchu are relatively easy
of access on the north, but the mass of Huayna Picchu is separated from
the ruins by another razor-like ridge impassable on the east side and having
only a footpath fit for goats and sure-footed Indians on the west side. This

24b. OUTER BARRACKS
LOOKING SOUTH
FROM THE CAMP

24a. CITY GATE
EXTERIOR
LOOKING NORTH

trail passes for more than a hundred yards along a horizontal cleft in the rock underneath an overhanging precipice of sheer granite and flanked by a similar cliff. Yet two men could defend it against an army. It is the only route by which Machu Picchu may be reached from Huayna Picchu.

So much for the northern approach to the citadel. The east and west sides of the ridge are sufficiently precipitous for fifteen hundred feet to be well-nigh unassailable. Rocks could easily have been rolled down upon invaders in the manner referred to by the *conquistadores* as a favorite method of Inca soldiers. If a path was maintained on each side, as is the case today, these paths, in turn, could easily have been defended by a handful of men. Wherever breaks in the precipices would give a foothold to intruders they were walled up and the natural defenses strengthened.

On the southern side rise the precipitous cliffs of Machu Picchu Mountain. In ancient times they were flanked by two paths which led, one on the west side along a great cleft in the face of a massive cliff, and one on the east side climbing the abrupt declivity by means of a stone stairway and circumventing the mountain by a trail which only goats could have followed with ease. Both of these paths led to the little ridge on which was the aforementioned fort, and which alone gave access to Machu Picchu Mountain from the plateau and the southern rim of the canyon. Both of them could have been readily defended in various places.

On the tops of both neighboring peaks of Machu Picchu and Huayna Picchu are the ruins of signal stations from which the distant approach of an enemy could have been seen and instantly communicated to the citadel. That on top of Machu Picchu was necessarily the more important and seems to have been occupied by a number of men who passed their spare time in building walls on the very edge of one of the most stupendous precipices in the Urubamba Canyon. If any of the workmen who built that wall slipped he must have fallen nearly three thousand feet before striking any portion of the cliff broad enough to stop him.

The builders of Machu Picchu did not rely entirely upon either their first or second lines of defense or their watchtowers, but constructed on the south side of the citadel two more lines—an outer wall and an inner wall. The outer runs along the ends of a magnificent tier of agricultural terraces. Close to the wall are the ruins of half a dozen buildings which may have been intended as barracks for the soldiers whose duty it was to protect the citadel on the only side where it was comparatively vulnerable. In case they should fail there was still the inner line of defense. At the

25b. **DEFENSIVE TERRACES**

Between Huayna Picchu
and Little Huayna Picchu.
East side.

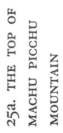

25a. **THE TOP OF
MACHU PICCHU
MOUNTAIN**

Ten thousand feet
above the sea
and four thousand feet
above the river.
Retaining wall at left.

26. OUTER BARRACKS (LEFT) AND THE PRINCIPAL AGRICULTURAL TERRACES SEMICIRCULAR TEMPLE AND BEAUTIFUL WALL IN FOREGROUND

narrowest part of the ridge, just before one reaches the citadel from the south, a fosse or dry moat was dug, its sides faced with stone. Above it the inner wall of the citadel extended across the top of the ridge and down each side until it reached precipitous cliffs which made the wall no longer necessary. On the very top of the ridge the wall was pierced by a large gateway built of massive stone blocks. The gate itself, probably a screen of heavy logs lashed together, could be fastened at the top to a large stone eye-bonder firmly embedded above the lintel and underneath six or eight feet of masonry. At the sides, the door could be fastened by a large crossbar whose ends were tied to powerful bar-holds firmly anchored in holes left in the doorposts for that purpose. Such a door might, of course, have been smashed in by an attacking force using a large log as a battering ram. To avoid the likelihood of this the engineer who constructed the fortifications brought forward a salient from the wall at right angles to the doorway. By this means the defenders standing on top of the salient could have rained down a lateral fire of rocks and bowlders on the force who were attempting to batter down the gate. The walls of the citadel were high enough so that they could not be scaled with ease. In fact, an attacking force which had been so fortunate as to overcome all the natural defenses of this powerful stronghold and had circumvented the defenders of the several Thermopylae-like passes would have found themselves in a very bad situation when rushing along the terraces toward the inner fortifications. At the end of the terraces they would have found it necessary to jump down into the dry moat and scale its farther side as well as the citadel wall, all the time subjected to a shower of stones from the slings of the defenders. Obviously the builders of Machu Picchu were very much afraid of being attacked by a superior force. It is difficult to imagine, however, that any attacking force could possibly have been large enough to overcome a vigorous defense even if the citadel were held by only a few score determined soldiers.

The City Gate shows evidences of being repaired. The top of the narrow ridge is at this point occupied by a large granite bowlder, which was worked into the fortifications, or, rather, the walls were strengthened by its being used as a member. As a result the outer gatepost of the massive entrance rests on an artificial terrace. This terrace has settled a few inches, due to erosion on the steep hillside. Consequently the wall has been thrown out of the perpendicular and has started to destroy the fine old gate. It will not be long before the great lintel will fall and carry with it the re-

27b. THE NARROWEST
STAIRWAY
IN MACHU PICCHU

27a. THE STEEPEST
STAIRWAY
IN MACHU PICCHU

paired part of the wall which is superimposed above it. One clearly gets the feeling, in looking at the entrance to the citadel, that it was rather hastily repaired at a period long subsequent to its original construction.

As can readily be seen from the folding plan of Machu Picchu (inserted in the pocket at the end of the volume), the city was well provided with terraces, stairways, and narrow streets. These divide it into compounds or clan groups, each composed of three or more houses.

Space was limited and the houses were crowded closely together, but an extensive system of narrow streets and rock-hewn stairways made intercommunication within the walls of the citadel comparatively easy. In fact perhaps the most conspicuous feature of Machu Picchu is the quantity of stairways, there being over one hundred, large and small, within the limits of the citadel. Some of them, to be sure, have but three or four steps while others have as many as a hundred and fifty. In several cases the entire flight of six, eight, or even ten, steps was cut out of a single bowlder. The stairways which connect the various agricultural terraces follow the natural declivity of the hill even where it is so steep as to make them seem more like a ladder than a flight of stairs. In several places a little garden plot was tucked into a terrace less than eight feet square behind and above a dwelling house. In order to make accessible little garden terraces like these, the owners constructed fantastic stairways scarcely wide enough to permit the passage of a boy. Within the citadel, however, and particularly in the narrow streets or alleyways, the stairs were constructed on a comfortable grade.

The stairway or flight of steps as an ornamental or ceremonial motif in Inca architecture does not seem to occur here, although it might well have originated in this locality. In the ruins of the monolithic gateway at Tiahuanaco, in Bolivia, in the curiously carved rock at Concacha, near Abancay, Peru, and on the famous carved rock called Kkenko, near Cuzco, are little flights of stairs which were carved for ceremonial, or ornamental, purposes and which serve no useful object so far as one can see. The stairways of Machu Picchu, on the other hand, with possibly one exception, all appear to be available for reaching locations otherwise difficult of access. While they are more numerous than was absolutely necessary, none of them appears useless, even today. The longest stairway, which may properly be described as the main thoroughfare of the citadel, commences at the top of the ridge at the terrace by which the main highway enters the walls and, roughly dividing the citadel into two parts, runs

28b. MONOLITHIC
STAIRWAY IN
ROYAL MAUSOLEUM
GROUP

Leading from beautifully made
houses in the upper part of the
group to more roughly constructed ones below, doubtless
occupied by retainers
or servants.
Note the difference in
finish between the walls
on either side
of the photograph.

28a. A SMALL
PRIVATE STAIRWAY
LEADING TO A LITTLE
GARDEN TERRACE
INGENUITY GROUP

all the way down to the impassable cliffs on the northeastern slope. This stairway was not only the principal street of the citadel but was also the site of its interesting waterworks.

There are several springs on the side of Machu Picchu Mountain, within a mile of the heart of the citadel. The little *azequia* or conduit which brought the water from the springs may still be followed along the mountain side for a considerable distance. It has been partly destroyed by landslides but may be seen where it runs along one of the principal agricultural terraces, crosses the dry moat on a slender stone aqueduct, passes under the wall of the citadel in a narrow conduit less than six inches wide, and is carried along one of the terraces of the citadel itself to the first of a series of fountains or little stone basins which are located near the principal stairway. As the builders had no pipes they conducted their small supply of precious water in very skilfully made stone conduits from one little reservoir to another. The first four are south of the stairway, and near the fourth the stairway is divided into two flights. At this point there begins a series of twelve. The *azequia* runs south from the last fountain and empties into the moat. The fountains are further described in the following chapter.

Possibly one reason for abandoning Machu Picchu as a place of residence was the difficulty of securing sufficient water. In the dry season the little springs barely furnished us enough water for cooking and drinking purposes for fifty people. In the earliest times, when the side of the mountain was forested, the springs would undoubtedly have done better; but with the deforestation which followed continued occupation and the resultant landslides and increased erosion of the surface soil, the springs must at times have given so little water as to force the dwellers in the citadel to bring the water on their backs for considerable distances. They had the choice of toiling up the steep slope for two thousand feet from the Urubamba River or of going back over the little paved road to springs in the mountains back of them, four or five miles away. They probably preferred the latter alternative.

It is significant that the sherds found near the City Gate represent forty-one containers of liquid refreshment as compared with four cooking pots, nine drinking ladles, and not a single two-handled or food dish. Evidently the dispensers of *chicha,* or native beer, were stationed here. The results are the more striking when compared with the finds in the southeastern quarter, where fifteen food dishes were found and twenty-four con-

29b. EAST CITY, EAST SIDE, WITH LONG STAIRS LEADING DOWN TO THE BURIAL CAVES

29a. STAIRWAY OF THE FOUNTAINS, THE MAIN STAIRWAY IN THE CITY

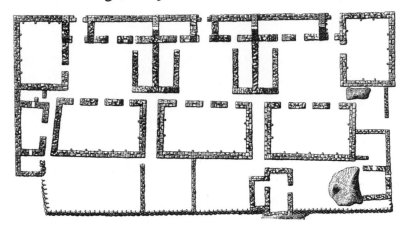

30a. PLAN OF THREE-DOOR GROUP

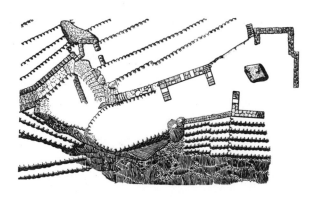

30b. PLAN OF INTIHUATANA HILL

tainers of liquids. Furthermore, in the latter case we find that in a building in the upper corner of this group, next to the main stairway and the water supply, the sherds show fourteen jars for liquids to four food dishes, as though this were a very wet corner.

The largest flat space within the limits of the citadel lies in a swale at the widest part of the ridge. This was carefully graded and terraced, and at the time of our visit had recently been cultivated by Richarte and his friends. In fact, one would have to go a good many miles in the canyon of the Urubamba to find an equally large pampa at an elevation of not less than seven thousand nor more than ten thousand feet. In other words, this little pampa offered an unusual opportunity to a people accustomed to raising such crops as flourished in Yucay and Ollantaytambo. The fact that it was possible for them also to cover the adjacent hillside with artificial terraces which would increase the potentiality of the region as a food producer was doubtless as important a factor in the selection of this site as the ease with which it could be made into a powerful citadel. One of the most carefully constructed stairways leads directly from the chief temples to the little pampa itself.

There is only one city gate, that mentioned on page 44. The northern, or Huayna Picchu, side was not defended by a transverse wall but by high, narrow terraces built on little ledges which would otherwise give a foothold on the precipices. Near these terraces there is a broad saddle connecting Machu Picchu with a conical hill that is part of a ridge leading to the precipitous heights of Huayna Picchu. South of the saddle, which was in 1911 covered with a dense forest, is a rude amphitheater. It had been terraced and there are five or six different levels, recently used for the small plantations of the Indians. On the surface of the ground, among the cornstalks, pumpkin vines, and onion patches, we found occasional pieces of pottery. Looking out on the amphitheater on the east side are twenty houses. Four of them appear to have contained windows. Two of these are marked by having three windows each, the third appears to contain only one, while the fourth is so much in ruins that it is difficult to say whether it has two or three. The houses on this east side of the amphitheater are nearly all made of stone laid in clay and only roughly finished. In the northeast corner there are two terraces with a marked difference from the others, in that the stones are much larger and more irregular. Most of the houses are built of rather small stones of a nearly uniform size. The terraces are built sometimes of large stones and sometimes of small.

31b. INTIHUATANA HILL
AND TERRACES
NORTH OF THE
SACRED PLAZA

31a. PRIEST'S HOUSE
ON THE
SACRED PLAZA

Interior of East Wall,
showing remarkable symmetry.
Behind it is
the bowlder with seven steps,
enabling the priest to ascend
to the platform on top
in order to salute
the rising sun.

Only one group of houses, that near the south end, appears to have been built with special care; in this the stones are fitted together without clay and the walls are in a beautiful state of preservation. A large group of houses here has three entrances, so we called it the Three-Door Group. In our excavation we found a rubbish pile in front of it, which, with what we collected inside, yielded pieces of one hundred and fifteen pots.

On the west side of the amphitheater are by all odds the finest and most interesting structures. Beginning with the northwest corner, after ascending a series of terraces one comes to a sightly spot on top of a hill which commands a magnificent view in all directions, including not only the city itself and the cultivated terraces but also the Grand Canyon of the Urubamba. I know of no place in Peru that has a more charming view. Many of the mountains sustain a cover of dense tropical vegetation from top to bottom; others are bare except for scant pasture; while still others consist of sheer granite precipices. On clear days snow-capped peaks may be seen both east and west, the finest being those of Salcantay and Soray, which are conspicuous from the lower Cuzco Valley.

On top of this little hill, from which the bridge of San Miguel may now be seen two thousand feet below, there was built a beautiful little temple near a very fine *intihuatana* or sundial stone, such as formed an important part of temples where the sun was worshiped. Similar stones may be seen in Cuzco, Pisac, and Ollantaytambo. The top of the bowlder was flattened off, leaving near the center a square upright portion to cause a shadow. *Inti* means "sun" and *huatana* is "a place where animals are tied." The *intihuatana* would seem to be "the place to which the sun was tied," so that it could not escape. A primitive folk so extremely dependent on the kindly behavior of the sun as were the Peruvian highlanders must have been in terror each year, as the shadows lengthened and the sun went farther and farther north, that he would never return but would leave them to perish of cold and hunger. Hence it seems likely that these short stone posts represented the post to which a mystical rope was tied by the priests to prevent the sun going too far away and getting lost. At the same time, it is probable that the priests knew from the shadow cast by this post the day on which the sun was likely to begin his southward journey. The *intihuatana* at Machu Picchu is cracked across the bottom but the crack seems to be comparatively new. The top of the stone is not so carefully finished as the rest and it is difficult to say whether it has been broken off or is in its original state. The height of the projecting block is a trifle over

32. THE INTIHUATANA STONE
"The place to which the sun was tied."
Looking west-northwest.

half a yard, thus making it the highest *intihuatana* stone found in Peru. The top of the stone shows evidence of a fracture but there is no indication that this was broken off in recent years. Squier reported an *intihuatana* stone in Ollantaytambo of about half a yard in height as having been destroyed by the Spaniards, and it seems to be a generally accepted fact that the Spanish priests took pains to knock off the top of the *intihuatana* stones wherever they were found.

Near this interesting and mysterious rock, which some people think is a sundial and others regard as having been made for idolatrous purposes, are the ruins of two stone structures built, like the rest, of white granite blocks, squared as nicely as could be done without the use of tools unknown to the builders, fitted carefully together without clay, and bearing the marks of extreme attention to detail. Both of these small houses are marked by one curious feature. As originally planned they had handsome though narrow doors; as left apparently by the builders the doors were filled up to two-thirds of the original height, leaving only windows. The best preserved house contains two fine niches and two windows, which are the same general dimensions, being about 3.2 feet in height and 1.5 feet in breadth. Both of the houses appear to have been originally one story and a half high with gable ends. They also have a peculiar feature common to a number of houses here in Machu Picchu in that, while the main portion

33. THE LITTLE TEMPLE ON INTIHUATANA HILL

of the walls is of stone laid without clay or mortar, the gables above are of much rougher blocks, not carefully fitted together but laid in clay and possibly plastered over. One's first impression is that houses containing two such different styles of architecture were built at different periods and that the later builders, fancying gable ends, had imposed their own type of ends built at much less trouble than those of their ancestors; but for a number of reasons I believe the two forms of construction here in Machu Picchu to be contemporaneous. A careful inspection of the walls reveals the fact that the lower portion does not end in a straight line but ends with rocks that were keyed and fitted into the upper and cruder portions. Furthermore, there exists between two of the houses a gateway made of splendidly cut blocks, matched without clay and joining together two houses each built of the two kinds of construction. As it is matched into the construction of each house, it would be reasonable to suppose that it was built contemporaneously with both houses. I had hitherto supposed from the nature of the structures on the islands of Titicaca and at Choquequirau that structures built of crude blocks laid in clay were of a much later period than those of a more finely cut stone keyed up without any clay or cement. It is evident, however, that the builders understood both forms of construction. This fact may be adduced as another reason for believing that Machu Picchu antedates the later Inca Empire and succeeds

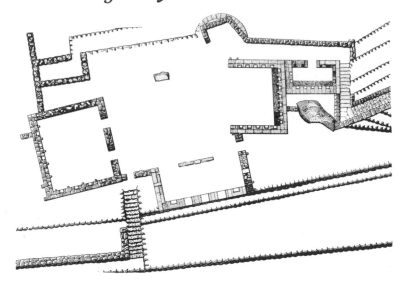

34a. PLAN OF SACRED PLAZA

34b. BIRD'S-EYE VIEW OF SACRED PLAZA AND SNAKE ROCK

Drawn by A. H. Bumstead.

the earlier megalithic period, containing as it does so many examples of both classes of construction. Nevertheless, it may all be late Inca.

The south end of this hilltop has been rounded and roughly faced with stones laid in clay, one of the larger of which has been curiously carved so as to leave a lug with a vertical hole pierced through it. The terraces below and around the hilltop are of rough stone faced nearly flat and laid in mud. On the south side thirteen terraces go down as far as it was practicable to make terraces, in other words, to the edge of the precipice. The hill itself is partly composed of huge, irregular blocks of granite. In many places where these overhang they have been propped up with stone walls, leading one to suppose that there might be graves within. Earlier excavators had been led to the same conclusion and, so far as I could judge, had encountered the same results, namely, that there was nothing behind the walls but earth and that the walls had been built chiefly to give a finished appearance to the rude bowlders. Our excavation on this hill yielded very poor results.

Leaving the hilltop and going in a southerly direction, one descends several flights of stone stairs and approaches a little flattened space which we have termed, for want of a better name, the Sacred Plaza. Before reaching it one passes on the left a very singular bowlder shaped more or less like a giant bivalve. Leading to the top are seven stairs cut in the soft disintegrating granite, and from the top one can get a charming view. Stones have also been fitted into the top of the bowlder so as to form a little platform on which three or four persons could stand and salute the rising sun. North of this bowlder and below it are the walls of a little house, about ten by fifteen feet in diameter, built in the best workmanship of the highest Inca style, that is to say, with carefully cut ashlars, many of them apparently rectangular, keyed together without cement. The lower tier is of particularly large, fine blocks about four feet in length and two feet in height; the upper tiers are smaller but all quite symmetrical. On the left of the door as one enters this house is a single gigantic block cut so as to form the entire lower half of that part of the front wall. Not only were the lower portions of two of the niches with which this house is lined cut out of this stone but in a spirit of almost freakish ingenuity or playfulness the builders carved part of the corner of the room itself in this extraordinary block, so that it even forms a very small part of one of the end walls. There is in Cuzco a stone made famous by early Spanish writers because it had fourteen angles; this stone has thirty-two angles. The little building

35. NORTHWEST CORNER OF THE PRIEST'S HOUSE
ON THE SACRED PLAZA

With the stone of thirty-two angles.

has another unusual feature—a long stone bench extending the entire length of the back of the house, made of beautifully cut ashlars. It may have been used as a couch. The building is lined with niches so nearly alike that the eye can scarcely detect any difference in shape or size. It adjoins on the south the main temple and may possibly have been the residence of the high priest. It should be noted here that the words "temple" and "palace" are used tentatively and merely record the impressions conveyed by a careful examination of the buildings.

The priests of the sun were, of course, most highly favored and it is not surprising to find the beautiful stone stairway which leads up to the *intihuatana* the most carefully constructed of any at Machu Picchu. The steps are about four feet wide, yet each of them was made of a single block of granite. There is a low parapet on each side of this stairway. North of the high priest's house runs a walk, and a balustrade overlooks the beautiful valley and the rapids of San Miguel. This sightly gallery connects at one end with the stairway leading to the *intihuatana* stone and at the other end with the Sacred Plaza.

Keyed into the priest's house and evidently built at the same time—for one of the lower stones forms a part of both edifices—is the Principal Tem-

36. STAIRWAY LEADING FROM INTIHUATANA HILL DOWN TO THE
PRIEST'S HOUSE ON THE SACRED PLAZA

The most carefully constructed one in the city, each step being
a single block of granite.

ple. This superb structure is entirely open to the Sacred Plaza on the south
and is enclosed on the other three sides by walls, twelve feet high, of remarkably beautiful construction. The lower tier of stones contains five
gigantic blocks, weighing several tons apiece; the three largest measure
13.2 feet, 10.2 feet, and 9.6 feet in length, respectively, each one is higher
than a man and nearly 3 feet thick. Yet they do not go more than a foot
underground and do not appear to rest on stone foundations. Above are
rectangular ashlars gradually diminishing in height until the top course
is reached, and this course is as fine as any of the others instead of being
rough as in all buildings which clearly supported a roof.

The interior of the Principal Temple was originally paved with coarse
white sand apparently laid down with a certain amount of wet clay to a
depth of five or six inches. Beneath this we found loose earth on top of a

37. ALTAR IN THE PRINCIPAL TEMPLE

jumbled mass of bowlders with many interstices, some of which admitted a crowbar for a distance of three or four feet, leading us to hope that we might find something as a result of further excavation, but in this we were disappointed.

At the base of the rear (north) wall of the temple and projecting three feet into the room is a nearly rectangular ashlar fourteen feet in length and a little over five feet in height, flanked by two similar ashlars about five feet long and four feet high. It can hardly have been intended as a couch, as it is so high above the ground as to be reached with difficulty and no steps were provided. It would seem, then, to have been a species of altar. Possibly offerings of food were placed on it or it may have been intended to receive the mummies of the honored dead, which could here be brought out and worshiped on days of festival. Above this there are seven niches and above the niches are six stone pegs, more or less squared off. Two of them are part of the same stone; of the other four, each has its own block. These compose the top layer of this side of the temple. The line of most of the stones is as straight as it was possible to make it without the use of instruments of precision. On each of the walls, about two-thirds of the way up, there is a row of five niches made as nearly alike as possible. None of the niches is at a height where it conveniently can be reached by a person standing on the ground, although this is a most unusual feature in ancient Peruvian architecture; in fact, I know of no other building where the niches are quite so inaccessible. It would seem as

38. THE HEART OF MACHU PICCHU: THE SACRED PLAZA

Principal Temple in the center, Temple of the Three Windows at the right. Above, to the left, Intihuatana Hill. Looking northwest.

39. WEST WALL OF THE PRINCIPAL TEMPLE

though they must have been designed for some ceremonial purpose, possibly to receive fragile offerings or an arrangement of little record stones which it was important should not be disturbed.

The entire east wall appears to have settled nearly a foot, carrying with it a part of the north wall. It is not strange that this settling should have taken place, for the wall appears to have only a dirt foundation. So perfectly keyed together was it, however, that it has settled as a mass without disturbing the arrangement of the stones except at the corner. Perhaps the most marked peculiarity of this ruin, whether it be temple or palace, is that the ends of both the east and west sides are not perpendicular; nor do they have the customary inward slope characteristic of nearly all ancient Peruvian structures. As a matter of fact, they form an obtuse angle. The lower half of the angle is in each case the edge of the single Cyclopean member of the lowest course in the end walls, which slopes inward toward the bottom. The upper half of the angle is formed of the six remaining courses and slopes inward toward the top. The point of the angle contains a hole cut into the Cyclopean ashlar of the lowest course, evidently intended to permit the admission of a large wooden beam which probably extended across the open front to the point of the angle in the front of the opposite end. My first impression was that such a log would have been used to support the roof of the structure, but the perfect finish of the topmost course leads me to believe that this building never had a roof but that these holes supported the ends of a log which in turn supported a screen that could be removed when it was not needed. Such a device would have permitted the interior of this temple to have been constantly exposed to the sun while at the same time it was screened off from the view of anyone in the Sacred Plaza.

Another interesting feature of the end walls is the presence in the end ashlar of the first course, immediately above the Cyclopean ashlar, of a very small bar-hold brought flush with the surface, as in the gateway to the Royal Mausoleum Group (see Fig. 28b). It is almost incredible that these bar-holds could have been intended to support a little pole stretched across the front of the structure, yet that seems to be the interpretation. Possibly it may have been in the nature of a taboo stick which would have prevented the interior from being desecrated. In any event, the presence of bar-holds in the end walls of a building is unique, unless one regards them as being the same thing in a different form as the eye-bonders inserted in the gable ends of houses for giving greater security to the roof beams. In such a case, however, it seems likely that another bar-hold or modified eye-bonder would have been placed near the top of the sloping wall. Two square projecting stones outside the end wall and near the front edge could have been used as roof-pegs to tie down the roof, although then it seems likely that their corners would have been rounded rather than square. On the whole, I am inclined to believe that this temple did not have a roof. If it were the place in which the mummies of departed ancestors were brought for purposes of worship—a custom known to have been practiced by the Incas—the presence of a roof would have been undesirable and would have interfered with the ceremony of giving the mummies a comfortable sun bath. Anyhow, no pains were spared to make this unique structure conform to all that was best and most solid in the architecture of the Incas.

The interior measurements of this building are twenty-six by twenty-one feet. There does not appear to have been any carving anywhere in the temple except that the sides of the two principal end megaliths were trimmed in such a manner as to give the effect of three tiers of stones instead of one single block. Furthermore, the large altar stone at the back has two projecting lugs at the base. They are not alike and are not symmetrically placed. In general, however, the temple gives evidence that the builders had a remarkable sense of symmetry: they did not absolutely match block for block but they came very close to it. The general effect of the symmetry combined with the exquisite fitting of the blocks is extremely pleasing. Few buildings in Peru give a finer example of the art of the ancient builders.

Below the plaza, on the west side, are rows and rows of beautiful terraces which extend down to the edge of precipitous cliffs. The uppermost terrace forms part of the plaza itself. It is broken by a semicircular bastion or bulwark, possibly intended as the base of a semicircular temple, which is a fine example of the perfection to which the ancient Peruvians carried the art of stonecutting (see Figs. 34a, 38). The bastion is made of large granite blocks cut to form a nearly perfect semicircle about ten feet in diameter and eight and one-half feet high. Above this is a low, crude balustrade not fitting exactly and made of rough stones laid in mortar. That it was never completed I judge from this rubble wall and from the fact that some of its ashlars still retain nubbins like those noticed at Rumiccolca,* which were probably used in putting the ashlars in place but which would have been removed by the workmen had the structure been completed.

On the south side of the plaza is a large rectangular building, of typical late Inca construction, built of small, roughly finished stones laid in adobe, having two doors, both in front, and no windows. Its inner walls were lined with symmetrically placed niches, the whole forming obviously an important residence but one which would have required only a few weeks or months to construct.

On the opposite and eastern end of the plaza are the ruins of the most interesting building of all, the Temple of the Three Windows (see Fig. 38). There are, it is true, several other buildings containing three windows and this one as a matter of fact contains five, but in the other buildings the windows are small and inconspicuous, being about 2.5 by 1.5 feet, whereas in this building, on the side overlooking the amphitheater and surveying beyond it a magnificent panorama of forest-clad mountains—one of the finest panoramas in Peru—are three conspicuously large windows, the largest, I believe, that have been found in any of the ancient Peruvian structures. The middle window is the largest, being 4.25 feet in height, 2.85 feet in width at the top, and 3.15 feet at the bottom. The northern window is 4.15 feet in height, 2.7 feet in width at the top, and 3.2 feet at the bottom. The southern window is 4.04 feet in height, 2.75 feet in width at the top, and 3.05 feet at the bottom. The southern window is 3 feet in depth at the bottom and 2.8 feet at the top. The middle window is

* Vide *Inca Land*, pp. 135-141.

40. THE TEMPLE OF THE THREE WINDOWS

Eastern Wall, overlooking the valley, thought to have been built
by the first Inca as a memorial to his ancestors.
See particularly Chapter IX.

the same. The northern window is 2.92 feet deep at the bottom and 2.64 feet at the top. From these dimensions and from the accompanying photographs a fair idea may be obtained of the size of these windows. The temple contains two other windows, one of which is practically in ruins, the other 2.2 feet in height with an average width of 1.7 feet.

The northern and southern ends of this building, which measures 38 by 17 feet, are built as follows: The lower half, of very large stones, is keyed together without cement, the upper half made chiefly of roughly finished stones laid in mud. As a result the upper portion has tumbled off the southern end of the building. The western end, opening on the plaza, is marked by a monolith about 7 feet high and 2.2 feet wide, containing a groove in the top, a monolithic pillar intended to support the front roof-plate of the building (see Fig. 38). The walls of this temple, like those of the Principal Temple, are on three sides only, the fourth side being left open to the Sacred Plaza with the exception of the unique monolithic pillar just referred to, a device not found in any other building in the cita-

41. TWO OF THE THREE WINDOWS IN THE TEMPLE
OF THE THREE WINDOWS

del. The building had a gable roof, the stones in the end of the gable being larger than customary but nevertheless laid in adobe instead of fitted together. As in the Principal Temple, Cyclopean ashlars were employed in the lower course, and the ends of the side walls, instead of being perpendicular, form an obtuse angle. Similarly, the point of each angle contains a cavity, evidently intended here to permit the admission of the end of a roof-plate. The top of the monolithic pillar located halfway between these two cavities was notched, as has been said, to permit a roof-plate to rest upon it. A curious feature of this building is that in the eastern wall as it was originally planned there were two large niches flanking the windows, the lower half of each of which has been filled up with a single granite block cut for that purpose. Also from the face of the southern wall in the interior of the building there project two nubbins, and on the exterior of both the north and south sides are projecting roof-pegs of characteristic cylindrical form.

In order to build this structure the architect was obliged to construct a foundation for the eastern wall down to the level of the next terrace. To do this, he used four large stones and built a wall which rises eleven feet from the terrace to the level of the window sill. The sill of each window forms part of a Cyclopean ashlar, a member of the lowest course of the back wall of the temple, and these ashlars in turn are part of the eastern retaining wall of the Sacred Plaza and its adjacent terraces. The walls of

42. TEMPLE OF THE THREE WINDOWS
Exterior of the eastern wall.

the temple are of massive blocks, some of them quite irregular, but all of them of well-selected white granite, beautifully worked.

The reason for one's great interest in this building lies in the fact that on its eastern side, overlooking the valley, the wall is really nothing but a stone framework for the three conspicuously large windows. Nowhere else in Peru, so far as we know, is there a similar structure conspicuous for consisting of a masonry wall with three windows obviously too large to serve any useful purpose yet most beautifully made with the utmost care and solidity, clearly a ceremonial edifice of peculiar significance. As has been said in *Inca Land*, it is the presence of this temple at Machu Picchu which better than anything else gives us a clue to the mystery of the citadel. This point is further discussed in Chapter IX.

Excavations in this temple yielded nothing. On the terrace under the three famous windows I felt sure there would be good sherds—those large ceremonial windows seemed to invite the throwing out of valuable offerings. And digging here yielded pieces of thirty-one pots. The round bastion west of the Sacred Plaza seemed to be the other dumping place in this quarter and contained sherds of thirty-five pots. Of the sixty-six pots found near the Sacred Plaza, fifty-six had to do with liquid refreshments!

CHAPTER IV

···•——◆——•···

THE ARCHITECTURE AND MASONRY OF
MACHU PICCHU AND ITS CLAN GROUPS

EVERY kind of stone wall known to the Incas may be seen in Machu Picchu, from the exquisitely finished wall of coursed dressed ashlars to walls little better than rubble. There are walls of Cyclopean masonry in which single units may weigh as much as twelve or fourteen tons. There are walls composed entirely of small blocks neatly laid in clay. There are walls whose construction must have taken years of patient effort and others which could have been built in a few days. In fact this great variety is one of the most fascinating and amazing features of the place.

A striking feature of the ruins is the large number of walls which seem to have been built in two distinct periods. In many cases the lower part of the wall is of carefully cut blocks beautifully keyed together with exquisite skill and patience, a process requiring a very long period of time. The upper part of the wall, on the other hand, is of roughly squared blocks laid in clay and probably once faced with thin stucco of adobe. In no other ruins that I have ever seen in Peru is this so striking a feature. It would seem to indicate that many of the buildings here had been repaired, or else completed in haste. Quite a number of the structures are of walls of uniform masonry but one continually gets the impression in walking through the citadel that it belongs to two distinct periods—the first a period in which the builders had an abundance of time, plenty of skilled hands, and sought solidity and permanence in their structures; and the second a period in which speed was an important element, and, as a result of the necessity for providing a considerable number of houses in a short space of time, hastily constructed walls were laid on ancient foundations and, this not providing enough room, other houses were hastily built on old agricultural terraces. (See Fig. 216a in Chapter IX.)

On entering the citadel, the first characteristic that strikes one is that a large majority of the houses were a story and a half in height, with gable

43. A SACRED ROCK

Surrounded by terraces faced with large rocks, illustrating
a difficult achievement in masonry.

ends. On the outside of each gable end may be seen a row of stone pegs
projecting a foot or so from the surface of the wall. This is a characteristic
feature of Inca architecture. At first sight I thought them to be merely
ornamental; they suggested the idea of being the petrified ends of wooden
beams, stringers, and purlins. This pleasant theory of wooden origin,
reminiscent of Doric architecture, was partly destroyed and partly con-
firmed one day in Ollantaytambo when I noticed wooden pins, similarly
placed, in the gable end of a modern adobe house, used as points to which
the roof was tied. Obviously, then, the stone pegs bonded into the gables
at Machu Picchu were not merely ornamental ends of structural beams,
but petrified roof-pegs, serving a useful as well as an ornamental purpose.

Also to be seen on the gables and elsewhere were eye-bonders, consisting of a stone slab about two feet long, six inches wide, and two inches
thick. About two inches from one end a hole was bored through from side to
side, probably by means of pieces of bamboo rapidly revolved between the
palms of the hands, assisted by the liberal use of water and sand. Such a
method required time and patience, but produced results as satisfactory as
may be secured by the use of a mallet and chisel and was less likely to split
the stone. The eye-bonder thus bored was set in at right angles to the edge
of the sloping gable wall in such a way as to be flush with the surface of

44. AN INTERIOR IN KING'S GROUP
Showing roof-pegs.

the incline, little spaces being left on each side so that the hole was readily
accessible for lashing the purlins to the steep pitch of the gable. At Machu
Picchu there were usually four of these eye-bonders on each side of the
gable, but Dr. Eaton later found that at Choqquequirau the builders used
nine instead of four, possibly due to the use of smaller purlins. Finally, the
thatched roof was kept from blowing away by being tied to the ends of the
projecting roof-pegs. So far as I have been able to learn, this method of
supporting the roof is purely of Inca origin. If used in any other part of
the world the fact is not known to those students of architecture to whom I
have presented the problem. It was due in part to the fact that the plateau
where Inca architecture flourished is treeless and wind-swept. Had there
been more trees they would not have had to learn to build stone houses, and
had there been more natural shelter against the wind, the roofs would not
have needed such careful tying down. (See Fig. 50a.)

The Indian huts in the Urubamba Valley of the present day are built
by planting upright posts in the ground and tying the principal beams to
them with fiber cords and lianas. In the absence of suitable lumber, the

45b. A FOUNTAIN

The basin is cut out of a single block of granite, with a drain hole drilled in one corner.

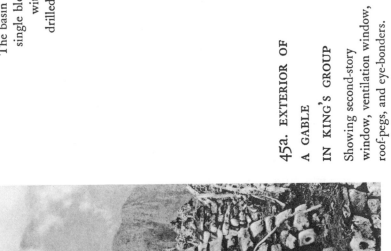

45a. EXTERIOR OF A GABLE IN KING'S GROUP

Showing second-story window, ventilation window, roof-pegs, and eye-bonders.

rafters are commonly made of the dried flower stalks of the agave, or century plant. These are tied together, in pairs, at the top, without the use of a ridgepole. The purlins, of small bamboo or large reeds, are tied on the outside of the rafters and not fastened beneath them, as with us. Bundles of grass for the thatch are tied onto the purlins. There are no struts or braces. There are no nails. The whole roof is really a flexible basket or cage, bound together with cords and set at a fairly steep pitch so that the thatch will readily shed the heavy rains. It does not appear likely that this style of building has changed much since the days of the Incas; probably the laborers and builders who constructed the palaces and temples of Machu Picchu lived in just such huts. One must also suppose that the agriculturalists who provided the residents of Machu Picchu with food lived for the most part in temporary grass-thatched wooden huts. There is not enough arable land in the valley to support a large population and the people of Machu Picchu must have had to occupy all the neighboring valleys wherever conditions of climate and soil were favorable to their crops.

In the center of the gable end of many houses at Machu Picchu is an opening which looks like a window but was probably intended to serve as a door to the upper story of the house. It could have been reached by means of a small ladder. That it was usually kept closed, however, is evidenced by the small vent or breathing hole which is often found a foot or two above its lintel. These little ventilating shafts in the gables probably meant that the attics were used, as in the Peruvian huts of today, for the storage of maize, the Incas undoubtedly having also learned that corn-on-the-cob keeps better in a well-ventilated space. Furthermore, the size of the little door which gave access to the "attic" was barely large enough for a man to crawl through, and the absence of anything like permanent stairs leading up to it would seem to indicate that it was not used frequently and was not intended for access to sleeping quarters. While access to the attic could have been secured by a ladder inside the house, this is doubtful. In the first place, the presence of such a ladder would have obviated the necessity for the doors found in the gable ends. In the second place, the opening in the attic floor would have let out the warm air in the main room and made it colder and more drafty, and if there is one thing the highland Indian dreads it is a draft of fresh air. The Incas, like their successors, the modern Quichuas, probably slept in a room whose doors and windows were closed as tightly as possible. Certainly we may be sure that an observer would have said of them, as Byron did of the modern Greeks, "They stare not on the stars from out their attics." The night air is very cold in the Andes, and has a penetrating quality which does not conduce to astronomical observations. Modern Andean shepherds do not sleep in the open but seek the shelter of windowless huts, and the ancient herders of llamas and alpacas probably did the same. Consequently it is not surprising to find that the Incas did not have that familiarity with the starry firmament which prevails in hot regions or semiarid pasturelands where the cool night air is grateful

46. DOORWAY IN A DWELLING OF ROYAL
MAUSOLEUM GROUP

after a torrid day. The Mayas in Central America, who developed such marvelously accurate astronomical knowledge, lived in a hot country at an elevation where it was pleasant to be out at night; and the shepherds of Palestine and Arabia would never have been so interested in the stars had they lived on the Peruvian plateau twelve thousand feet above the sea.

The doors of the houses were high enough for the tallest Peruvian to enter comfortably without bumping his head. As in ancient Egypt, the sides slope, the bottom being wider than the top. The lintel is generally duolithic, although in a few of the most important structures the lintels are monolithic. The walls of the houses are all of granite. Most of the ashlars could have been quarried a few rods from each house, but in some of the structures evidence is shown of very careful selection of the material. The granite of the ridge varies from a reddish to an almost pure white, and the

47. INTERIOR OF A DWELLING OF ROYAL MAUSOLEUM GROUP
Showing niches and pegs in walls.

most beautiful walls are those built of carefully matched blocks of white granite.

The exterior of the house walls is without ornamentation but the interior is almost always broken by niches, about three feet in height, ten inches in depth, and two feet in width, narrower at the top than at the bottom, so placed in the wall as to be nearer the floor than the ceiling. Originally designed probably for ceremonial purposes, possibly to receive the carefully dried mummies of the departed, they came eventually to be recognized as a great household convenience. Crudely made niches can be seen today in the huts of modern Indians where they take the place of shelves, cupboards, and bureaus. Stone pegs usually were placed between the niches and on a level with their lintels.

So far as we know, the Incas used neither chairs nor tables. The modern Indian who wishes to be comfortable seats himself on a pile of sheepskins; the builders of Machu Picchu probably squatted on the ground or rested on thick rugs made from the wool of the llama, or blankets of alpaca. It may almost be said, then, that the niche was the principal article of furniture. Their smaller cooking utensils and the dishes out of which they ate were probably kept in the niches. Larger utensils and water jars stood on the floor, the aryballi with their pointed bottoms supported by three or four small stones, or, if the floor was covered with gravel, resting comfortably in slight depressions. Things which were better when kept

48b. CITY GATE
INTERIOR
Cf. Fig. 50b.

48a. THE LOCK-HOLE
SHOWN IN
FIG. 55
With the cover removed
to show the
saucer-shaped depression
in the cap-stone,
into which
the bar-hold fitted.

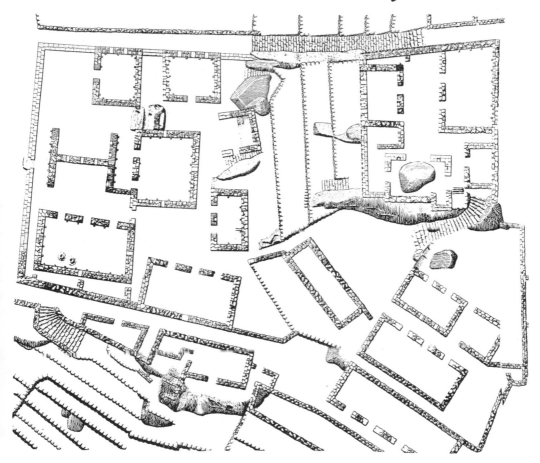

49. PLAN OF INGENUITY GROUP AND PRIVATE GARDEN GROUP

hung up were in the "attic" suspended from the rafters, or in the room below they could have been suspended from stringers or in some houses hung
from stone pegs which projected from the walls between the niches and on
a level with their lintels.

Since the citadel stood on a side hill, nearly all the houses were built
on terraces, with their doors facing the hill, thus admitting but little light
to the interior. As a consequence, and particularly where the outer wall of
the house was flush with the retaining wall of the terrace, two or three
small windows lighted up the interior and gave a pleasant outlook over
the Grand Canyon.

Some of the houses were lined with such beautiful stonework as to
require no other finish. In most instances, however, the rough stones were
covered with clay stucco and probably all the houses whose walls were
built of rough stones were so lined. In a few houses a little of it still re-

mains but for the most part the clay surface has entirely disappeared. Yet there is no evidence here, as there is at Racche in the temple of Viracocha,* that the beautifully finished stones were ever covered with adobe.

As has been said, the houses usually were arranged so as to form part of a compound or clan group. Sometimes the group is a row of houses on a single terrace, sometimes the rows are on two or more terraces. If space permitted, the group was arranged about a central court. To this compound there was usually but one entrance, a gateway whose façade had a reëntrant angle, as though the doorway had been let into the back wall of a large niche. In every case the entrances to compounds were found to have been furnished with the means of fastening a bar across on the inside. The crossbar was lashed to the stone bar-holds which, when the gateway was built, had been firmly set into the gateposts. The more common method of anchoring the bar-holds was to cut a cubical cavity in the top or corner of one of the larger blocks in the gatepost and set a stone cylinder into saucer-shaped depressions cut into the ashlars below and above the cylinder. Thus the bar-hold would be so firmly keyed into the wall that it would be able to resist at least as much pressure as the wooden crossbar which was lashed to it. It is possible, however, that the bar-locks supported nothing more than a "taboo stick." There is a reference to this subject in the famous will of Don Mancio Sierra Lejesema,† the last survivor of the companions of Pizarro in the conquest of Peru. In his "True confession and protestation in the hour of death," made in Cuzco on the fifteenth of November, 1589, and addressed to his sovereign, King Philip II of Spain, he declares that before the Spanish Conquest crimes were so little known among the Incas "that an Indian with one hundred thousand pieces of gold and silver in his house left it open, only placing a little stick across the door, as the sign that the master was out, and nobody went in. But when they saw that we placed locks and keys on our doors they understood that it was from fear of thieves, and when they saw that we had thieves amongst us they despised us." One must, however, deny the statement that an Indian in the time of the Incas ever had "one hundred thousand pieces of gold or silver" in his possession, since neither private property nor gold or silver coins were known to the Incas. On the other hand, the observation

---

* Vide *Inca Land*, p. 129.

† This is Prescott's spelling in his quotation from the preamble of the will, in Spanish. Markham's spelling in *Incas of Peru* is Mancio Serra de Leguisamo, but in his translation of the *Travels of Cieza de Leon* he spells it Marcio Serra de Lejesama. The date is given by Prescott as September 15, 1589; by Markham in the former of the two works mentioned as September 18, 1589.

50a. PROBABLE METHOD OF USING THE EYE-BONDERS AND
ROOF-PEGS FOUND IN THE GABLE ENDS
OF INCA HOUSES

50b. DRAWING TO SHOW HOW THE CITY GATE MIGHT HAVE BEEN
FASTENED TO THE BAR-HOLDS AND THE EYE-BONDER

51. ONE OF THE BOWLDERS IN INGENUITY GROUP

With little platforms for the reception of offerings.

of the old *conquistador* that it was the Inca custom when the master of the house was out to place "a little stick across the door" seems to indicate the use of "taboo sticks." The fact that we could not discover any devices for fastening these sticks across the doorways of private houses shows that further discount must be made of Don Mancio's powers of observation. Nevertheless he could hardly have invented the stick idea, and it is possible the clan group were protected against intruders merely by the fear of stepping over a barrier sanctified by custom and fortified by superstition.

The lintels to some of these clan-group gateways have fallen down in the course of time but in the majority of the places where they remain an eye-bonder was found anchored in the wall on top of the lintel at right angles to it and projecting sufficiently so that the hole in the eye-bonder was outside of the surface of the lintel. It is entirely possible, therefore, that the taboo stick theory is not correct and that some form of gate or door was used, which may have consisted of a wooden frame or screen made of logs tied together with rope, braced with crosspieces, and kept in place by two logs crossing each other at right angles, as shown in Mr. Bumstead's drawing (Fig. 50b). An upright post, probably set into a shallow hole in the ground in the middle of the entrance, could have been fastened at the top to the eye-bonder over the lintel. None of the doors to individual houses had this locking device but all the entrances to the family or clan

52. ONE OF THE SACRED ROCKS

Surrounded by a stone platform. This particular bowlder is fifteen
feet high and thirty feet long, but only two feet thick.

groups had it, and the same device occurs in the gateposts of the City Gate. From these facts the conclusion may be drawn that while there was common ownership within the family group which occupied the compound, and hence no desire to provide any device for securing doors to houses, there was no intention of allowing free access at all times to outsiders.

Within the enclosures of most of the clan groups at Machu Picchu are generally to be found large bowlders or crags, in which seats or small platforms were usually cut. We learn from the early Spanish writers that the Incas were ancestor worshipers and supposed that their most distinguished departed forebears took up their residence in large rocks. Hence it is to be presumed that these bowlders were really altars, the center of ancestor worship, and that the seats or little platforms cut in their surfaces were intended for the reception of offerings, probably of food and drink.

Each of the compounds, with one exception, differs from the others either in the arrangement of its buildings or in some distinctive feature of its architecture. One of them is characterized by very unusual niches. In one of the houses there are two niches large enough to permit an Indian to stand in them, and in the back wall of each niche is a small window at the height of an Indian's face. The shrine of this group, which we called Unusual Niches Group, was built on a picturesque crag, the side walls of

53b. THE SNAKE WINDOW
IN THE
SEMICIRCULAR TEMPLE
Cf. Fig. 64.

53a. THE TEMPLE
BUILT
ON A ROCK

One of the buildings
in the Unusual Niches Group,
with its wall
laid on a foundation of rock
that is tilted nearly forty degrees
from the horizontal,
and without the use of
either mortar or cement.

54. NICHES WITHIN NICHES

In the Unusual Niches Group, with bar-holds for closing them.

the temple being locked into the sloping surface of the rock in a very interesting manner, as is shown in the photograph (Fig. 53a). Into the top of the rock the usual stone platform was cut. Above it were three niches, each large enough to receive a huddled-up Peruvian mummy. It was the custom in mummifying a body to draw the knees up to the chin so as to make the mummy take up as little room as possible. Mummies had multifarious wrappings and look not unlike small barrels, the final wrapping in some cases consisting of yards and yards of braided rope. Each of these niches was large enough to receive such a bundle. Furthermore, each had two unusual features, bar-holds on both sides of the entrance to each niche and three little inner niches, one placed on the back wall of the niche and one on each of the two side walls. It seems to me probable that the large niches were intended for the reception of the mummies of chiefs; that the little niches inside of each niche were for the reception of offerings, articles presumed to be of value and interest to the departed; and that by means of the bar-holds taboo sticks could have been fastened in front of each niche to ward off any interference with the mummy or its articles of value. The long stone platform carved into the solid rock immediately below the niches was probably intended to receive offerings of food and drink; or the mummies may have been placed there to dry in the sun.

Another clan group, characterized by particularly ingenious stone-

55. THE MOST INGENIOUS LOCK IN MACHU PICCHU

Ingenuity Group. Here the lock-hole was cut out of the same
block of stone as the bar-hold.
Cf. Fig. 48a.

cutting, I have called Ingenuity Group (for plan, see Fig. 49). Here the
bar-holds of the principal gateway were themselves cut out of the heart
of solid granite ashlars. The top of the bar-hold was set into a saucer-
shaped depression in a member of the next course above, but the base of
the bar-hold formed a part of the ashlar in which it was cut. Access to the
bar-hold was gained by cutting a square hole in the center of the face of
the ashlar. Surely it was not only an ingenious but a patient and devoted
stonecutter who would have taken the trouble to make such a neat con-
trivance for securing permanency in the bar-holds of his compound. Excavations in the principal house of Ingenuity Group yielded pieces of eight
pots and brought to light the tops of two granite bowlders which originally
projected above the level of the floor. These bowlders were carved into
useful kitchen utensils, unbreakable and always in place,—mortars, where
maize could be ground and potatoes mashed under the smooth-faced
mullers or rocking-stones which have been in use throughout the central
Andes since time immemorial. Near the mortars we actually found one
of the ancient mullers which had been rocked here centuries ago. The
wife of the chief of Ingenuity Group must have enjoyed a sense of su-
periority over her neighbors who, in making their corn meal, had no such

56b. A MONOLITHIC STAIRWAY

With not only the steps,
but the balustrades as well,
cut out of a single stone.
It leads from Ingenuity Group
to Private Garden Group.

56a. "BUILT-IN" MORTARS

Carved out of bowlders
in the floor of a house
in Ingenuity Group.
Lying near one of these
was the original rocking muller,
which the boy
in the photograph is holding.

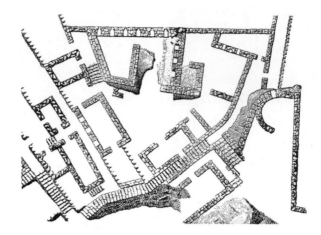

57a. PLAN OF UNUSUAL NICHES
GROUP

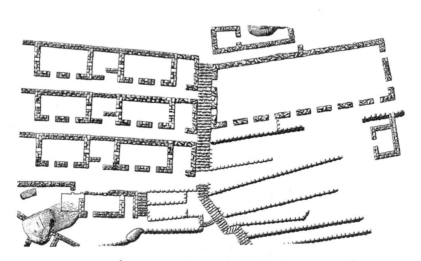

57b. PLAN OF HOUSES EAST OF
INGENUITY GROUP

permanent conveniences built into their kitchens. This group also contains several stone benches. No other houses of this group yielded any potsherds, but one had a stone couch, built up in a corner, as though someone here preferred not to be always sleeping and sitting on the ground.

In this group is the only example in the city of a large gabled building divided into two sections by a party wall rising to the peak, pierced with three windows. This type, so rare here, is common enough at Choqquequirau and Ollantaytambo. On the rougher, interior walls of some of the houses of this compound several square yards of surface still remain covered with reddish clay. One of these houses had been selected a few years ago by Richarte or one of his friends as a good structure to be repaired and roofed for use, but was abandoned, perhaps because it proved too large for the necessities of a modern Indian family. It was certainly much too far from water. It may have served as a temporary structure for use while engaged in cultivating the near-by pampa.

Subsidiary to Ingenuity Group and opening through it is another compound which we named Private Garden Group (for plan, see Fig. 19). Access to the small garden terraces near its houses could be had only by passing through the compound, although each terrace wall except the lowest was provided with a flight of steps, each step made of a projecting stone bonder.

One of the stairways in Ingenuity Group is fantastically wedged in between two huge granite rocks which are so close together that it would have been impossible for a fat man to use the stairway at all. In another flight, one of those leading from Ingenuity Group to Private Garden Group, not only the steps of the stairway but also the balustrades were cut out of a single ledge. Considering the fact that the only tools obtainable were cobblestones of diorite and other compact pebbles which could be obtained in the bed of the roaring rapids two thousand feet below, it must have taken somebody who had spare time a good many months to carve these steps out of the living rock. At any rate, the worker had the satisfaction of knowing that his work would achieve something as near immortality as anything created by the hands of man. (See Fig. 56b.)

The walls of the buildings of Private Garden Group are of very roughly squared stones laid in clay in irregular courses, yet the terrace on which they were built is faced with unusually large ashlars nicely joined, presumably the work of an earlier period. Before the more recent wall was constructed a small conduit was cut into the top of one of the fine old

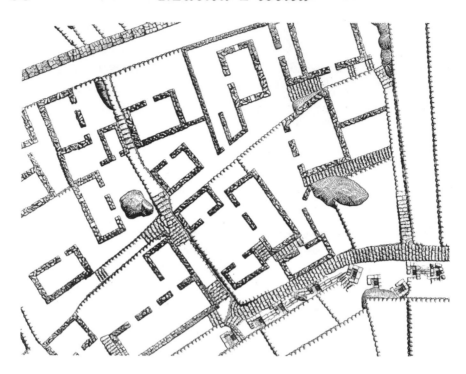

58. LOWER NINE FOUNTAINS AND AZEQUIA

The little stone-lined aqueduct may be traced
from the lowest fountain to the moat.

blocks of the retaining wall so as to permit the courtyard of this compound to be properly drained. The builders of Machu Picchu were careful about drainage and guarded against the accumulation of ground water wherever it was not wanted. If the top of the retaining wall of a terrace was level with the surface of the ground, no pools would collect and conduits were not provided. If it was necessary to continue the retaining wall above the level of the ground, for purposes of defense, as in the principal wall of the citadel, or as a screen, as in the walls of certain courtyards, small channels or conduits were always constructed so as to insure good drainage.

The basins of the Stairway of the Fountains, already referred to on page 48, are usually cut out of a single block of granite which was placed on a level with the floor of a little enclosure into which the water carriers came to fill the narrow-necked water jars. Frequently one or two little niches were constructed in the side walls of the enclosures as a shelf for a cup or possibly for the stoppers of the bottles, made of fiber or twisted bunches of grass. Sometimes a small lip was cut in the stone at the end of the conduit so as to form a little spout, thus enabling the water to fall clear of the back wall of the fountain. In other cases the water would usually pass through the narrow orifice with sufficient force to reach the opening of the jar without the necessity of the carrier dipping the water from the basin. In times of water scarcity, however, we may be sure that the latter method was followed, and that the reason for the sixteen basins was not only in order to permit many jars to be filled at once but to keep the all too precious fluid from escaping. There never could have been very much water on the mountain side. The *azequia* is narrower than any I have ever seen anywhere else, being generally less than four inches in width. (See Fig. 58.)

The little stone basins are about thirty inches long by eighteen inches wide and from five to six inches in depth. In some places both the basin and the entire floor of the fountain enclosure are made of a single slab of granite. Sometimes holes were drilled in one corner of the basin to permit the water to flow through carefully cut underground conduits to the next basin below. In case of necessity these holes could easily have been plugged up to permit the basin to fill. The conduits run sometimes under the stairway and sometimes at its side. It is perhaps worth noting that the modern Peruvians call these fountains *baños,* baths, but it does not seem to me likely that they were used for this purpose. On account of the rarefied air, the cold, and the rapid radiation, even Anglo-Saxons do not need to bathe frequently in the Peruvian highlands and the Indians of today never bathe. It is hardly to be supposed, therefore, that the builders of Machu Picchu used these basins for such a purpose. On the other hand, the Incas were fond of making easy the work of the water carriers and of providing them with nicely constructed fountains.

The highest of the fountains is in a remarkable group which, for convenience, I have called the Group of the Royal Mausoleum. Its most striking feature is a semicircular temple perched on top of a great rock, in the construction of which great care and ingenuity were used to secure solidity and permanence. A portion of the top of the rock was cut away so that the ashlars of the lower course, which are more irregular than any others in the structure, could be keyed into the ledge. They are held firmly in place by a hooklike portion of the great rock, which was left when part of the surface was cut away. The second course is also slightly irregular in order to enable the largest ashlar to be heeled into a corner of the underlying hook which was left projecting above the first row of ashlars for

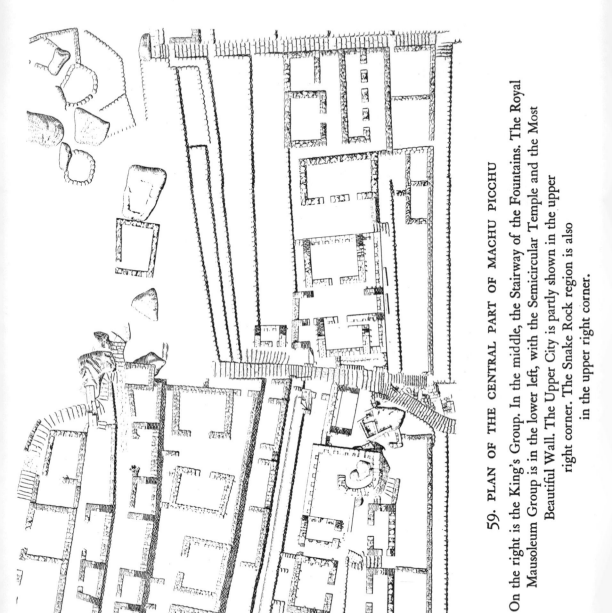

59. PLAN OF THE CENTRAL PART OF MACHU PICCHU

On the right is the King's Group. In the middle, the Stairway of the Fountains. The Royal Mausoleum Group is in the lower left, with the Semicircular Temple and the Most Beautiful Wall. The Upper City is partly shown in the upper right corner. The Snake Rock region is also in the upper right corner.

60. CORNER OF THE ROYAL MAUSOLEUM GROUP

Where the Semicircular Temple joins the Beautiful Wall, commanding
a magnificent view of the canyon. Note the altar within
the temple, partly destroyed by fire.

this purpose. Having thus assured themselves of a stable foundation tightly
locked into the living rock, the builders then proceeded to lay the ashlars
in regular courses. Modern builders would hardly think it possible to
anchor a masonry wall to a rocky crag without the use of metal clamps
and the best grade of cement, yet the builders of Machu Picchu used
neither. In fact, although they were unfamiliar with the principle of the
arch and its keystone, they understood the art of keying a wall together
by using irregular members better than any other builders in the world—
then or now. The walls of this temple follow exactly the rather flat curve
of the rock, the line of general inclination of the wall being perfect in
every block. Each ashlar has been cut with such exquisite care that the
temple seems to have grown naturally on top of the granite ledge. The
stonecutting reaches a perfection which has never been surpassed and is
only equaled in the celebrated wall, also a flattened curve, of the Temple
of the Sun, now the Dominican Monastery, in Cuzco (see p. 232).

Under the ledge is a cave which seems to have been enlarged and fitted
up as a royal tomb. The entrance to the cave is lined with irregular ashlars
fitted into the natural fissures of the ledge in a manner which surpasses belief, and the walls of the tomb itself are lined with nicely cut ashlars. On
the far side of the tomb is a stone bench which may have been intended as

61. INTERIOR OF THE CAVE UNDER THE
SEMICIRCULAR TEMPLE

Royal Mausoleum Group, possibly the burial place of Pachacuti VI,
last of the Amauta dynasty. See page 223.

a resting place for mummies. In the walls of the tomb are four large niches, two of them on the same level as the bench. None of the other tombs found in the caves of Machu Picchu compares for a moment with this one in beauty or splendor. Obviously, this cave was intended to receive the mummies of the rulers of the citadel—possibly that one in particular whose memory was worshiped at the stone altar within the Semicircular Temple overhead.

In honor doubtless of this same exalted personage, the most experienced master mason of the time constructed the most beautiful wall in America, built in the form of a try-square, and connecting the temple with the priest's house. This wall is made of carefully matched ashlars, of white granite especially selected for its pure color and fine grain. The interior surface of the wall is broken by niches and square projecting stones or pegs. The exterior is perfectly simple, yet we grew more fond of it than of any other structure at Machu Picchu. At first sight it would appear to be merely a simple wall of carefully dressed ashlars laid in regular courses, not absolutely perpendicular but sloping gently inward as it rose from the ground. The lower courses, of particularly large ashlars, give a look of massive security to the foundations, while the upper courses, gradually de-

62b. THE MOST
BEAUTIFUL WALL
IN AMERICA
NORTHWEST CORNER

62a. A DETAIL
OF THE
BEAUTIFUL WALL

Showing the ingenious
stone fitting, which,
unaided by mortar or cement,
kept the ashlars keyed together
at the point
of greatest strain.

creasing in size toward the top, lend grace and delicacy to the structure. Apparently of rectangular blocks, there is not a mathematically correct right angle or straight line in the entire wall, the builder having no instruments of precision. Nevertheless, the effect is softer and more pleasing, if less splendid, than that of the marble temples of the Old World. Since this wall was obviously built with the utmost care by an artist who desired it to be a permanent object of beauty, it was necessary that there should be no cracks in it, that the seams between the closely fitting ashlars should never open. Yet at the south end of the wall was the priest's dwelling, a two-story-and-a-half house, its second floor opening onto the terrace which supported the Beautiful Wall, its lower floor opening onto the next terrace below. In the course of time such a house, whose attic was entirely above the level of the Beautiful Wall, would tend to lean away from the wall, and the seams would open. Consequently the stone mason ingeniously keyed the ashlars together at the point where the greatest strain would occur, by altering the pattern from one which is virtually rectangular to one containing hookstones, thus making a series of braces which would prevent the ashlars from slipping and keep the house from leaning away from the ornamental wall. The result was successful: although this is a land where earthquakes are not uncommon and the builders used neither cement nor metal clamp, each ashlar still fits snugly into its neighbors and there is scarcely a place where a pin could be inserted between the stones (Fig. 62a).

Keying or locking a wall by the irregularity of its own well-fitting members may be said to have been a lost art, even in Peru, since the days of the Spanish Conquest. Attempts to restore one of these old lashed-in masonry walls are never completely successful even though all the units exist. I believe that part of the secret was the use of a very thin film of the finest clay which, although eventually of the thickness of a sheet of paper, prevented the outer faces of the ashlars from chipping and flaking at the point of contact. It is also true that the ashlars are never mathematically correct geometrical figures. One never finds cubes or rectangular parallelepipeds. Although the outer face of the ashlar may look like a parallelogram, examination will show that it never is a parallelogram as accurate as those found commonly in modern stone structures. The interior angles are even less likely to be mathematically rectangular. It need hardly be said that a granite wall composed of mathematically correct parallelepipeds would not last long in an earthquake country unless good cement

63a. SEMICIRCULAR TEMPLE AND BEAUTIFUL WALL, LOOKING TOWARD KING'S GROUP AND STAIRWAY NEAR PRIVATE GARDEN GROUP

63b. ROYAL MAUSOLEUM GROUP ON THE LEFT, WITH SEMICIRCULAR TEMPI OVER ROYAL BURIAL CAVE; ON THE RIGHT, STAIRWAY OF THE FOUNTAINS; KING'S GROUP, WITH HIGH GABLES ON THE EXTREME RIGH

or metal clamps were used, and even then, a vigorous shake would be sure to open cracks in the walls. The only modern wall which can withstand an earthquake is one which is a unit in itself, either of some flexible material or of reënforced concrete. So successful, however, were the builders of this citadel in keying their walls together into a solid mass that the only cracks observable in the best walls are those caused by settling. The foundations usually rested on earth, and not on carefully prepared rock.

The slope of this Beautiful Wall is characteristic of practically all the walls in the ruins and even of the vertical lines of doors, windows, and niches. All are "Egyptian style," narrower at the top than at the bottom. The origin of this would seem to lie in the fact that a sloping wall is easier to build than a perpendicular wall, yet the builders of this citadel had sufficient skill to have enabled them to construct perpendicular walls whenever they so desired. The custom was therefore probably due to the fact that the walls which first required the most careful workmanship were the retaining walls of agricultural terraces, where such a slope is a distinct advantage.

As has been said, the Beautiful Wall connects the priest's house with the temple on top of the rock over the cave tomb. The temple contains the family altar—actually the uppermost part of the great rock on which the semicircular building rests and beneath which there appears to have been a royal mausoleum. The altar is carved into seats or stone platforms.

When subject to great heat the surface of granite bowlders flakes off in shells around the point where the greatest heat strikes the stone. An examination of the top of the bowlder which occupies most of the space within the Semicircular Temple and of the adjacent walls shows that at some time or other a really extraordinary amount of heat must have been applied. Absence of ashes and pieces of charcoal would indicate that this took place a very long time ago, probably long before the building of the valley road and the advent of the first modern Indians. It is difficult to account for all the flaking which has taken place unless it was caused by repeated fires or by one in which the fuel was often replenished, and it is impossible to believe that the damage was done by burning an ordinary thatched roof. Were it not that the upper courses of the Semicircular Temple indicate the former presence of a roof one might suppose that this had been verily a place of burnt offerings.

In this temple are three windows. Two of them look out over the valley; each is about the size of an ordinary niche, about two feet in height,

64. A CLOSER VIEW OF THE SNAKE WINDOW
Cf. Fig. 53b.

the façade being decorated with four nubbins, one at each end of lintel and sill. These may have been supports for an exterior blind; they may have been merely ornaments. There are no others like them.

The third window in the Semicircular Temple is larger than the others and offers much food for thought and speculation; in other words, it is what archaeologists commonly call "problematical." Its beautiful monolithic lintel was cracked by the heat of the fires which took place long previous to our visit, and part of it has fallen—further evidence that it was no small conflagration that so ravaged the temple. The sill of this window is most unusual, broken as it is by two flights of steps, facing each other. These steps contain a little labyrinth of holes and very small passages or channels less than an inch in diameter which lead to cavities cut out of the blocks in the interior of the wall. The openings to these channels vary in size; some are two inches in diameter. Other similar holes lead nowhere, and some of the passages have less conspicuous openings. The channels are large enough to permit the passage of a chameleon or other small lizard. Lizards, however, are not common at Machu Picchu. The holes within the wall are unnecessarily large for lizards' nests but they are of the right size for a comfortable nest for a small snake. As has been said, there are many snakes in this vicinity, in fact they are sufficiently numerous to have given it a bad reputation among the natives. Moreover, several of the large rocks within the city have carvings on them which represent serpents, and one of the pots, a lebes-shaped kettle with band-shaped handles (Fig. 71), is decorated with two snakes in relief, an example of the so-called Barbotine technique. Although I admit that this curious window offers a problem extremely difficult of solution, it seems to me barely possible that the priest of the Semicircular Temple kept a few small tame snakes and that he may have used their chance exits out of one hole or another as a means of telling omens and possibly of determining the proper course of future events. If the snake theory prove untenable, it may be suggested that possibly the spirits of the ancestral gods who were worshiped in this temple were supposed to speak through these openings, although in this case it is a little difficult to understand why cavities were left at the ends of the passages. Another possible theory is that *chicha*, the most highly desired native beverage, may have been offered to the spirits by being poured through these openings into the interior of the wall, where the god of the temple might presumably have dwelt. In this event, however, it is a little difficult to see why small exits were left, through which the *chicha* could have run out beneath the lower steps. Altogether the problem is a fascinating one and is still unsolved. On several of the Inca walls in Cuzco may be seen carved snakes, both incised and in relief. In the Temple of the Sun, now the Dominican Monastery, which it will be remembered has a semicircular building similar to this, in that it follows the lines of a flattened curve, I noticed holes similar to these. They are in a portion of the wall which cannot be further examined but it is presumable that they also lead to inner cavities. At Machu Picchu we should never have discovered the inner cavities and the little labyrinth of tiny passages had it not been for the ruinous state of the window sill. Owing to the conflagration already spoken of, the steps of the window sill were badly cracked; some of them, indeed, had fallen down and were found in the course of our excavations.

There are two gateways to the Royal Mausoleum Group. The inner one is a beautiful specimen of stonework and seems to have had a stone roof (see Fig. 28b). Its bar-holds are integral parts of the stone blocks of the gateway as in the Ingenuity Group, but here the bar-hold is carved at the surface of the ashlar instead of being cut out of its interior. This group is further distinguished by containing the only house in the citadel consisting of two and a half stories. Notwithstanding the skill with which most of the stones in the temple, the wall, and the two-story house were finished,

65b. DOORWAY IN THE KING'S GROUP

Noteworthy for its monolithic lintel, which weighed about three tons.

65a. GATEWAY TO THE INGENUITY GROUP

Showing steps and re-entrant angles. Exterior view.

the gable end of the house is of rough stones laid in adobe and the ashlars in the uppermost two courses of the Semicircular Temple are roughly finished and not fitted together. This is characteristic of every structure that was undoubtedly roofed. No matter how fine the walls of a house, that portion of the wall which would come immediately under the eaves and the gable ends is never nicely fitted together but always laid in adobe. This may have been to facilitate fastening the rafters to the wall, or it may have been due to the fact that the earliest houses did not have gable ends. (I do not remember seeing a single ancient Inca gable in the city of Cuzco, although they are common in Ollantaytambo and other places.)

Our excavations in this group yielded practically nothing, but on the terraces just below, the old rubbish piles contained pieces of more than two hundred pots. A few had been thrown over into the dry moat. Not a house in the three best groups contained a thing; evidently the former owners were good housekeepers and insisted on broken pots being taken away to the rubbish piles.

Across the great stairway from the Royal Mausoleum Group is a compound which I have called the King's Group because of the extremely solid character of the walls which enclose it, and also because it seems as though no one but a king could have insisted on having the lintels of the doorways to his houses made of great solid blocks of granite each weighing about three tons. In the other compounds the houses almost invariably have duolithic lintels, but in this group the chief had sufficient power to overcome the mechanical difficulties involved in placing a monolithic three-ton lintel on top of his doorposts and fitting it accurately to them. Had he possessed cranes, pulleys, and steam winches, he would have found it no easy task, but since he had none of these things and must have built up a solid inclined plane side by side with the wall as it rose, to permit him to locate these great blocks with levers, it staggers the imagination to realize what a prodigious amount of patient effort he employed. The gables of the houses in this group are also unusually steep. No buildings in Machu Picchu except the temple opposite had such fine walls as the King's Group, yet the stones of the gables were not fitted together but were laid in adobe, according to the usual custom (see Figs. 44 and 45a). Nothing was found in the excavation in this group, but fragments of many pots were taken from the stairway just outside.

CHAPTER V

⸺◆⸺

THE RESULTS OF A STUDY OF THE
BURIAL CAVES

THE day after Richarte and his friends had reported the discovery of "eight burial caves," Dr. Eaton and I followed them across the city and plunged down the wooded slope on the eastern side of the ridge until we reached an artificial cave where our guides proudly pointed to a skull. As Dr. Eaton says in his report:

In this cave and in a good many others similar to it, human remains were well protected by the bowlders from rain and surface water, sufficient ventilation being had through the interstices of the loosely constructed wall to insure the preservation of the bones, long after the mummy wrappings and softer human tissues had disintegrated. The protecting wall was stout enough to keep out all the larger mammals that might otherwise enter and scatter the contents of the grave, and . . . the burial place was so well screened that chance visitors to the region might pass within a few feet of the cave without seeing it.*

When the protecting wall had been carefully removed the bones of its sole occupant were found to be

those of a woman about thirty-five years of age. The skull, which had fallen on its side, is of the broad and short type (brachycephalic) that is generally regarded as characteristic of the Peruvians of the middle coast region. The burial had evidently been made in the contracted position, that is to say, with the legs flexed and the knees drawn up close under the chin. In fact the larger bones of the legs still protruded from the ground in that position. . . . A long narrow splinter of stone that had probably been dislodged from the front wall rested across the lower jaw. Other bones lay on the ground just where they had fallen when the skeleton dropped apart. No metal articles were found with the remains, and no pottery was obtained inside the cave, but the sherds of the following earthenware vessels were found at the surface of a pile of earth and small stones that partially concealed the protecting wall: Two beaker-shaped ollas or

* "The Collection of Osteological Material from Machu Picchu," *Memoirs of the Connecticut Academy of Arts and Sciences*, Vol. V, May, 1916.

66. CAVE NO. I AND FIRST SKELETON FOUND AT
MACHU PICCHU

After partial excavation, showing skeleton in position.

cooking pots, fire-blackened on their bases and sides from long use, one large two-handled dish and a medium-sized dish of the same form.

In the second cave I found fragments of two small adult skulls but no pottery or bronzes. In the third cave, my joy knew no bounds when I was able to lay hands for the first time at Machu Picchu on a perfect piece of Inca pottery. It was an excellent specimen of a two-handled dish, nicely decorated. This cave was divided into two parts by a stone wall. The outer section contained the skeleton of a "woman of about thirty-five years of age, the skull being of the oblong type usually found in the mountain regions. While the skeleton is of robust proportions, necrosis of the right maxilla has been associated with alveolar abscess, and the left femur shows an extensive (syphilitic) periostitis."

Encouraged by what we had found in the first three caves the work was continued until our ambitious Indian guides had covered every accessible—and many seemingly inaccessible—parts of Huayna Picchu and Machu Picchu Mountains and the ridge between. As the burial caves were more or less covered with dense tropical jungle, the work of visiting and excavating them was extremely arduous, but practically every square rod of the side of the ridge was explored, the last caves opened being very near

67. CAVE NO. I

From a distance of twenty feet, to illustrate the difficulty of finding
the burial places. Entrance near the center of the photograph.

the Urubamba River. In some of the caves only the most fragmentary
skeletal remains were found; in others only the larger bones and a skull or
two. Dr. Eaton says:

The imperfect state of several of the human skeletons found at Machu Picchu
appears to have been due to some cause other than the natural process of decay,
and offers an interesting problem in connection with the mortuary customs of
the place. The most plausible way of accounting for the loss of certain parts
from a skeleton, as a skull, a lower jaw, or bones of a limb, is on the supposition
that these portions may have become separated and misplaced or lost, either
during the removal of the mummies from temporary mortuaries to their final
burial places or else during some festival, when, according to custom, the mummies were taken from houses and graves, and after being washed and perhaps
decked in new clothes and wrappings were given places of honor as silent witnesses of various ceremonies.

Other caves contained not only nearly complete skeletons, but pots in a
more or less perfect state of preservation, and occasionally pieces of bronze.
In this way a large and valuable collection was made of human skeletons,
pottery, and other artifacts of various materials, including some of the
tools probably used by the Inca or pre-Inca stone masons in the more intricate parts of their work. The custom seems to have been, whenever possible, to bury the dead in the sitting position, with the knees raised. In a

68. CAVE NO. 10, BY FLASHLIGHT

very few instances bodies were interred in crudely fashioned "bottle-shaped graves."

Usually the last residents of Machu Picchu buried their dead in caves. Since the number of available places was limited, they used both natural and artificial caves. Projecting ledges, overhanging bowlders, and other rock shelters were taken advantage of in the effort to secure a relatively dry, safe place for the reception of the mummy bundle. The front of the cave was sometimes, though rarely, closed by a roughly built wall of rocks and earth. When this wall was in good condition the bones of the skeleton were generally found lying on the surface of the cave floor, or in the shallow humus, just as they had fallen when the mummy wrappings decayed. Near the bones were often found artifacts, usually pottery, more rarely bone implements or pieces of bronze. When the wall was in poor condition so that treasure hunters or wild beasts, bears or members of the cat family, could have entered, the bones and potsherds were likely to be found strewn about the cave or even outside the protecting wall. Sometimes the bodies had been actually buried underground, and then the front of the cave would be merely marked by a low wall or rough terrace. Some caves were divided into two or more compartments by thin partitions of irregular rock walls.

The region near the first burial caves we opened I shall refer to as Cemetery No. 1. It lay halfway down the mountain side, northeast of the city, on the edge of a precipice eight hundred feet above the river. Under the bowlders and ledges of this region the remains of about fifty individuals were found. Nearly all of them have been determined by Dr. Eaton to be female, only four being clearly male. In the first twelve caves to be opened in this cemetery all the bones appear to have been those of women, and it would almost seem as though it was a women's cemetery.

A thousand feet south of the first cave, in a region east of the city, and from two to six hundred feet below the end of the principal stairway, we found another group of burial caves, Cemetery No. 2. It lies near the end of the outer city wall; in fact, one of the caves was only about a hundred yards from the lowest house. Here the remains of some 50 individuals were found. Of those taken out under Dr. Eaton's supervision, only 4 or 5 appear to have been male, and 15 more caves opened after his departure contained the remains of 2 men, 13 women and 3 babies. Hence in this cemetery the females seem to outnumber the males about 8 to 1. There was also evidence of earlier burials having been disturbed to provide room for later ones, probably due in part to the convenient location near the foot of the main stairs.

Cemetery No. 3 is on the northern slopes of Machu Picchu Mountain, above the ruins. At the nine-thousand-foot contour is a very large cave, thirty feet long and fifteen feet wide, which, although containing a walled-up grave, seems to have been used as a primitive dwelling or rock shelter. There was no protecting wall in front of it, but the sides and back had been nicely finished off with neatly laid stone walls. These walls may have been intended to give a sort of finish to the cave or possibly to act as partial insurance that the huge bowlder, a portion of whose flat under surface forms the roof of the shelter, would not settle down on the occupants. We thought at first that the back wall was merely a partition, setting off another mortuary chamber, but nothing was found behind it. Had this immense rock shelter been used as a mausoleum we should undoubtedly have found bones lying about on the floor, in addition to the large number of potsherds which were in evidence. Since, however, no human bones were found except those in the walled-up grave at one end of the cave, it seems to me quite likely that this fine dry cave should have been once occupied as a temporary shelter for workmen engaged in neighboring quarries, or carriers who had occasion to use the old Inca road not far away. Another suggestion is that it may have been a "mortuary chapel" used for ceremonies in connection with neighboring burial caves, more than a dozen of which were discovered in this immediate vicinity.

Late in the season I was conducted by Richarte along a narrow and dangerous trail under the cliffs, on the west side of Huayna Picchu, to a very large cave, nearly ninety feet in length and partly lined with walls of cut stone. It could have been used as a shelter for a considerable number of people, and it might have been used as a burial cave. On account of its accessibility from the lower slopes of Huayna Picchu, which can easily be approached at low water, it had probably long been known to Melchor Arteaga and other Indian treasure hunters of the neighborhood. Nevertheless it was new to Richarte and he was greatly excited by its discovery, thinking that it was going to yield him a rich return in the way of bonuses and prizes. Greatly to his disappointment, although a grave or two were found near by, the cave contained nothing at all, not even a bone. The entire absence of skeletal remains would seem to indicate that it had probably been used as a rock shelter by workmen engaged in cultivating the fields of Huayna Picchu rather than as a burial cave.

Of the last ten graves to be found, only one was within the limits of any of the three cemeteries; in fact eight of them were from widely separated locations far from the city. That the hunters were finally driven to go so far afield and penetrate such difficult areas would seem to indicate that the three cemeteries had been thoroughly explored and all caves within easy reach of the city carefully examined. A careful count of the skeletal material found in the various caves and graves seems to show the remains of 173 individuals. A comparison of the three important burial cave regions or cemeteries leads to the following conclusions, based upon the reports of the field parties and the study of their finds. In Cemetery No. 1 skeletons represented 52 individuals, of whom 4 were certainly of the male sex. In Cemetery No. 2 we found the remains of 49 individuals, of whom 3 and possibly more were males. In Cemetery No. 3 were 43 individuals, of whom 11 were males. Within the limits of the city or on its terraces were found 8, of whom 3 were males. Scattered at various points over the mountain side and not included in any of the other groups were found 21 individuals, of whom 4 or 5 were males. With the 52 individuals in Cemetery No. 1 were the remains of some 85 pieces of identifiable pottery. With the 49 individuals in Cemetery No. 2 were the remains of some 162 pots. With the 43 individuals in Cemetery No. 3 were found the remains of some 101 pots. With the 21 individuals whose graves were widely scattered there were found pieces of 16 pots.

The cemetery containing the largest number of pots per person is the one nearest to and most accessible from the ruins of the city. It would seem

69. A BOWLDER, WITH PLATFORMS FOR OFFERINGS
Lying over one of the burial caves.

likely that this would be the one most used, yet only about the same number (49) of skeletons were found here as in the slightly more remote No. 1 (52). On the other hand, about twice as many pots were found here. The reason for this would seem to lie in the possibility that many of these potsherds represented the garniture of burials which had taken place so long ago that all of the bone material had disintegrated. This hypothesis is borne out by the fact that in the rocky region south and southwest of the Sacred Plaza, probably an ancient burial ground from which nearly all the skeletal material had disappeared, a very large number of potsherds were found, from which we have been able to identify 521 different pots, including specimens of every one of the 18 principal types known to Machu Picchu. Although nearly all the burial caves contained pieces of pottery none of them yielded a fragment of a three-legged brazier. Probably the people whose bones were found in the caves did not use the braziers, the metal workers being undoubtedly men.

The art of trepanning seems to have been rather widely practiced in ancient Peru. Consequently there is considerable food for reflection in the fact that none of the more than one hundred burial caves opened on the sides of Machu Picchu and Huayna Picchu contained a single trepanned skull. Yet practically all the large burial caves which we have opened in the Urubamba or Pampaccahuana valleys within a distance of thirty miles contained a number of trepanned skulls.* Evidently the warriors whose wounds required this treatment did not live at Machu Picchu and were not buried in the neighboring caves, most of the skeletons found here being those of women or children. In the first 52 graves opened under the supervision of Dr. Eaton only 10 contained male skeletons. After Dr. Eaton's departure, the work was continued by the same Indian helpers under Mr. Erdis' supervision. As the latter's presence was required within the city walls, the location of most of these later discoveries could be known only approximately from the accounts given orally to Mr. Erdis at the end of the day. In the first 25 caves thus investigated the remains of 10 male individuals were found, or as many as in the first 52. In their second 25 they found only 5 male skeletons. The reason for this curious result seems to lie in the fact that the Indian helpers, Richarte and Alvarez, anxious for gratuities and thinking that the three cemeteries had been pretty thoroughly explored by Dr. Eaton, immediately went further afield after he left and found a number of caves scattered over the mountain side and variously described by them as being "about 500 yards southerly from the camp," "500 yards southeasterly from camp," "600 yards south of our camp and above the level of the rock-sheltered terrace," "halfway down the mountain side, northeast of the city, and near the foot of Huayna Picchu," "two-thirds of the way up Machu Picchu mountain," "halfway up Machu Picchu mountain," "one mile southeast from the city, in a saddle of the Machu Picchu mountain," and "at the foot of the hill east of the city." In these lonesome spots, most of them at a considerable distance from the regular cemeteries, they found a dozen male interments. When they wearied of the superhuman efforts required in the location and investigation of caves scattered widely over the jungle-clad, precipitous slopes, many of which yielded no results, they returned to the more accessible cemeteries and succeeded in finding a score or more of graves which had escaped their first efforts. Yet only two of these contained remains which could with certainty be referred to men.

Still more puzzling was the discovery by Mr. Erdis of two burial caves only two hundred feet from the Main City Gate and lying west and northwest of it, the only graves found on the western side of the city. Both these caves contained the remains of men.

Very little skeletal material was found within the city, though a female

---

* It should be noted that many of the so-called "trepanned skulls" are claimed by competent surgeons to show more evidence of disease than of surgery.

skull was discovered under a bowlder about 250 feet south of the Principal Temple. We did find, near the Sacred Plaza, several caves which probably contained mummies at one time or another, and a stone-lined bottle-shaped grave, but all were empty. It is impossible to say whether they were despoiled by the first treasure seekers who visited the city in the middle of the eighteenth century or whether they were emptied long before that. I incline to the latter view because of the extreme unlikelihood of treasure seekers caring to remove every single bone, and the fact that in this humid subtropical climate mummies and mummy wrappings would not last long enough to make them commercially valuable, as they are when found in the cemeteries of the arid Peruvian coastal desert.

The bones of the men who built Machu Picchu have disappeared. Some may have been buried elsewhere. Of those who died in this immediate vicinity, probably all vestige has been lost. The bones of the more recent dwellers in the citadel show them to have been mostly women, since of all the remains that we found only 22 could be definitely called adult males. On the other hand, 125 were women and children. These were divided as follows: adult females, 102; young females, 7; infants, 5; young males, 4; young persons of unknown sex, 7. The sex of 17 adults could not be determined. Cemetery No. 1 contained only 2 adult males, Cemetery No. 2 contained 4, Cemetery No. 3 contained 4. Evidently, then, men were not absolutely excluded from these burial regions. On the other hand, female remains were found in the more scattered graves. There is nothing to lead one to suppose that we overlooked a "men's cemetery." The truth seems to be that although it must have required an enormous amount of powerful labor to construct the temples and palaces, fountains and stairways, the last people to live here were men "of inferior physical development" and women, many of whom, representing persons of both highland and coastal descent, pertain to what may be termed "a refined, high-bred physical type." Dr. Eaton is

strongly inclined to the opinion that during the late pre-Columbian and early post-Columbian periods of occupation, the Inca Empire maintained at Machu Picchu, one of those convent-like establishments known as Acclahuasicuna, and that the female skeletons found in such predominance are largely the remains of Virgins of the Sun and priestesses engaged in the service of the temple. Another hypothesis is that the human remains obtained here represent a population in which the normal proportion of the sexes was modified by the withdrawal from the community of most of the active males, to take part in military operations. . . . With few exceptions the men buried here were individuals of inferior physical development, men who fell far short of the generally accepted definition of the warrior type. This, however, is a condition that would as naturally obtain in a priest-ridden holy city as in a city depleted during war-time of its able-bodied fighting men. On the whole the first hypothesis advanced is probably the more credible of the two. . . . Viewing human nature broadly and without inquiring too intimately into the duties and manner of life of the Virgins of the Sun, no insurmountable obstacle to the acceptance of this theory is raised by the occasional occurrence of infantile remains. It is probable, too, that other women of high rank, not connected with convent or temple, were buried in the caves of the mountainside. . . . It is only a very few years since any American skeletal material known to be syphilitic would have been regarded by the majority of pathologists as undoubtedly post-Columbian. Through the scholarly researches of Doctor Iwan Bloch it now appears that syphilis is a disease of great antiquity in the New World, and that it was brought to Europe from Haiti by Columbus' crew on their return from the First Voyage. Therefore the fact that bones from either North or South America show syphilitic alterations cannot be accepted as satisfactory evidence that they belong to the post-Columbian period.

The persons whose bones we found were not the builders. They were probably the so-called Virgins of the Sun, selected from among the most attractive damsels of the Inca Empire to be the personal attendants of The Inca. This conclusion, for which we are indebted to Dr. Eaton's investigations, makes all the more interesting the garniture of the graves, the personal possessions of the priestesses. The condition of the caves opened by the Indians after Dr. Eaton's departure cannot be determined but may be assumed to be in general like that of those he saw opened. A certain proportion of the burial caves which he himself was able to describe showed evidences of having been visited before, as long ago as the days when the city was still occupied. The object of these visitors was to make room for later burials and they ruthlessly swept the earlier occupants into a corner. If they had so little respect for the bones, they may have had less for the garniture of the graves, and attractive pots and bronzes may have been removed. Other visitors were probably the treasure seekers of the generation past. Señor Lizarraga, for instance, is known to have sold a pot or two which he said came from Machu Picchu, but the difficulty of the climb up to the ruins and the low price of pots probably dissuaded him from making any serious effort to locate graves. The Indian Richarte and his friends had small inducement to disturb any graves until the days of our arrival and the opportunity of securing liberal gratuities. They could not have sold more than one or two ollas without being detected by their land-lord, who would have immediately claimed anything of this kind. The most frequent visitors to the caves on the mountain side were undoubtedly wild animal prowlers searching for food and shelter, and especially the spectacled bears, which are still common in this vicinity.

Of the forty caves or locations where Dr. Eaton secured human skele-tal material, twenty-six had probably been visited previously and twenty-one contained graves, perhaps thirty in all, which had not been disturbed. Six or seven suggested that bones had been moved to make way for later burials. The undisturbed graves can give us very important information and deserve special notice. In the first cave no pottery was found inside with the bones, but broken pieces of three beaker-shaped ollas and two two-handled dishes were found in the refuse outside or among the stones and earth of the protecting wall. They may have been the remains of earlier burials. In the second case of an untouched cave, two skeletons were found, probably female. There was nothing with them. In the third cave two chambers had been constructed, both containing female skele-tons; one had a broken beaker-shaped olla, the other a fine two-handled dish, but this was all. Another cave, near by, had the remains of a pelike-shaped jug near the bones of a woman. In this group of untouched graves were the remains of six women. Two of them seem to have had no posses-sions; only one had a dish in good condition.

In another grave, which did not appear to have been disturbed by human beings, was a female skeleton and the remains of two two-handled pots. The best one, a perfect specimen of a deep dish of fine red ware, "lay on its side near the skull." Near it was the undisturbed grave of a young person, sex unknown, with no possessions at all. While the protecting wall was too low to prevent entry, the proximity of an open cave with a fine dish in it would seem to indicate that this locality had not been visited and that the young person really had no personal dishes.

In "a small chamber at the rear of a large natural cave" with the skele-ton of a woman "about fifty years of age" was a plant-spine needle, a child's jawbone, an imperfect beaker-shaped olla, and a deep plate with broken handle, also "several fragments of llama bones, representing food for the dead." In another grave, apparently undisturbed, a "small adult female" was buried beneath a mass of earth and stones, with a broken beaker-shaped olla. In an adjoining cave was the skeleton "of a woman about fifty years of age" accompanied by "a heavy bronze pin about 11 cm. long, which had been interred with the remains." In the cave was a beaker-shaped olla. It is interesting to note that in these last three graves the occupants were women and each was provided with a cooking pot.

In the next undisturbed burial cave the occupants were persons of more importance. Both were small adult women, buried at a depth of "nearly five feet." Over their bones, but well concealed "beneath the earth and cobbles of the floor" was a complete set of pots suitable for two ladies. Although broken, probably by the manner of the burial, they are very significant. There are two beaker-shaped ollas, one high and one low; two two-handled dishes, one deep and one shallow; two deep plates; two pelike-shaped jugs; and two other containers for liquid refreshment, an aryballus and a small jug. It is evident that these were ladies of property, since their pots include examples of every one of the types which we associate with the women of Machu Picchu.

The next complete and apparently undisturbed grave was that of "a young person, probably female, of about sixteen years of age." There was no pottery, nothing but the skull of a little agouti which may have been the young lady's pet or may have been offered as food for her spirit.

In front of a rock-sheltered terrace, a thousand feet higher than the City Gate and at some distance beneath the surface of the ground, was found the "skeleton of a delicately formed woman," probably of high rank. "Close to her bones were her small personal belongings, her pottery and the skeleton of her dog," an Inca collie. Her pottery included a pair of perfect jugs, with human faces partly modeled and partly painted on the necks, and a fine beaker-shaped olla. Fragments of three aryballi, three beaker-shaped ollas, three two-handled dishes, one pelike-shaped jug, and one deep plate were also found in this grave, as though testifying to the wealth and high estate of the deceased. Even more striking is the witness of her other personal belongings, which included two large bronze shawl pins, two plant-spine needles, a fine concave bronze mirror, two small bronze spoons and a pair of bronze tweezers, these last probably worn as pendants. In view of the richness of the material buried with this lady and her evident importance—no other grave contained anything like as fine garniture—and in view of our good fortune in finding this grave undisturbed although located in the most striking cemetery at Machu Picchu, it is worth noting, particularly for the benefit of our Peruvian critics, that not a single article of gold was found here (or anywhere else). Gold must indeed have been extremely scarce if none could have been spared for such a *grande dame* as was here interred. Perhaps whatever gold she may have possessed had been confiscated and sent to form part of the ransom of the unfortunate Atahualpa, whose failure to fill a room full of gold for Pizarro cost him his life!

Another undisturbed grave contained two female skeletons, a beaker-shaped olla, a deep plate, and a small "neatly decorated aryballus." In a cave from which pottery on the surface might easily have been removed was the undisturbed grave of a "young woman." On the surface of the ground near by lay a broken beaker-shaped olla. In the grave, with the bones, were found the young woman's two shawl pins. It would seem as though she must have been a person of consequence, for these were of silver. Near the grave was a large flat muller of rare shape, used for grinding meal, probably for ceremonial purposes. Not far from here, another grave, which had no pottery in or near it and which was at one end of a bowlder which had been visited, was found to contain the bones of a woman who was buried with a bronze knife, a bronze shawl pin, and two silver pins of similar size and shape. Among the Indian women of Peru and Bolivia today shawl pins of silver are often the most valuable of their personal belongings.

A single undisturbed stone-lined grave or cyst was found to contain the bones of a woman and four oblong stone pendants, probably pieces of a necklace. Near by were found the remains of two beaker-shaped ollas, a two-handled dish, and a jug, all of which articles we have learned to associate with the women of Machu Picchu. Necklaces of durable material do not seem to have been common. Equally striking is the fact that "under a great overhanging bowlder," with the bones of eleven people, were no objects of value. The sherds of only a single pot, a two-handled dish, were found with the bones of an adult woman, "on the topmost shelf of the cave." These eleven persons evidently must have been very poor. The presence of five skulls ignominiously thrown into "a narrow recess" at one end of the cave, and the absence of any potsherds, would seem to point to the conclusion that these were people of no consequence, perhaps slaves.

In another locality a large bowlder covered the remains of three women and a child of six years. The bones were in three connecting chambers and the lower two did not appear to have been much disturbed. With the bones was a perfect specimen of a drinking ladle and the nearly complete remains of three beaker-shaped ollas, four two-handled dishes, a two-handled bowl, and a fragment of a large amphora.

The last cave examined by Dr. Eaton contained five undisturbed graves. "The depth of these graves was such that the skulls which were in place with reference to the rest of the skeletons were found from fifteen to eighteen inches below the floor of the cave." The bones were of two males and three females. A considerable amount of pottery was recovered, a perfect jug lying close to the skull of one of the women. A long bronze "champi," probably a crowbar for the work of a builder, was found near the skull of one of the men whose burial seems to have been "considerably older" than some of the others in this cave. A hammer-stone and an ingot of bronze found here may have belonged to the men. Among the pots recovered from the excavation of these five graves were four beaker-shaped ollas, a pair of attractive ladles or plates of similar style and pattern, a pair of two-handled dishes, five pelike-shaped jugs, and six deep plates or drinking ladles.

Since there is no means of being sure that the material brought in by the Indians was always actually found with the skeletal material, or of knowing actually how many separate localities were excavated by them, or how many places were visited more than once, it would be dangerous to attempt to draw conclusions from their finds except as regards the general locality whence they came. One locality about which there can be little doubt, "one mile southeast from the city, in a saddle of Machu Picchu mountain," not sufficiently near any other finds to make it likely that the material collected here by the Indians might have become confused, contained the bones of a man and a woman, both of small stature. Their property as represented by the artifacts consisted of two two-handled dishes, a diota-shaped olla, a deep plate, a wooden deep plate (rare), a wooden spindle-whorl, a stone counter, two small bone awls, and seven "polishing stones." A few llama bones and the lower jaw of an agouti represent the funeral "baked meats." If they used the olla for cooking, the dishes for serving their stews, the two plates for drinking the soup (no one had soup spoons in those days and "fingers were made before forks"), we have their entire kitchen furniture. The woman, like all Indian women in the Andes today, had her spinning and weaving to do. The man was a stone mason but possibly he was fond of wood-working; he did some hunting. His wife was provided with a wooden spindle-whorl and one of them had a wooden soup plate. They were temperate folk. They had no jugs. They were poor. They had nothing of metal, no silver or bronze. They may have been llama drivers. They were buried not far from the old Inca stone-paved road which led around the slopes of the mountain to the open country and the llama pastures beyond.

To summarize the results obtained in the undisturbed graves of women, several contained nothing whatever in the way of pottery or objects of value; eight contained a single pot. Of these four were beaker-shaped ollas, three were two-handled dishes, and one was a pelike-shaped jug. Of those which contained more, one grave had a deep plate in addition to a beaker-shaped olla; one contained an aryballus in addition to the last two types. One contained two beaker-shaped ollas, a two-handled dish, and a jug. One had three beaker-shaped ollas and a pair of two-handled dishes. One contained the bones of two women who had a fine set of pots. Several had pins of bronze or silver and needles of plant spines. Finally there was the lady of great distinction who had a dog and a large set of bronzes and pots.

The conclusions which we may draw from the results of Dr. Eaton's careful excavations are as follows: Burials were usually made in a contracted position. Mummy wrappings had long since disappeared. The women had few durable ornaments. The number of pots placed with a body varied with the importance of the individual. Youths rarely had anything; some women had nothing; a few women had a full assortment of such ware as is usually associated with woman's work, jugs for the manufacture and dispensing of *chicha,* beaker-shaped ollas for cooking purposes, two-handled dishes for stews, and drinking ladles or deep plates for individual service. Most women, however, had only one or two pieces. None of the few burials of men indicate them to have been of much importance. It is unfortunate that we cannot be sure just what dishes they owned, if any. It is significant that the builder's hammer-stone, the bronze crowbar and, later, another hammer-stone, a "small polishing stone, a stone knife or scraper" and two large hammer-stones, each weighing not less than fifteen pounds, were found in graves containing the bones of men, probably builders.

Reference has already been made to a cave only "two hundred feet" from the City Gate, which was opened under Mr. Erdis' supervision. It contained the well-preserved skeletons of two men, one "about twenty years of age," the other "a small man approaching middle age." These men were not builders, no hammer-stones or crowbars being buried with them.

The younger man had an elaborately carved "grey talc necklace ornament" of unique design, a number of bone beads, and "pieces of what appears to be a bead made of fused green glass"! The older man had a few ornaments, small stone tokens and bronze necklace pendants. Also he had a jug, the only jug, by the way, that was not found associated with women's bones. His bones were "free from decay." The muscles of his "left thigh still adhere to the bone." There were even a few "pieces of cloth and cord made from brown llama wool." Evidently this was one of the most recent of all burials. It is curious and significant that these two men should have female ornaments as well as a woman's jug. Their unusual place of burial, their feminine adornments, the absence of masculine possessions, the extraordinary presence of a mass of desiccated muscle tissue on the older man's thigh, the little jug, all point to something peculiar about these two. Why were they buried in this unusual place? Were they unwelcome visitors who came to the outskirts of the sacred city and were buried near the gate without being admitted to the society of the Virgins of the Sun? It seems to be an insoluble puzzle. And what about that bead of fused green glass? Where did the young man get that? It is probably of European origin. To be sure, it is only a little thing, but it would seem to say that the young man came here after the Spaniards had reached Cuzco. Were these men spies, sent by the Spaniards to try and locate the refuge of the Virgins of the Sun who had escaped from the holy city? Did they bring presents for the sacred women, necklaces and a jug and a precious glass bead, the like of which none of them had ever seen before? Who can tell?

This brings up the question as to how recently Machu Picchu was occupied. It will be remembered by readers of *Inca Land* that our excavations in the fortress of Uiticos, the last Inca capital, resulted in the finding of a number of iron articles of European manufacture, including a buckle, a pair of scissors, several saddle ornaments, and three jew's-harps, mementos of the days of the Spanish Conquest. Had Machu Picchu been known to the conquerors or been occupied by Inca soldiers who had opportunities, as did the followers of the last Inca Manco, to waylay Spanish travelers, we might expect to find similar foreign artifacts here. It is all the more striking and significant, therefore, to note that after the most thorough and painstaking search in all the one hundred caves or graves which contained objects of interest, as well as in the many other caves which yielded only negative results, only two others contained objects which could be surely assigned to the post-Columbian era. Furthermore, in no case was the object one that might not perfectly well have been brought to the caves long after the burials had taken place and Machu Picchu been abandoned as a place of residence. In a cave halfway down the mountain side, east of the hut of Richarte, at a considerable distance from the city and the principal cemeteries, was found "a piece of rusty iron, . . . little more than a thin rust flake about 3 cm. long and 1 cm. wide. It looks as if it might be the shard of a knife blade." There is no reason why it may not be from the knife of a treasure hunter, particularly in view of the fact that no objects of bronze or pottery of marketable value were found in this cave. The presence of several artistic little carved stone chips of animals in silhouette makes it seem likely that other attractive articles were once here. On the other hand, it may have belonged to one of the occupants of the neighboring grave. The knife blade, if such it was, may have been used to carve the little stone tokens. In the only burial cave near this one was found a well-preserved example of typical coast pottery, a stirrup-shaped spherical bottle, totally unlike anything of Inca workmanship; also more carved animals. The contents of these caves as well as their location would seem to dissociate their occupants from those who were buried in one of the regular cemetery areas. On the other hand, the use of the green chloritic schist as the medium for perpetuating the appearance of certain animals would seem to identify the individuals as permanent residents rather than as transients.

The only other cave containing anything of post-Columbian origin was "about five hundred yards from the camp in a southerly direction and a little above the level of the Rock-Sheltered Terrace." In other words, it lies fairly near, if not actually in, Cemetery No. 3 where many of the chief people of Machu Picchu were buried. This cave contained two peach stones and a beef bone, "a fragment from the shaft of a bovine tibia," as Dr. Eaton describes it. In view of the complete absence of beef bones in any other cave I am inclined to assume that the peach stones and the bone were the remains of some visitor's lunch. We have seen that Machu Picchu was reported to exist as an interesting archaeological site as early as the unsuccessful attempt of Wiener to visit it in 1875. We know that Lizarraga had been treasure hunting on these forest-clad slopes at least ten years before our visit to this cave. It is also significant that neither at this cave nor at another whose location is recorded in the same general terms and which was probably close to it, did our workmen find any pottery, bronzes, or other artifacts of commercial value. It seems possible that the absence of funeral offerings may be traced to the successful hunter who brought the peach stones and the beef bone. Except for the bead of fused green glass, none of the burial caves near the city or in Cemeteries Nos. 1 and 2 contained any evidence that the persons buried there had had any contact with the Spanish conquerors. It seems reasonable to conclude, therefore, that the last occupants of the citadel perished before the Spanish Conquest or sought refuge here and perished without having been visited by any Europeans. Such a conclusion, based of necessity on negative rather than positive proof, fits in with the assumption made in *Inca Land* that Machu Picchu was in its last stage the home and refuge of the Virgins of the Sun, priestesses of the most humane cult in aboriginal America, who fled from the sacred city of Cuzco at the time of Pizarro's invasion. There is no evidence in the Spanish chronicles to show that either Augustinian missionaries or Spanish soldiers ever reached Vilcabamba the Old, "the largest city" in the province, in which was the University of Idolatry, "where lived the teachers who were wizards and masters of abomination," as Father Calancha describes it. So far as we can learn from the printed record and the mute story of the burial caves, Machu Picchu may have been the site of that hidden and sacred city.

CHAPTER VI

⚫━◈▶━⚫

THE POTTERY OF MACHU PICCHU, ITS FORM, DESIGN, AND FREQUENCY

THE pottery of Machu Picchu is characterized by simple, graceful lines like that of ancient Greece. Some of it resembles in its simplicity and utility modern vessels at present in use in French kitchens, as has been called to my attention by M. Georges Pelissier of Paris. It is strikingly different from the ancient pottery of the northern Peruvian coast, where one finds the human body represented in many forms, some of them extremely degenerate. Portrait busts, manikins in every conceivable attitude, persons afflicted with dreadful diseases, comedy and tragedy, all are found represented in coastal ceramic art. The lack of any such tendencies in the pottery of Machu Picchu leads to the conclusion that there existed a prejudice against the use of the human form in decoration among the Incas. This was probably due to the necessity which existed among the Peruvian highlanders of always having their bodies well clothed. Probably in the earliest times this was not so, since the Indians of the southernmost part of South America who live amidst the snow and ice of Tierra del Fuego are scarcely clothed at all. Once clothing had been invented, however, and its use furthered by the domestication of the Peruvian cotton plant and the wool-bearing alpaca, comfort would dictate that it be continually used. As a result of this, custom would in time decree that any exposure of arms or legs was indecent. The growth of such strict ideas of decency would promote a sense of shame which would lead to the practice of using geometric patterns and designs in pottery decoration rather than the human form. On the warm sands of the tropical coast lands garments were frequently discarded, and fisher folk and bathers accustomed the native artists to the shape of the human body, but on the lofty Andean plateau the natives never discard their clothes. The dry, rarefied air causes bodily heat to radiate and be lost so quickly that even the Anglo-Saxon, with lifelong habits of cleanliness, finds it easy to go for weeks without washing his body or changing his clothes. When washing

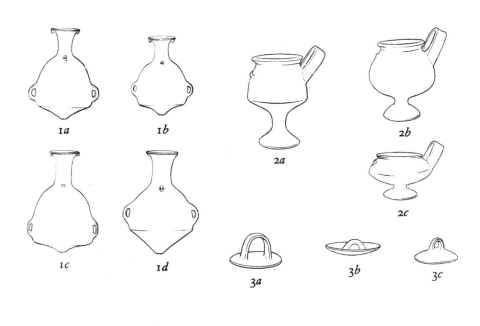

1, aryballus; 2, beaker-shaped olla; 3, pot covers; 4, two-handled dish; 5, two-handled bowl.

70. TYPES OF POTTERY

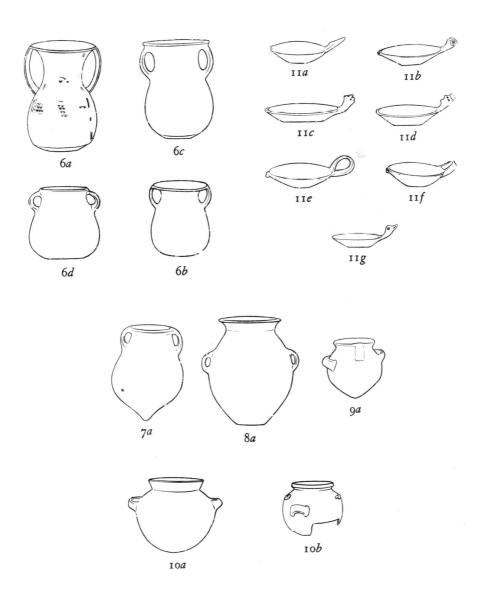

6, pelike-shaped jug; 7, diota-shaped olla; 8, pithos; 9, hydria-shaped olla; 10, lebes-shaped kettle; 11, drinking ladle.

71. TYPES OF POTTERY

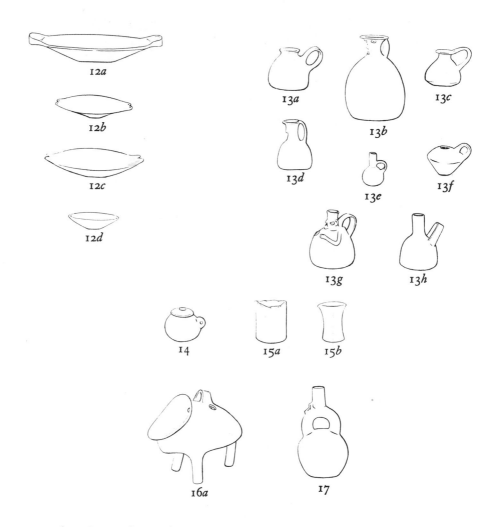

12, deep plate; 13, jug; 14, jar; 15, cup; 16, three-legged brazier; 17, stirrup-shaped bottle.

72. TYPES OF POTTERY

73

a. Small aryballus, restored from fragments of about one-third of original. White ware, decorated with maltese cross design in black and red; neck, alternate lines of black and red; panel, broad lines of red edged with black; crosses, black; cross-hatched triangles red; rope nubbin very simple, undecorated. Ears not punctured. A unique piece. Height, 21 cm.; diameter of bowl, 14.5 cm.; diameter of neck, 3.3 cm. *b*. Photograph of above. *c*. Fragment of above, showing profile of rope nubbin.

74

Aryballus restored from 102 sherds found in excavations near the head of the Main Stairway. Two-color ware. Neck, showing unusually short and narrow for size of jug. No white appears to have been used in decoration. Design in black over a rich red background. The pattern is the familiar Inca assemblage of horizontal lines of red pyramids separated by vertical lines of concentric diamonds. Rope nubbin narrow. Height, 38 cm.; diameter, 29.5 cm.

one's hands at a high elevation one frequently experiences a slight chill as the water touches the wrists near the large arteries of the arm. Possibly all this may explain why the paintings used in the decoration of Inca pottery resemble the culture of the Arabs rather than that of the Greeks, even though the shape of the vases is as graceful as those of Greece.

All the pottery found at Machu Picchu appears to have been handmade with the exception of two or three very recent fragments evidently belonging to the modern Indians. It seems likely, however, that a primitive form of potter's wheel was used in the manufacture of a large part of the ancient utensils. The method may have been such as we observed in use at the base of Mt. Coropuna in 1911, where the potters employ rough clay plates on which to build up their creations and on which the pots are allowed to dry in the sun before being baked in a fire. The clay plate is revolved with the left hand while strips of wet clay are applied with the right hand. We found that the pottery was baked in a shallow depression in the ground covered with llama dung, fired by bunches of dried grass laid on top.

We have been able to identify the remains of about 1,660 pots. One-fifth were found in burial caves, and four-fifths in the city. Nearly all of them were in a damaged condition; many of them were beyond repair. Burials in rocky caves did not conduce to the life of the pot. It has been suggested by Dr. Eaton that the small bears which are common in this vicinity may have deprived the spirits of enjoying some of the funeral baked meats and that the pots were thus broken by the clumsy thieves. Most of the pottery of which we found sufficient pieces to enable us to restore it with reasonable certainty occurred under rocky ledges or in caves where portions of the roof might have fallen in. Some of the fragments of individual pots were found in more than one cave, indicating either that the ceremonial burial offerings had been fragmentary or else that the bears had smashed the dishes and carried off some of the more succulent portions to neighboring caves.

Most common of the vessels found at Machu Picchu was the aryballus,* a bottle-shaped jar, which had, as a rule, two pierced earlike nubbins attached to the rim, a single, incised, conventionalized animal-head nubbin attached to the shoulder of the vase, and two band-shaped handles

* For definitions of this and the other types of pottery discussed in this chapter, see the author's article on "Types of Machu Picchu Pottery," *American Anthropologist*, Vol. XVII, 1915, pp. 257-271.

75

One of a pair of small, attractively made, and highly polished jugs from a burial cave. Three-color ware. Sides of handle pierced, as though for suspending jug by string. Rim, black; neck, red; eyes, mouth, and teeth, black on white background; nose, red. Panel on bowl outlined with black border, and showing "necklace" design of red strings and black disks on white background; remainder reddish yellow. In other jug, face slightly different, pupils of eyes smaller, black on white background, this in turn on black background; rest of neck red; mouth with horizontal line, giving effect of two rows of teeth; twenty-four pendants to necklace instead of twenty-three. Height, 14.5 cm.; diameter of bowl, 11 cm.

76

Small aryballus, source unknown, purchased in Cuzco. Inserted here to show origin and development of the "necklace" pattern, which occurs so frequently in designs of Cuzco style.

77

Necklace of small copper disks, nearly round, but not perfectly so. Diameter varies from 1.2 cm. to 1.3 cm. Holes irregular, carelessly punched, and varying from 0.15 to 0.25 cm. in diameter. Disks all of about same thickness, varying slightly according to the amount of corrosion, the thinnest about 0.02 cm. Average weight per disk, 0.13 gr. Color, dark green to brown. Thirty-nine disks were found a foot underground near the top of the Stairway of the Fountains and were possibly strung as shown in cut. In restoring the necklace, the design shown on Figs. 75 and 76 was followed. The strings had all disappeared.

78

78a

Aryballus, restored from a few fragments. Three-color ware on a yellowish red base. This remarkably intricate pattern appears to have attracted so much attention from children and others interested in pretty potsherds that the pieces were widely scattered and it was im-

Fragment of neck of fine, large, three-color ware aryballus, decorated with twelve rows of small black diamonds on red background, edged with black lines and separated from each other by white lines. Diameter of neck, 14.7 cm.; diameter of rim, 31 cm.; thickness of shoulder, 2 cm.; thickness of neck, 0.75 cm.

possible to make a thoroughly trustworthy restoration of the shape. Fragments of at least four aryballi of this design were found. The unusual feature of the decoration is the use of small red crossed lines near the outer edge of the panel. Black lines are much more common.

79

Probable method of carrying an aryballus, showing use of the rope nubbin. Drawn by A. H. Bumstead.

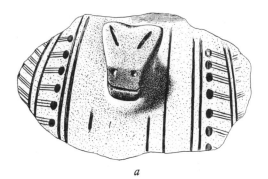

a

b

c

d

e

f

80

Fragments of aryballi. *a*. Probable three-color ware. Much weathered. Necklace design, black on red background; some evidence of white on side bars. Rope nubbin of unusual shape, somewhat resembling a llama's head. *b*, *c*. Fragments of large aryballi. *d*. Three-color ware. *e*. Rope nubbin; decoration red on black. *f*. Portion of very large aryballus found near Snake Rock. Three-color ware. Horizontal panel of red and white diamonds on black background.

81

Aryballi. *a.* Restored from fragments of about one-half of original. Three-color ware, highly polished. Background a rich, dark red; conventional pyramid and diamond pattern, the pyramids arranged in horizontal rows on sides, separated by vertical band of black diamonds on white background, and white bars. Height, 25 cm.; diameter, 17 cm. *b.* Restored from fragments of about one-third of original, found below the three windows of Principal Temple. Two-color ware; no evidence of white; design in red and black on a polished yellowish background. Conventional pattern of double "necklace" design separated by red bands and bar and cross pattern. One of the commonest and most characteristic forms of Inca or "Cuzco" style. Height, about 65 cm.; diameter, about 40 cm. *c.* Three-color ware from burial cave. Design a very curious and most unusual combination of Greek fret panel pattern and vertical diamond design; background a rich, dark red. *d.* Inca *pithos,* or wide-mouthed aryballus, restored from very large number of pieces; probably three-color ware.

attached vertically to the lower body below the ears (Fig. 70, type 1). The base was always pointed. The aryballi were usually decorated by means of paint and sometimes by what is technically known as a slip, or paste with which the body of the vessel was coated. The principal part of the decoration nearly always occurs on the same side as the nubbin. The aryballus was intended to be carried on the back and shoulders by means of a rope passing through the handles and around the nubbin, and when being so carried the decorations would be plainly in view. The side of the jar which rubbed against the back and shoulders of the carrier, on the other hand, usually had no pattern to be damaged by abrasion. (Fig. 79.)

The designs are nearly always geometrical and conventional. They include squares repeated one within the other, crosshatching, rows of triangles, parallel lines, rows of lozenges, elaborate scrolls, conventionalized moons, checkerboard patterns, and a conventionalized necklace consisting of a large number of disks each suspended by separate strings from the principal cord, possibly a representation of the Royal Fringe of Sovereignty—the crown of the Incas—sometimes applied horizontally but usually vertically in a double row. The nubbin or hook, placed on the shoulder to prevent the carrying rope from slipping, was usually decorated with two eyes and a mouth, very crudely made. Sometimes more pains were taken, ears, lips, teeth, and even nostrils being added. Rarely, however, was any attempt made to give a pleasing expression; usually the face is brutal and repulsive. Possibly there was a subconscious idea that the ill-natured demon who caused precious fluid to be spilt from jars would be frightened away by the sight of an uncouth animal, its head projecting out at him from the front of the jar.

The aryballus comprises 28 per cent of the total of the pots whose remains were found at Machu Picchu. The huge aryballi, of which about 150 specimens are represented in the sherds from the city, were naturally enough found hardly at all in the graves, since they were obviously community vessels rather than personal. Similarly, the pot covers or lids which may often have been used with them were found in the city rather than outside. Of ninety-seven which have been identified, only six came from graves; and these may have been used with the cooking pots. Of the smaller aryballi the sherds show that both in the city and the caves the percentage was about 19 per cent of the total. In other words, about one pot in five was a container of water or *chicha* for individuals or families. The aryballus is the most easily recognized of all as a typical Inca vessel,

a *b*

c *d*

e

82

Fragments of aryballi. *a.* Two-color ware; black and white on yellowish background. Panel has white border edged with black lines, and contains five Maltese crosses, the one at the extreme right having a very unusual form. *b.* Much weathered three-color ware. *c.* Large aryballus found in excavations in the city. Three-color ware, bar and double cross pattern. Lines black on white background; the broad black bands edged with red. Rope nubbin painted white and well rounded. *d.* Large aryballus of three-color ware. Rope nubbin incised. *e.* Two-color ware, resembling Fig. 74. Design entirely in black on red background. Rope nubbin narrow, concave; very simple and useful in form; no attempt at representation of animal's head.

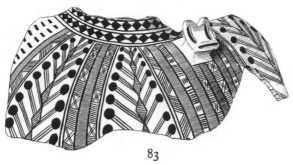

83

Fragment of large aryballus from burial cave. Three-color ware. An unusual arrangement of the necklace design, painted with black on a yellowish white background; vertical bars red. Rope nubbin, a crude concave face painted white.

84

Fragment of very large aryballus. Three-color ware. Design rather crudely put on and looks like later development of conventionalized necklace pattern; strings of disks four in number, and pattern employed in unusual manner on shoulder, where there appear to be also small ladders which may be remains of conventional teeth originally accompanying the face when this design was first used. Narrow bands around neck white, the broader ones black or dark red on white background; broad bands separating designs on body of aryballus red. Rope nubbin gone. In most specimens rope nubbin appears to have been built into jar, but in this pot it was stuck on afterward and readily came off. Diameter of neck, 14.5 cm.; height of rim above shoulder, 26 cm.; thickness of rim, 1.5 cm.

85

Fragment of large aryballus. Three-color ware. Rope nubbin of unusual form, the only specimen that has ears, eyes, nostrils, and mouth represented.

86

Fragments of aryballi. *a.* Three-color ware. Conventional necklace, bar and cross pattern, the bars in red, the crosses in black on a white background; vertical lines red edged with black; necklace lines and disks black. *b.* Medium sized; much weathered; rope nubbin small and crudely incised. *c.* Three-color ware, somewhat similar in design to Fig. 84, but here the round disks have been left off and only the three connecting lines remain; the teeth, however, are well figured. The rope nubbin, a somewhat more realistic head than the average, is painted red on white background. *d.* Three-color-ware neck. White Greek fret bordered with black on red background. Diameter, 2.1 cm. *e.* Much weathered. Rope nubbin narrow, oblong, two narrow incisions. *f.* Ring-shaped base of aryballus. *g.* Three-color ware. Rows of large black diamonds separated by red bands edged with narrow black lines on a yellowish background. The rim is unusually narrow in proportion to the width of the neck. There may have been ears, but no fragments of them were found. Diameter of neck, 11.9 cm. *h.* Much weathered, from burial cave. Ears rudimentary, not pierced. Diameter of neck, 5.9 cm. *i, j.* Unusual patterns.

87

Rope nubbins from aryballi. *a*. Has modeled ears, pierced eyes, and incised mouth; much weathered. *b*. From very small three-color-ware aryballus, 12 cm. in height, found in a burial cave. Unusual in being pierced with single hole. *c*. Three-color ware. The only rope nubbin with any indication of teeth. *d*. From large aryballus. Unusually flat; eyes pressed in with fingers; nostrils pierced; mouth molded. *f*. Much weathered, large aryballus. Eyes deeply pierced, one to depth of 1.5 cm.; mouth deeply incised. *g*. From large aryballus. Single eye pierced in middle of forehead. *h*. White design on red. *i*. A grotesque head, concave, deeply incised. *j*. Painted black on red background; ears and mouth hastily and deeply incised. *k*. Rounded and incised with three vertical lines. No attempt at representing animal head. *l*. Painted red. Eyes deeply incised, nostrils pierced, mouth incised.

consequently its frequency here places the Inca stamp indelibly on Machu Picchu.

We have been able to restore the necks of at least fifty-seven aryballi. Of these, seven, or 12 per cent, are at least 14 cm. in diameter and belong in the same class with those shown in Figures 78a, 84, and 116. Thirty-eight, or two-thirds, are at least 7 cm. in diameter, and probably represent aryballi larger than the example shown in Figure 117c, where the diameter of the neck is only 6.7 cm. Fourteen of the necks, or one-quarter, are less than 6 cm. in diameter. Only five, or less than 9 per cent, are less than 4 cm. in diameter or as small as examples shown in Figure 73. The average of the fifty-seven necks is 9.05 cm., and there are thirty necks larger than this mean.

One of the most common of all types of Machu Picchu pottery is a deep ladle or plate, probably a drinking ladle, having a handle on one side and a double nubbin on the rim opposite (see Fig. 71, type 11). We found pieces of nearly three hundred examples. They somewhat resemble the Greek patera in form, the handle sometimes being a broad loop but more often a conventionalized animal or bird head. The exterior of the plate was not decorated, but the interior, the side which the user would look at and would gradually discover as he drank his beer or his soup, was nicely and often elaborately decorated with patterns similar to those used on the aryballi and two-handled dishes. The drinking ladles differ but little in size, the average being about an inch and a half deep and six inches in width.

These drinking ladles may have been for soup or stew. Throughout the Andes soups and stews are still favored as the most common form of food. In a country where there is too little fuel to use it for bodily warmth and where drinking cold water is likely to be followed with disastrous results, it is very natural that the craving of the body for additional heat and liquid should be gratified by soup and beer. On my first South American expedition one of the first things which struck me as differentiating the Andes of eastern Colombia from the plains of Venezuela was the fact that hospitable repasts were likely to consist of three or four kinds of soup to one of anything else.

The decoration of the ladles is usually such as to cause a smile. Just as the aryballi nearly always had a conventionalized animal's head carved on the nubbin, so the handles of the drinking ladles or dippers are frequently fashioned into the form of birds' or animals' heads. Was this to

88

Aryballus rope nubbins. *a*. Much weathered. *b*. Flat. Ears, eyes, and mouth modeled to resemble a bear. *c*. Three-color ware. *e*. Remotely resembles head of an animal. Mouth underneath is unusual feature. *g*. Much weathered. Ears and mouth molded, eyes incised. *j*. Marked with eyes but no mouth—an unusual form. Thickness of fragment, 0.8 cm. *k*. Double long incisions for eyes and ears; mouth modeled. *l*. Much weathered.

a   *b*

c

d   *e*

89

Drinking ladles. *a, b, e,* three-color ware. *a.* Restored from sherds found in the niche behind the great Irregular Ledge. Handle, a much conventionalized bird's head, probably painted white on top and black on upper part of sides of head and neck. Bowl, edged with row of black triangles on white background, bordered with black line; interior painted rich red crossed with double black lines. Contrary to usual custom, the nubbins are not pierced. Height, 4 cm.; diameter, 15 cm.; height of beak, 8 cm. *b.* Roughly made. Bowl red, V's white containing small black crossed lines. Height, 5 cm.; diameter, 14 cm. *c.* One of pair found in burial cave. The conventionalized bird's head handle is painted white on top, but appears to have had no suggestion of eyes or mouth. The rim is decorated with triangles painted in black or brown on white background, giving appearance of white triangles. Rows of conventionalized alpacas in the central design are painted black or reddish brown on white background. Carefully made. Height, 3.5 cm.; diameter, 12.5 cm. *d.* One of three from burial cave containing the bones of three women. Of the others one is of same size, one slightly larger. In each the head is unusually narrow and eyes protrude. There appears to be no painted design and the customary nubbins on the edge of the ladle opposite the bird's head handle are missing. Height, 3 cm.; diameter, 13.5 cm. *e.* From burial cave. Loop handle, rim edged with black; inside, a ribbon of black triangles on red background edged with two black lines. Bowl crossed by broad band containing fret in black and white on red background, edged with black lines. Handle, bars and double crosses in black on red background; painted on upper side only. Very fine workmanship. Height, 3.5 cm.; diameter, 16.5 cm.

help the drinkers to "enjoy themselves"? Did the shape of the head or the nature of the bird or beast have any significance? Today the Indians have a few primitive secret societies which are distinguished on the occasion of a public festival by wearing fantastic uniforms. They are very conspicuous at the Copacabana fair, described in *Inca Land*. It might seem as though the ducks' heads belonged to the members of one society and the llamas' heads to another.

We found also that these plates or drinking vessels were often made in pairs, and in one instance three of a kind were found in a cave with the bones of three women. The usual rule, however, seems to have been two, since they occur in pairs in a dozen of the graves. The first idea that suggests itself is that they were made to order for a man and his wife, though pairs were sometimes found in the grave of a lone woman. The very rare design figured on page 139, with the interesting filleted human head, was found, according to the Indians, in the grave of a woman, "placed about six inches from the skull, one on each side." Pieces of a similar pair were found on one side of the Sacred Plaza. This woman may have been a person of distinction, possibly a priestess, since her grave yielded an unusual number of ornaments, including a thin bronze disk, several bone pendants, some pierced teeth, two bronze bells, and a number of wampum beads of shell or limestone. Dr. Eaton describes the woman as "about thirty years of age, and as far as may be conjectured from the symmetry and delicate contours of the cranial and facial bones . . . of decidedly attractive appearance."

The different types are not limited to any one cemetery or group of caves. The duck's head, more or less conventionalized, occurs in all and is about as common, proportionately, in the city as in the graves. The plumed bird's-head handle occurs twenty times in the city and only once in the graves. On the other hand, the plain loop handle is more common in the graves than in the city, twice as frequent as one would expect from the general average, and it does not occur in graves which lacked female remains. Was the plain loop considered more suitable for women? Was the plumed bird or the animal head more appropriate to masculine hunters and herders?

Remains of a large number of drinking ladles, quite a considerable part of which were in good condition, were found in the burial caves. The rarest forms are those in which the handle takes the form of a horizontal or vertical loop. The original form of the drinking ladle may have been a

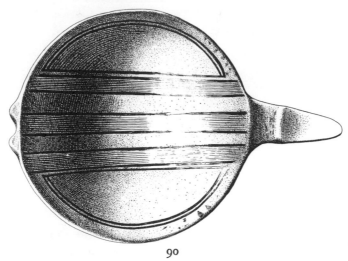

90

Three-color-ware drinking ladle, restored from fragments. One of pair found on north side of Main Stairway. Bird's head handle, white on top, black on sides, turned up at unusual angle. Rim, black or very dark red. Bowl, yellowish bordered with row of black triangles on white background, edged with two black lines; center crossed with three broad red stripes, separated by two broad white stripes edged with narrow black lines. Nubbins not pierced. Height, 3.5 cm.; diameter, 16 cm.

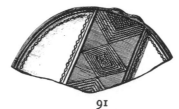

91

Fragment of three-color-ware ladle. Dark red band on which are placed black lines and concentric black diamonds, centers decorated with white dots on red background; on each side of broad red band, undecorated spaces bordered with trellis-work in black and red.

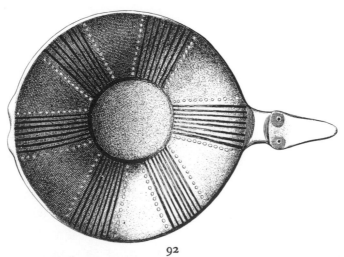

92

Three-color-ware drinking ladle, restored from fragments of pair found in burial cave. Bird's head painted white on top, black on sides; eyes painted in circles of red with black centers. Rim edged with black. Bowl painted a rich dark red, decorated with six-rayed sun, the rays consisting of black lines and white dots. Height, 3.5 cm.

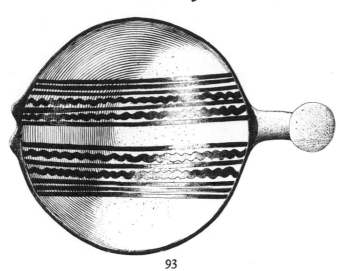

93

Drinking ladle with mushroom-shaped handle. From room in House of Two-Bowlder Metate, Ingenuity Group. Somewhat weathered, but otherwise uninjured. Three-color ware. Rim probably edged with black. Bowl crossed by two bands of straight black and wavy red lines on white background. Head of handle had white tip. Height, 4 cm.; diameter, 15.5 cm.

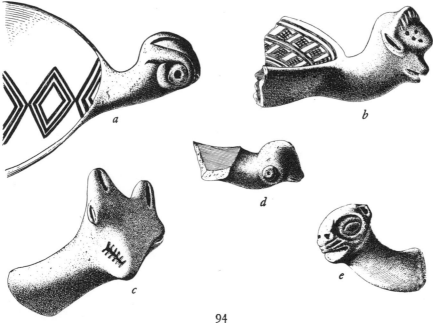

94

Fragments of drinking ladles. *a.* Much weathered. Probably three-color ware. Head represents crested bird, decorated in relief; nostrils pierced. Height, 3 cm.; diameter, 13.5 cm. *b.* Three-color ware. Handle, a carefully modeled alpaca or llama head with decorated headgear; eyes raised and incised; mouth incised; nostrils pierced; headgear incised; head probably painted white on top with black spots. Rim and neck, black. Bowl, much conventionalized red alpacas on a white background. *c.* Possibly represents young llama. Ears, eyes, and teeth incised. Much worn by handling after fracture. *d.* Eyes put on in relief and then pierced. Mouth, incised. Neck and sides, painted white. *e.* Much worn after fracture, as though it had been used for a plaything. The incised whiskers would seem to indicate some member of the cat family.

two-handled saucer; when one of the handles broke off, it was still convenient to use the other handle, but the stumps of the loop handle remained, and these are continued in nearly all the ladles found. No matter what may be the form of the handle on the opposite side of the plate, there are almost always two little round nubbins with indentations on the other side. They are purely ornamental, as in no case do they pierce the dish and become holes, and they look like the echo of a time when these plates were made with two handles. Here again is the striving after balance and symmetry. It may have been an early discovery that the loop form of handle of the ladle, particularly in its horizontal position, was not convenient, as only one or two examples of these exist in our collections. The vertical loop is somewhat commoner, but even this was soon found to be not necessary, and there developed a straight projection, frequently fashioned to represent the head of a bird or animal, and nearly always containing a convenient depression into which the first joint of the thumb fits very neatly when the hand is holding the dish with the fingers underneath it. In a few cases the handle has disappeared entirely, leaving its remnants on both sides of the ladle or plate in the form of a pair of semicircular projections with indentations. In one specimen the indentations have disappeared.

The forms of decoration selected for the drinking ladles are many and varied. A rare design, of which a pair was found in bad condition, had for a handle the form of a human head (see Figs. 95 and 97). This dish was originally painted white, divided into four sections by broad red bands.* On one of these bands is painted in black and white a row of five conventional diamonds, made up of concentric lines, black and white with a red center, the other band having conventional rows of red triangles, decorated by white lines. This continuation of concentric diamond squares, flanked by rows of triangles, is one of the two most common and characteristic forms of Inca decoration. The unique feature of these ladles lies in the handles, which are in the form of human necks and heads. The headdress or crown is painted white with a black spot in the center, which may indicate that the crown was a fillet and the black is the hair showing in the middle. The hair is painted black, the eyes and mouth white. The ears are pierced. The chief interest lies in the peculiar form of headdress,

---

* In describing the colors of the pottery, the attempt has been to state what they appear to have been rather than what they actually are in their present faded and weatherstained condition. The black has generally become dark brown; the white frequently a cream color, sometimes yellowish with age. The measurements of pots are given to the nearest half centimeter.

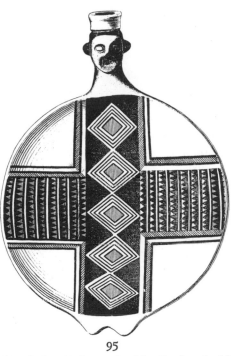

95

Three color ware drinking ladle with human head handle, from burial cave. Handle, cap, or fillet, white with black center; hair and top of ears, black; face, red; eyes, white with red pupils; mouth, white; ears, pierced, black above and red beneath; neck, red. Rim, black edged with black. Inside of ladle, divided by cross bars into quadrants, which appear to have been of white edged with black lines and diagonals, but the decoration is so weather-worn that one cannot be certain of this; the vertical cross bar has fine adjoining concentric diamonds of black and white lines with red center, the whole on dark red background; horizontal cross bar, rows of red triangles on black background, separated by white lines. The nubbins opposite the handle do not appear to have had holes pierced in them. A very rare design. Depth of ladle, 3 cm.; diameter, 16.5 cm.

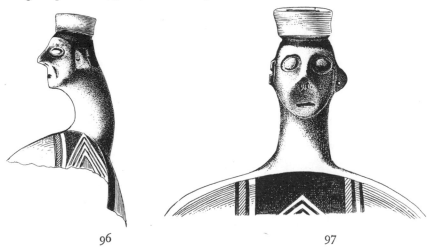

96

Profile view of handle of drinking ladle in Fig. 95.

97

Fragment of another drinking ladle with human head handle. Found in same cave as Fig. 95. The white cap may represent a white fillet, the black spot in the center representing hair.

which I have not been able to find represented in any other Peruvian mountain pottery. The expression on the faces is not quite alike, that shown in Figure 95 seems to be smiling, while that in Figure 97 is much more haughty. Unfortunately the dishes are badly weathered and it is impossible to be perfectly sure of the entire scheme of decoration.

Figures 92 and 127g represent slightly different versions of the use of the concentric diamond squares. The latter shows this occurrence in connection with the leaf pattern, while in Figure 123d the leaf pattern occurs in connection with the binding design. Figure 123d was a portion of a large ladle with a horizontal handle. The clay has baked a light yellowish red, and the decoration consists of heavy red lines running across the dish, dividing the conventional basketry binding pattern, which was not entirely completed by the artist, the whole being flanked on either side by the leaf pattern. The dish is bordered with black lines and black triangles, and appears to have been painted white, though this is uncertain. In Figure 123b we have the remains of a ladle whose main design was a red disk or sun on a white background, an unusual pattern.

Figure 124 shows designs on saucers. In Figure 89e we have a fine example of the ladle with the loop handle, the handle decorated with the conventional binding pattern of black stripes on a red background, the main design of the dish being a possible representation of the rainbow, which occurs quite frequently, notably on the aryballus shown in Figure 117c. The only white used in the design of this dish appears to be in between the black lines of the rainbow or Greek fret. In Figure 93 we have a purely conventional mushroom-shaped handle, with the wavy-line design in black, red, and white, somewhat similar to that shown on the deep dish in Figure 109a.

The most common form for the handles of the ladles to take at Machu Picchu is that of birds' heads, more or less conventionalized. In the example shown in Figure 89d the head is very thin, the eyes protrude, and there are no reminiscent stumps of another handle. These stumps have sometimes been spoken of as the tail of the bird; but they occur in many dishes where there is no bird's head. Furthermore, in one cave we found three of these ladles with similar birds' heads and no reminiscent stumps. These dishes have been so completely weathered that the design has practically disappeared. Figure 101h shows another very narrow bird's head, much conventionalized, the eyes being represented by incised rings. In Figure 101d the head is painted half white and half red, with a black band

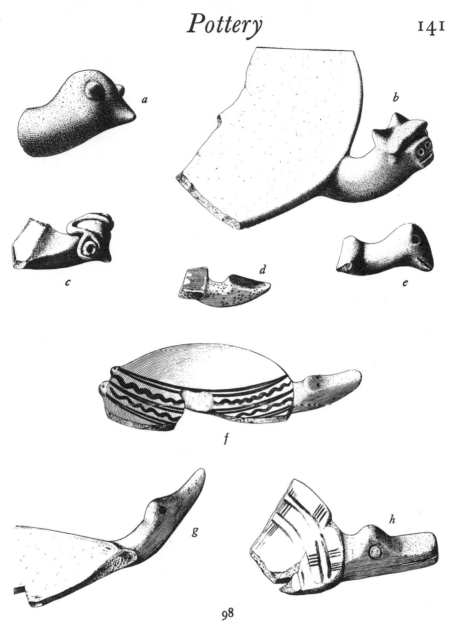

98

Fragments of drinking ladles. *a*. Bird's head handle, with protruding eyes. Much weathered. Beak small and pointed. *b*. Much weathered. Head nicely modeled so as to bring out the overhanging forelock of the alpaca; eyes and ears raised; nostrils pierced; mouth incised. *c*. Much weathered. Eyes and crest laid on in unusually heavy relief. Mouth incised. *d*. Three-color ware. Sides and neck, black dots on a white background; top of head red. *e*. Much weathered. Eyes deeply pierced; beak incised on sides. *f*. Weathered. Bird's head, eyes pierced. Brownish straight and wavy lines on a white background. *g*. Probably three-color ware, much weathered. Handle unusually long and pointed. Eyes pierced. *h*. Probably three-color ware, much weathered. Eyes and mouth incised; beak unusually broad.

around the collar, the eyes being incised and also painted with a black band. In Figure 101k the head is unmistakably that of a duck, the eyes are painted in brown, the pottery is of a whitish clay, and there is a band of brown extending along the middle of the head to the extremity of the beak. Figure 98h shows a duck's head with the eyes and mouth incised. In Figure 100b the decoration of the bird's head has been lost by weathering and the neck is unusually short. Figure 98g represents about one-third of a ladle, showing almost indistinguishable traces of a black and white design, with an unusually long, narrow bird's head for handle, the eyes in this case being punctured with a round instrument. In Figure 99e the head is very crudely modeled, the eyes and mouth being only roughly indicated. In Figure 99f we have the remains of a zigzag pattern in black, red, and white across the dish, the bird's head having an incised mouth and punctured eyes. Figure 89c represents one of the most attractive ladles. The handle is a conventionalized bird's head, the top painted white, no indication of eyes or mouth being given; the dish is deep and decorated with a reddish-brown design which seems to consist of two rows of highly conventionalized alpacas. The rim of the dish is decorated with the well-known triangles. Figure 89a shows another example of the conventionalized bird's head decorated with a band of black. The interior of the ladle was painted red and a white band encircled the edge, on which were painted black triangles. A pair of black lines running crisscross through the center of the dish complete the design. In Figures 98d, 99d, and 99h, we have other examples of the highly conventionalized bird's head with the convenient notch for the thumb. Figure 99h is a fragment of three-color ware, the band around the edge of the dish being white. It is perhaps a piece of the mate to Figure 89a, although found a foot underground in an excavation near the Sacred Plaza, while the latter was found in a burial cave on the mountain side above the city. Owing to its burial underground, the colors of the design are rather better preserved than in its mate. In Figure 99d, the conventionalized bird's head was painted white on top, decorated with black stripes. Figure 98d, found in the rubbish on the north side of the Main Stairway, shows a very unusual decoration, the neck and sides of the bird's head having been painted white and then having received a liberal supply of black dots. The top of the head is painted red. Figure 90, another find on the north side of the Main Stairway, was nearly complete, with a conventionalized bird's head, three broad red bands running across the dish, and the usual white band around the edge

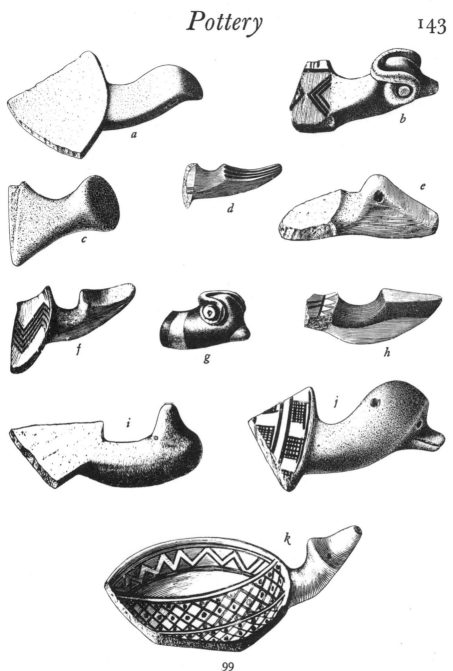

99

Fragments of drinking ladles. *a*. In form of conventionalized snake's head. Much weathered. Eyes incised. *b*. Much weathered crested bird's head handle. Three-color ware. Eyes incised. *c*. Simplest form of handle. Much weathered. *d*. Three-color ware. Top of head, three black lines on white background. Sides and top of neck, black. Interior of bowl, red with black lines. *e*. Much weathered. Eyes pierced. Beak incised at end. *f*. Three-color ware. Eyes pierced. Beak incised. Head painted red. Bowl probably red, crossed by zigzag of black and white lines, edged with black lines. *g*. Represents crested bird's head. *h*. Possibly mate to Fig. 89*a*. As it has been protected from weather, colors are much brighter. *i*. Very unusual. Beak of conventionalized bird's head points upward. *j*. Three-color ware, much weathered. Beak incised. Two pairs of eyes, both pierced. *k*. Three-color ware of complicated design. Handle, eyes and beak pierced. Bowl, bordered with wavy white line on red background edged with black lines; crossed with two bands of trellis-work composed of red or black lines, white diamonds, and red dots. Height, 3 cm.

of the dish, decorated with black triangles. Owing to much weathering, it is impossible to say what was the design between the red bands, or whether anything occurred on the flanks. In Figures 91 and 98f, we have the unusual feature of the eyes of the bird's head being placed on top, incised in 98f and painted in 92. The remainder of the design in 98f appears to be reddish-brown lines on a white background, the wavy line resembling those shown in Figure 93. A pair of ladles, a restored example of one of which is shown in Figure 92, were found in Cave No. 74. The top of the bird's head was painted white, the eyes made of painted red rings, in the center of which a small black dot lends a realistic expression to the face. The neck of the bird is white, the side of the head is painted black. The attractive six-star design in the dish is an unusual pattern, the background being red, the lines black with dots of white. Figure 99k shows another unusual design, with the zigzag line around the edge of the saucer in white, white squares painted on a red background, and then black or red dots superimposed on them. Figures 99a and 100e show further shapes and styles, all of conventionalized birds' heads. Figure 98a has curiously protruding eyes and a very pointed snout. Figure 133 is hollow, may not be the handle of a ladle at all, and appears to represent an animal with horns.

While the preceding heads have been mostly those of flat-billed, duck-like birds, Figures 98e, 99j, 100a, and 100g show an attempt to represent round-headed, shorter, pointed birds of various kinds. Figure 100a is in the very rare white ware and was found at the same place as the pretty plate shown in Figure 115f. The design is in three colors, the background being white, the triangles red, and the interior of the design alternately black, red, and white, as shown in the drawing. In Figure 99j the design of the plate appears to be a reminiscence of the llama or alpaca form shown in Figure 89c. In Figure 98b we get the only attempt to represent the nostrils. In Figure 94a is shown another style of bird's head, the one represented here and in Figures 98c, 99b, g, and 100h appearing to be a crested bird of the jungles. The different ways in which this crest was put on are shown in the various examples. In Figure 100h the background is of black, the nose, eyes, and neck being touched with white. In Figure 99g similar colors were used. In Figure 99b are shown the remains of the concentric diamond square design. In Figure 98c, as in so many cases, the weathering has entirely destroyed the design. In Figure 94d we have one of the few attempts to show the modeling of the bird's beak; in this instance the neck was painted white, but the rest of the design has been lost. Figures 99i, 100e,

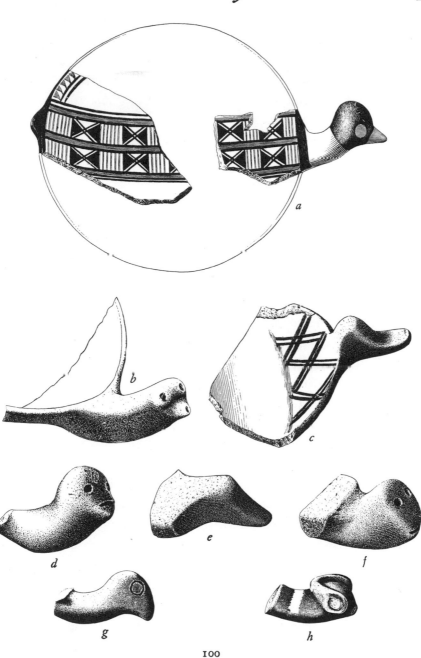

100

Fragments of drinking ladles, much weathered. *a*. Three-color ware on white base. Bird's head well rounded; eyes and beak, white touched with red. Rim, black bordered with red triangles edged with black lines. Bowl, crossed with the common bar and double cross pattern, the three latitudinal lines being red with black borders, the bars red on white background, the double crosses black. *b*. Neck unusually short. *c*. Head red, forehead white; eyes and mouth, pierced. Rim, red; bowl, white. Height, 3.5 cm.; diameter, 15.5 cm. *d, f*. Made in form of animals' or birds' heads. All show signs of much handling since fracture and appear to have been used as toys, amulets, or tokens. *e*. Bird's head of unusual shape and very short neck. *g*. Parrot-like in form; eyes incised. *h*. Represents crested bird's head, painted black on white base.

and 100f show further ramifications of the effort to make the handle of the ladle resemble a bird's head. Many other examples might be given, but these are enough to show the fact that there was no slavish adherence to any set pattern. As shown in Figure 99c, the potter occasionally contented himself with a very simple handle without making any effort to imitate anything.

Animals' heads occur, but not nearly so frequently as birds' heads. Figure 94b shows a ladle in which the handle represents the head of a llama with his hair braided. The design in the dish itself is a section of conventionalized llamas in two rows, painted in red on a white background. The head is nicely made, even the nostrils and a realistic mouth being provided in addition to carefully modeled protruding eyes. In Figure 98b the overhanging locks of the alpaca are carefully modeled, but the design on the dish has been lost. Figure 101b gives us an amusing caricature of a llama in black pottery. In Figure 94e, judging by the incised whiskers, we may have a member of the cat family; at all events, the sherd shows signs of use, and was probably a plaything of some little child after it had been broken off from the ladle to which it originally belonged. The same is true of Figure 94c, which appears to represent a young llama. In fact, it is significant to note in this connection that animals' heads and bodies were almost always found widely separated from the dish to which they originally belonged. This may have been due to their being the product of an earlier generation of potters and to their being designed as playthings for children, or tokens of grown-ups. Whatever the cause, the fact remains that we were unable to find enough pieces of any animal, apart from some ladles with birds' heads, to warrant us in restoring examples. Figure 101e shows a very unusual, short head; the design appears to be that of an animal with a spotted face, a diagrammatic representation of which seems to have been used to decorate the interior of the dish. Figure 101a shows a very realistic, fierce-looking jaguar. Figure 101c is of a sherd that had been used so much as a plaything that the ears have become broken and the fracture well rounded. The same remark applies to Figures 100d, f, and 101g, i, which, so far as one can judge from the specialization of the fracture, were used as toys. Figure 100c shows a beast or bird with a curiously stocky neck, Figure 89b an unusually deep ladle with a conventionalized animal's or bird's head, the design being V-shaped lines of white on a red background. In Figure 109b, we have what is probably the remains of a dish without a handle, although with a pair of nubbins. The design is quite intricate. On

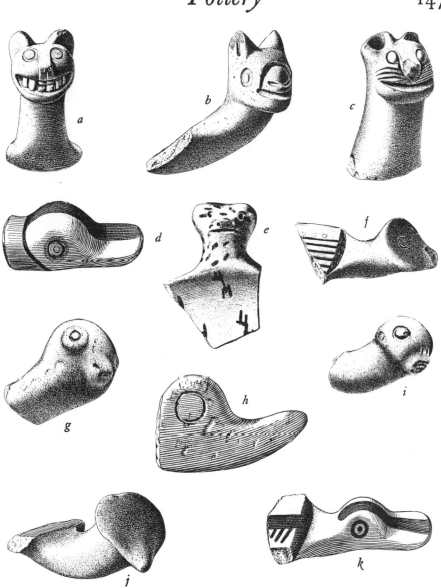

101

Drinking ladle handles. *a*. Much weathered. Realistic representation of cougar or jaguar, nicely modeled. *b*. Much worn and fire-blackened. Realistic representation of a llama, much incised. *c*. Much worn and handled since fracture. Possibly used as toy or amulet. Seems to represent some member of cat family. *d*. Three-color ware. Eyes incised and edged with red. Right half of bird's head white; left half, red. Eyes white. Collar black. *e*. Red ware. Bowl decorated with black, conventionalized animals. Eyes and nostrils pierced; mouth incised. Head painted red, faces upward, decorated with black spots, as though to suggest an ocelot or wildcat. *f*. Three-color ware. Eyes incised and placed in front. *g* and *i*. In form of animals' or birds' heads. Show signs of much handling since fracture and appear to have been used as toys, amulets, or tokens. *h*. Much weathered. Narrow bird's head with incised eyes and sharp pointed beak. *j*. Shows tendency toward simplification in the shape of the handle, culminating in Fig. 93. *k*. White ware; eye brown, but may have been originally painted black. Well-modeled duck's head decorated with a single brown band.

a red background the artist used white circles and white dots with black borders and black lines, with a very pleasing result. In Figure 123a we have an example of a similar plate which was found in perfect condition. The design shown in the drawing is in red, black, and white, the background being red, the dots and some of the spaces being filled with white, and most of the lines being black. The parrot is outlined in black, and filled in with white, the center consisting of crossed black lines, showing a little red background and giving the plate a spotted appearance.

A third common Machu Picchu type of vessel is the beaker-shaped olla, or cooking pot (see Fig. 70, type 2), of which we found pieces representing some two hundred examples. They vary in size from a little miniature three or four inches high to a very large olla eighteen inches high. They were usually, however, not over nine or ten inches in height. Many were found in the women's graves. All were very much fire-blackened, but none gave any evidence of having been painted; since they were constantly used in fire, there was no object in decorating them with painted designs that would get smudged and burnt off. Owing to the hard usage to which these cooking pots were subjected, we found none in perfect order. In some instances we found enough pieces to enable us to restore the pot completely, but in a large majority of cases this was not true. These pots may have had clay covers, although we were not so fortunate as to find any covers actually with the pots found in the graves. Mr. Dorsey in his report on excavations on the Island of La Plata* gives a picture of a beaker-shaped olla with a cover, which he discovered there. In general, the pots were made thin and of common clay.

In Figures 102, 104, and 106e I have attempted to give a clear idea of the restored beaker-shaped olla in its different manifestations. The covers used for the purpose were not found with the pots, but, as they fit them fairly well, have been employed in order to give a better idea of how the cooking pot looked. The beaker-shaped olla shown in Figure 102 has a height of 20 cm. and a width of about the same. Eighty-one pieces of this olla were found by Dr. Eaton in Cave No. 39, constituting about eight-tenths of the pot. Some pieces are very badly fire-blackened. The cover shown in Figure 104 is an exceptionally large one, as is the beaker, which was found in Cave No. 69 in a badly damaged condition. Nearly all of the pieces were recovered, however, and the pot is one of the best examples that we have of

---

* *Archaeological Investigations on the Island of La Plata, Ecuador,* Field Columbian Museum, "Anthropological Series," Vol. II, No. 5, 1901.

102

Roughly made beaker-shaped olla or cooking pot found in burial cave. Reddish clay, burned black by use over fire. Appears to have had crescent-shaped relief ornament opposite the handle. Height without cover, 20 cm.; width, 19.5 cm. Cover found in an adjoining cave, of similar material and workmanship, but may not belong to this pot, although it appears to fit very well. Height, 5.5 cm.; width, 11 cm.

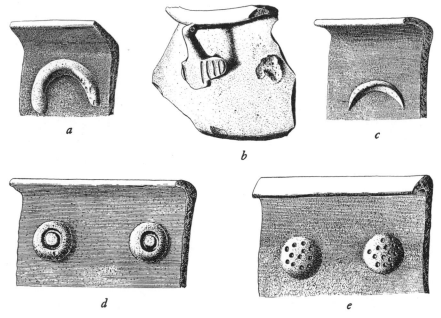

103

Various types of ornament used on beaker-shaped ollas or cooking pots. The series also illustrates the development of various decorative forms and the different styles of lip used in these ollas. In no case is there evidence of the design having been painted on, the decoration consisting entirely of reliefs or incisions. See also Figs. 105–107.

Machu Picchu kitchenware. The pot in Figure 106e was found in fairly good condition at the foot of the Great Ledge. The side away from the handle is more blackened than that toward the handle, and lends color to the belief that the arrangement of the long looped handle on one side proved to be convenient in extracting the pot from the fire.

Each beaker-shaped olla has a single foot or base. In many specimens the base of the pot has become broken off; but apparently this did not prevent the use of the olla, which was propped up in the fire by stones. Each has a single loop handle attached to the shoulder. On the opposite shoulder is the only decoration, consisting of a low relief which may be thought of as an effort to give balance and symmetry to the pot or as the echo of the base of another handle. If we knew the history of this cooking pot we should probably find that it followed a long process of evolution, beginning with the introduction into the fire of a simple two-handled pot. Somebody discovered that by adding a base or foot to it the pot would stand better among the embers of a small fire. Later the discovery was made that only the handle nearest the cook was really necessary; the other handle got too hot to be of much use and was finally abandoned, its place being taken by a little ornament in low relief attached to the pot just before it was baked. These bas-reliefs were made in various forms, some of which are illustrated in Figures 103, 105, 106, and 107. Figure 107e shows a bas-relief ornament which retains the recollection of a time when there were two large handles to the cooking pot. Figure 107g gives an example of the reduction of this handle to its lowest possible terms, merely a lump of clay impressed on the pot after it had been fashioned. Figure 107h is a little more elaborate reminder of the old handle. Figure 106g shows that when the handle broke off, naturally two lumps were left at its base, and these are preserved in the form of low bosses. This is perhaps the most frequent form of the decoration on the beaker-shaped olla. Figures 103e and 106i show some effort to decorate these bosses by incising a number of dots, and they also show the different styles of lips used for the mouth of the olla. Figure 103d shows the two bosses incised in such a way as to produce the effect of a pair of eyes. In Figure 106h the eyes, instead of being round, are mere slits. In Figure 107b the bosses are incised to make two crosses. In Figures 107a and d the bosses are joined and in Figure 107c only one is used.

Having once developed the principle of embossed ornamentation for the cooking pot as a result of the projections remaining after the handle

104

Beaker-shaped olla or cooking pot, of reddish-brown clay, from burial cave. The decoration appears to be a spotted serpent, with two heads, in relief. Beautifully made and exceedingly delicate. Height, 20.5 cm.; width, 25 cm. Cover probably does not belong to this olla; restored from sherds within the city. Height, 4.5 cm.; width, 18 cm.

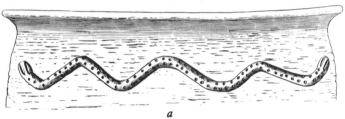

a

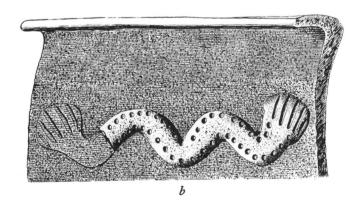

b

105

Various types of ornament used on beaker-shaped ollas or cooking pots. Spotted snake design.

had broken off, it was a simple step to elaborate this ornamentation according to the fancy of the potter. In Figure 105a we see this carried to the extent of a representation of a two-headed, spotted snake, with two rows of incised points for the spots. Figure 107f gives an example of the use of one row of larger incised points. Figures 105b, 106a and f show other developments of this motif. A further conventionalization of the snake is to be observed. There appears to be no rule as to whether the ends are to be turned up or down, and in Figure 106b we get what appears at first to be the letter W but is in reality merely a crude attempt at a snake. In every case it appears that the decoration was laid on in the form of an extra strip of clay after the pot was finished; consequently it frequently has been knocked off in the course of time. In Figure 106d the snake design is reduced to its lowest elements, and in Figure 106c the snake appears in an almost embryonic form. In Figure 103a, c, a crescent shape is developed, which, it is interesting to note, appears to be entirely confined to a single group of graves, those connected with Caves 1 to 6 and in that vicinity. This suggests that the decoration indicated the family or clan to which the article belonged, but we have been unable to carry the proof of this any further. Owing to the fragile character of this cooking pottery and the rough usage which it received, much of this evidence has been destroyed. Figure 103b gives the most elaborate example of cooking-pot decoration which we have found; it evidently consisted at one time of a pair of birds, rather crudely made, their beaks taking hold of the lip of the olla, while their feet were planted in the original location of the second handle. Figure 128 may be another example of olla decoration, but as we have been unable to get any pieces to go with it we are still in doubt as to how it should be classified.

A few examples of beaker-shaped ollas were found at Pachacamac by Dr. Uhle; but they showed no signs of use and appeared to have been made as offerings rather than to have been buried with the people who used them, as at Machu Picchu. In every case the beaker-shaped ollas of Machu Picchu show signs of use.

An extraordinarily large proportion of the beaker-shaped ollas are from the caves, where they constitute some 21 per cent of the total finds. In the city, on the other hand, they only represent 10 per cent. Why should they be twice as common in the caves as in the city? Was the beaker-shaped olla a later form? Was it more common in the days when Machu Picchu was occupied chiefly by women, the women of the burial caves? Or is the cooking pot so essentially a woman's possession that greater preponderance

a-d, f-i. Various types of ornament used on beaker-shaped ollas or cooking pots. *e.* Beaker-shaped olla or cooking pot. Reddish clay, blackened from fire use, particularly on side opposite handle. Decorated with spotted snake in relief. Found in burial cave. Height, 11 cm.; width, 15.5 cm. Cover probably does not belong to this pot; restored from fragments found in the city. Height, 2 cm.; width, 10.5 cm.

of women in the graves accounts for the greater percentage of beaker-shaped ollas? It is just as easy to identify an old olla of this type as a new one, the shape being unmistakable. In the prolific Snake Rock region this type constitutes only 13 per cent, yet in Cemetery No. 1 it constitutes 27 per cent. Among the very numerous discards from the Royal Mausoleum Group, representing some two hundred pots, the beaker-shaped olla forms only 6 per cent. In the northeast quarter of the city, among some 161 finds it forms a little less than 6 per cent. Yet in Cemetery No. 2, among 162 pots this cooking pot forms 18 per cent of the total. It would seem as though a pot subjected to such rough usage as these ollas must have had, in daily contact with the stones of the fireplace and the fuel, would have been frequently broken, and that pieces of it would have been very common in the rubbish piles of the city and less common in the cemeteries, instead of the reverse. Its presence in the cemeteries, in a proportion to the other pots of about one in five, seems reasonable enough. That the skeletons of some 141 adults should have associated with them some seventy-three beaker-shaped ollas, or one cooking pot for every two people, is not strange. But why should pieces of this rather fragile pot, made thin so as to permit the fire to heat the contents quickly and keep the pot from unnecessary cracking, a pot exposed to the daily perils of the fireplace, be relatively so much rarer in the rubbish piles of the city than in the garniture of the burial caves? Its rarity in certain sections of the city, sections that are clearly residential, would seem to suggest that the ollas in the graves came from these sections. Its entire absence from the stuff thrown out of the Temple of the Three Windows and its virtual absence from the Sacred Plaza would seem to indicate that it did not figure in the ceremonials there. An unclean cooking pot, fire-blackened, had no place in such festivals. May this not give us the key to the mystery? Is it not entirely possible that Machu Picchu, with its wonderful temples, its royal mausoleum, its ceremonial wall with three windows, and its marvelously beautiful walls, may have been an Inca Mecca, a shrine periodically visited on the occasion of certain great festivals? We know from the chronicles that these feasts were very "wet"; while the Incas did not countenance drunkenness as a habit they permitted the monthly festivals to be very merry. Molina says, "They passed the day in eating and drinking and enjoying themselves," and according to Garcilasso, "After the eating was over they brought liquor in great quantity." This would account for many things. The women who prepared the food were sober and handled the beaker-shaped ollas with reasonable care. Of

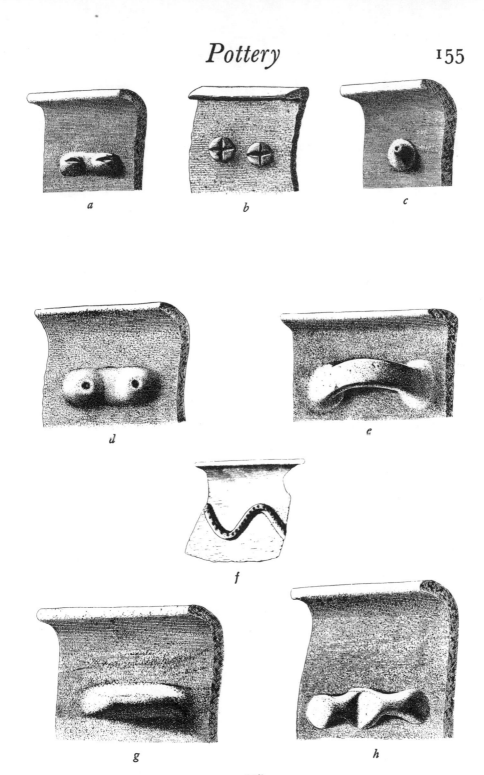

107

Various types of ornament used on beaker-shaped ollas or cooking pots.

course some got broken, but not a great many. Then came the "liquor in great quantity." Toward the end of the festival those who were "enjoying themselves" had unsteady hands, jugs and jars were accidentally dropped and broken, just as drinking vessels have been broken in drinking bouts from time immemorial. Hence perhaps we ought not to be surprised to find that in the rubbish piles of the city pieces of vessels intended to contain liquids are far more common than pieces of cooking pots.

A fourth, very common, form frequently found associated with beaker-shaped cooking pots is the deep two-handled dish in which the width is greater than the height (see Fig. 70, type 4). The handles, band-shaped, are attached horizontally below the rim. This type was found almost as often as the smaller aryballi, 271 examples being identified. It formed about 16 per cent of the total and was about as common in the caves as in the city. It seems to have been the usual container for stews and porridges, the more substantial parts of the ancient fare. Nearly all the two-handled dishes show signs of paint or slip decoration with the conventional geometric patterns, frequently in three colors. Both sides of the dish were decorated alike so that if, as seems likely, it was intended to be used by more than one person at the same time, the persons sitting on opposite sides of the dish would each have the benefit of attractive decoration. In one group a pair of miniature two-handled dishes, obviously intended as an offering rather than for use, were painted inside on a white slip that covers the entire dish. In these specimens, found in a burial cave with the skeleton of an unusually tall woman, possibly the high priestess, the design is an attractive pair of butterflies painted in three colors (Fig. 122). The other articles in this cave were also of superior quality.

We found fragments of two-handled dishes whose handles were made in the form of fierce-looking carnivorous animals attached vertically, connecting the rim of the dish with its body, the heads rising above the level of the rim, glaring at each other with open mouths and bared teeth, the animals' tails turned to the right (Fig. 136). None of these were found in any of the graves but fragments of a number occurred in the excavations in the citadel. They evidently were of great age and the paint had disappeared. A fine specimen of this type from the Titicaca Basin is in the American Museum of Natural History in New York. One of the handles of a deep dish was found representing the head of a laughing fox or coyote, exquisitely modeled; the spirit in which the modeling is worked out is most delightful (Fig. 120b). The decoration of the two-handled

108

Two-handled reddish clay dishes of three-color ware, found in burial caves (*b-f*). *a*. From House of the Two-Bowlder Metate, Ingenuity Group. Rim, red on top edged with single black line. On each side a band of twenty-two red lozenges on white background, bordered by three horizontal black lines above and below and a single vertical black line at each end. A common type. Height, 8.5 cm.; width, 14 cm. *b*. Restored from fragments. Rim, red on top, white stripe underneath, bordered by black lines. Each side decorated with double black rectangle, roughly painted on, enclosing string of twenty double-hatched lozenges of reddish brown on white background. Height, 10 cm.; width, 17 cm. A common type. *c*. Slightly irregular in form but carefully made. Polished and decorated with high degree of skill. The whole dish, both outside and inside, is covered with light red paint. Rim, dark brown lip edged with black above a white band, edged with black, completely encircling the dish. Handles, bar and cross pattern of black lines on dark red background. Sides, symmetrically arranged series of very conventional Inca pattern which may be described as follows: On each side, five panels, the center one consisting of two vertical bands of bar and cross pattern bordered by double black lines, filled in with dark red; the four outer panels containing the conventional necklace or "fruit tree" design in black, each panel bordered by double black lines filled in with dark red. The bottom is decorated by a dark red band, 1 cm. in width, surrounding the edge, an unusual feature. Height, 6.5 cm.; diameter, 12.5 cm. *d*. Restored from fragments constituting about one-half of the original. Reddish-yellow clay. The whole dish, both outside and inside, covered with cherry-red paint. Lip, a band of black triangles connected by a continuous black line at the outer edges. Handles, probably cross and bar pattern with black bars. Sides, a row of white triangles pointing alternately up and down, separated by four oblique black lines, enclosed in a single black rectangle. An unusual pattern. Height, about 9 cm.; width, about 15 cm. *e*. Brownish-red clay, painted red. Rim, black and white zigzag on a red background edged with narrow black lines. Handles, bar and cross pattern, the triangles formed by double crosses filled with white dots. Sides, a solid black panel edged with narrow black lines, on which are painted seven rows of seven red rectangles edged with white, alternately arranged on black background. A very unusual pattern. Height, 8 cm.; diameter, 12.5 cm. *f*. Rim, red on top, white underneath, bordered with black lines. Handles, cross and bar pattern, consisting of vertical lines interrupted by X-shaped pattern of double lines in imitation of basketry, black on white. On either side of handles are vertical bands decorated with cross and bar pattern set vertically, reddish-brown bars and black crosses on white. These vertical bands are connected by horizontal bands of lozenge pattern like *b*. Height, 7 cm.; width, 12 cm.

dishes was usually sober and not frivolous, except in the dishes with the two animal handles. This type, however, has a rim which makes it look more like a drinking vessel than a food dish.

The common forms of deep dishes are of heavier construction than the ollas, and they rarely show any signs of having been used in the fire. They are made broad and open so that the hands of the diners may readily extract the delicacies of the pot.

The commonest forms of decoration of the deep dishes are shown in Figures 108 and 109. In Figure 108b the design is in three colors. The lip is painted black, underneath it is a band of white edged with a black line. The principal design has black lines; the small diamonds are composed of thin lines of red, crisscrossed on a white background, edged with heavier lines of black. In Figure 108f the design is in three colors, the lip black, a white band underneath it, edged with a black line, the principal lines of the main design being in heavy black, the smaller lines in red on a white background. In Figure 108a the design is painted in the usual three colors, the straight lines black, the diamonds red on a white background. Figure 109c, the first pot to be discovered, was found in Grave No. 3 on a little ledge, and was in practically perfect condition except that the design was somewhat weathered. It is in three colors, the heavy lines in black, the smaller lines red on a white background. In many of these deep dishes a broad band of white was apparently drawn first, then heavy black lines were used as borders, and finally red and more black lines completed the ornamentation. Sometimes the decoration runs completely around the pot under the handles, as shown in this figure, but more commonly the handle is too low to admit of this and the decoration stops at the handle. The designs shown in these figures are clearly derivatives from basketry patterns, this being particularly true of the design on the handle shown in Figures 108f and 109c. This handle design, consisting of crosses and bars, a well-known basketry type, is used in the vast majority of cases where handles are decorated. Evidently first developed in the binding of the handles by cord or withes, it took the fancy of the early pottery decorators, and occurs again and again in different forms of pottery, sometimes as one of the principal features of the design.

Figure 109c shows the handle design carried out as the main design of the pot. Figure 109e has a design in three colors, chiefly on a white background bordered with heavy black lines, the vertical lines being red and the cross lines black. In Figure 108d basketry binding design is employed for

a

b

c   *d*   *e*

f

109

Two-handled three-color-ware dishes. *a*. Restored from fragments of about one-half of original, found in burial cave. Yellowish clay. Rim, chocolate-brown band edged with black line. Sides, double rectangle of black lines containing two wavy brown lines on white background. Rudely executed. Height, 14 cm.; width, 18.5 cm. *b*. Brownish clay, restored from sherds found near Snake Rock. Whole dish appears to have been painted red. Rim, white zigzag line; handles, red and white concentric diamonds on red background. Over handles, a fringe of inverted black triangles edged with double black line. Between handles, band of white concentric circles on black background, which design is repeated at bottom, where it completely encircles the dish. Sides, a large, double, white zigzag line filled in with red, interspersed with concentric white squares, also filled in with red. An unusual type. Height, about 9 cm.; diameter, about 18 cm. *c*. Dull red clay, from burial cave. The first pot to be found in perfect state of preservation. Lip, red edged with black; handles, bar and double cross pattern. Encircling body, below handles, is band of fifty-four black, cross-hatched lozenges on white background bordered with two horizontal black lines. Height, 11 cm.; width, 15 cm. *d*. Brick-red clay, restored from fragments of about two-thirds of original found in burial cave. Rim, edged with black; handles, probably decorated but impossible to say how. Sides, probably a white band above succession of vertical rows of black lozenges, edged with narrow black lines separated by vertical red bands. Height, 8.5 cm.; width, 12 cm. *e*. Yellowish clay, from burial cave. Lip painted red, over which are black crossbars edged with single black line. Sides, cross and bar pattern set horizontally, consisting of reddish-brown bars and black crosses on white background, enclosed in a double rectangle of black lines, the whole crudely painted on without much skill. The pot itself roughly finished, showing marks of scraper; not polished. A common type. Height, 11 cm.; width, 16 cm. *f*. Reddish-brown clay, restored from a few sherds found near Snake Rock. Careful workmanship. Lip edged with black; handles, bar and cross pattern edged with black; sides have vertical bands near handles, connected above by a similar horizontal band consisting of triple zigzag black lines filled in with white on rich red background. Within this pattern are two large panels whose design has been almost entirely lost, separated by a vertical band of triple black zigzag lines filled in with white on red background. The whole inner pattern is bordered by a network of black on white, except at the bottom. Carefully made and polished. Height, about 13 cm.; diameter, probably about 18 cm.

the main ornamentation of the deep dish and another familiar basketry pattern has been used to decorate the interior of the lip. The design is in three colors; the pot was a deep red and on it are painted white triangles bordered with black lines, and on the rim black triangles. In Figure 109a the design appears to be either that of a rainbow or of snakes, representing rain, thunder, and lightning. It is crudely applied and of frequent occurrence. The design was apparently originally in black, red, and white, the pot itself of a dark yellowish brown. The straight lines are black, the crooked ones white on a black background. Figure 109d shows another geometrical pattern, evidently developed from basketry. The design consists of heavy vertical bands of red and white and on the latter were painted black lines and black diamonds. In Figure 108c we have an example, the only one in the collection of deep dishes, of one of the two most common designs found on Inca pottery of various forms. The central portion has been developed from the handle decoration, and the right and left sides are either crude representations of fruit trees, or else a development from the ancient necklace pattern referred to elsewhere. Both sides are similarly decorated. The design is in three colors, black, white, and red. The heavy vertical lines are in red, edged with black. The only white of which evidence remains was in a band going completely around the pot, just under the lip, which was painted black. Figure 109f shows another development of the rainbow, snake, or lightning pattern. The design is in red, black, and white, the pot itself being of red clay. Figure 109b, another unique design, is more fanciful. This pot was found in very bad condition and was blackened as though it had been used in the fire; deep dishes may have been used for cooking, although the evidence seems to show that the majority of them were not so used.

In Figure 108e we have an extremely attractive little dish, found in a niche near a grave. It was nearly whole when found and has since been restored. The decoration consists of small red squares edged with white, arranged with considerable regularity on a black background. The rim is decorated with a white line edged with black on a red background. The handles have, in addition to the conventional binding pattern, white dots on a red background, while the crossbars are of red edged with black. Owing to the lack of hard usage which these dishes received, and the fact that they appear to have been commonly placed in the graves, probably with a full complement of food for the departed, more reasonably complete examples of them were encountered than of any other kind of pot.

110

Jug, bought in Cuzco, but said to have been purchased by owner from muleteer who lived in the valley near Machu Picchu and who declared that he had found it there. Handle, red; rim, red. Front design, black and red on reddish-yellow background; no trace of white; trellis-work and circles, black; vertical and horizontal bands, red. Underneath the handle on the back of the jug, two dark red lines crossed. Nubbin, painted red. Height, 21.5 cm.; diameter of bowl, 17.5 cm.

111

An unusually tough piece of pottery found in burial cave in perfect condition and transported to New Haven without cracking; a section of the ceiling of the room in which it was stored fell on it with such force as to smear it with white, but without cracking it, although the pot next it was smashed into a hundred pieces. Black ware. Vertical handle. Face carefully modeled. Figure slightly humpbacked. No other examples of this coastal type were found at Machu Picchu. Height, 17 cm.; diameter of bowl, 13.5 cm.

A slightly different form of dish, perceptibly shallower and flatter, was so weatherworn that it is impossible to say whether it ever had any decorative design or not. There is no evidence of one. An interesting feature of this dish is that it was broken in use and holes were drilled so that the two pieces could be securely fastened together. Evidently the dish was not used for liquids, but probably for parched corn or peanuts.

Another common Machu Picchu type is a pelike-shaped jug almost unknown in other parts of South America (Fig. 71, type 6). Seventy-eight specimens were found, varying in height from eleven inches to twenty inches and in width from about four inches to six inches. Each has a pair of handles attached vertically, connecting the rim and shoulders of the jug. One pair was found decorated in a manner resembling a two-handled dish; as a rule, however, they do not seem to have been as elaborately decorated as the dishes. About one-third of the pelike-shaped jugs came from the burial caves, and all but one of these from the three chief cemeteries. Not one can be positively associated with a male skeleton.

Ordinarily one-handled jugs also seem to be in this class (Fig. 72, type 13). Of the seventy-three specimens, nearly half come from the burial caves. In one of the cases where there could be no room for doubt, a *chicha* jug, with a grotesque face, was found buried close to the skull of a female skeleton. In another, two jugs were found buried close to a distinguished lady. Of the thirty-one jugs associated with burials, ten came from Cave No. 1 and ten from Cave No. 2. Only two were found in caves with men only, and of these one is more of a round-bottomed flask than a jug and the other cannot positively be assigned to the grave where the man was buried. In other words, strange as it may seem, jugs, both of the one-handled and two-handled varieties, belonged properly to the women. Undoubtedly, then, it was the women who made the *chicha* or other beverages, as is the custom in Peru today. One of the jugs had a handle decorated with the head of a fierce puma or jaguar, partially hollow so that a string could be passed through the teeth in such a manner as to support the jug from a peg. Several jugs are decorated with the human face in low relief, or sometimes partly in relief and partly painted. One amusing specimen, decorated with a human face in relief, is humpbacked and has human arms in relief, the hands resting comfortably on the well-developed paunch (Fig. 111).

The rarer types of pots present many problems. Extremely rare is the little jar in Figure 72, type 14, only two examples of which were

112

Jug. Vertical handle broken off and nubbins polished off. Three-color ware; rim, black; neck, red inside, white outside. Decoration is rather unusual variation of necklace, bar and cross pattern. Lines all in black on yellowish background. Vertical bands red. Design runs almost all the way around the jug, connected by three black lines under the handle. Full pattern is shown in Fig. 113. Height, 13 cm.; diameter of bowl, 11.5 cm. This jug, evidently the property of a wizard or medicine man, was found in a burial cave and contained a large variety of objects, including bone, charcoal, seeds, herbs, etc.

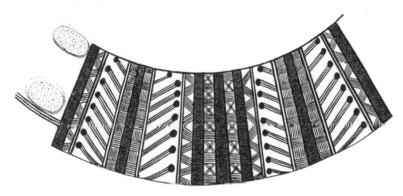

113

Pattern on bowl of jug above.

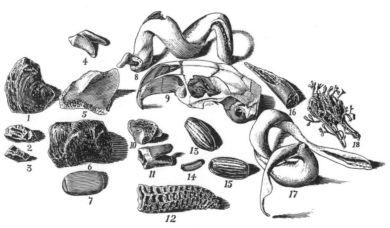

114

Partial contents of jug shown in Fig. 112. 1 and 6, pieces of charcoal; 2 and 3, silver or lead ore; 4, human tooth; 5, charred bone; 7, 13, and 15, seeds; four others are not figured; 8, twisted rawhide; 9, skull of small rodent of genus *Abrocoma;* 10, fragment of bone; 11, human tooth showing signs of decay; 12, very small corncob, length, 3.8 cm.; 14, tooth from small skull; 16, charred fragment of wood; 17, rawhide; 18, dried moss. Besides the articles figured there were two other fragments of charcoal. Nos. 4, 5, 10, and 11 "belong to two of the human skulls taken from this grave."

found. By a strange coincidence, the first grave I ever opened in Peru (I had done some excavating in the Hawaiian Islands) at Choqquequirau, as described in *Across South America,* contained one of these little unguent jars. One of the two at Machu Picchu was near the Snake Rock; the other was in the grave of an unusually interesting and peculiar young man who had some ornaments but no appropriate masculine possessions. Equally rare is the stirrup-shaped spherical bottle, a common enough coast type, of which only two specimens were found here (Figs. 72, type 17, and 115a). One came from the rubbish pile in front of the Three-Door Group, the other from a grave "halfway down the mountainside . . . southeast from the city." This again is an unusual locality. The associated bones are probably female, and the artifacts included some unique stone tokens.

Almost equally rare is the hydria-shaped olla (Fig. 71, type 9), of which only three examples were found, one near the Snake Rock, one on the main stairs, and one, the only complete specimen, in the grave on the other side of the Urubamba River near Heald's bridge. Here again one of the rarest forms is in unique surroundings. None of these three types occurred in any of the regular cemeteries or burial cave groups, and they apparently were not in the possession of the ordinary people. Where did they come from? How did they get here? The jar is an Inca type. The bottle is a coast type. The hydria-shaped olla is fire-blackened, probably a cooking vessel, like the beaker-shaped olla and the diota-shaped olla. It is of crude workmanship and may be a jungle type.

Of lebes-shaped kettles (Fig. 71, type 10), sherds representing seven pots were found. Although this is a rare shape it is apparently represented in seven different localities, widely scattered. One of its forms (type 10b) is excessively rare, only a single specimen having been found. Equally rare is the two-handled bowl (Fig. 70, type 5), of which nine examples were found, widely scattered. Rare also is the wide-mouthed aryballus, or pithos (Figs. 71, type 8, and 81d), with nine specimens, four in the Snake Rock Cemetery and five in the burial caves. In one of these caves was buried the skeleton of a "very young, perhaps new-born" child. Urn-burial was practiced in Peru, examples being known from widely separated sites, and it would appear as though the pithos were the type of jar made for that purpose. Bones of infants would not be expected to last very long in this climate, so it need not surprise us that in only one case at Machu Picchu were they actually found in the urn.

Pottery

a. Stirrup-shaped bottle. *b.* Portion of jug in white ware decorated with black and red vertical bands. Height, 10 cm.; diameter, 11 cm. *c.* Fragment of pot. *d.* Jug, decorated with red incised band. Very rare. *e.* Pot handle decorated with incised and concentric diamonds, bars, and double crosses. Very rare. *f.* Deep plate, from near Snake Rock. Pure white clay. Design, concentric circles of reddish-black crescents, alternately opening up and down. A unique pattern. Height, 3 cm.; diameter, 12.5 cm.

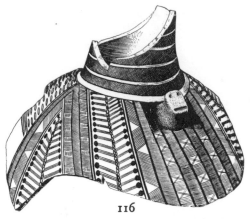

116

Fragment of large aryballus. Narrow bands around the neck white, broader bands of fine black lines crisscrossed on red background; central decoration of broad red bands between lines of bars and crosses, which are fine black lines on red background. Rope nubbin painted red. Interior of jar a peculiar bluish gray, the firing not having materially altered the color of the clay. Diameter of neck, 14.6 cm.; thickness of material in neck, 1.2 cm.

a

b

c

117

Aryballi of three-color ware, from burial caves. *a.* Partly restored. Panel contains zigzag of black and white lines on red background, surrounded by white border crossed and edged with black lines. Entire bowl, except base and under handles, painted red. Rope nubbin painted white, decorated with black spots. Shoulder pierced with four holes, possibly made in repairing the aryballus when the neck first broke off, or in order to suspend it. *b.* Front panel, two rows of black diamonds and one of red diamonds separated by black lines. Sides of shoulder, red band bordered with black and white lines. Rope nubbin undecorated. Diameter, 14 cm.; height to base of neck, 15.5 cm. *c.* One of the few pots found in fine condition. Three-color-ware aryballus from burial cave. Neck and ears, white; panel, black and white fret on reddish-yellow background; border, broad red band surrounded by two narrow black lines. Rope nubbin black or dark red. Height, 39 cm.; diameter of bowl, 24 cm.; diameter of neck, 6.7 cm.; height of rim above shoulder, 12.5 cm.; diameter of rim, 14.5 cm.; thickness of rim, 0.8 cm.

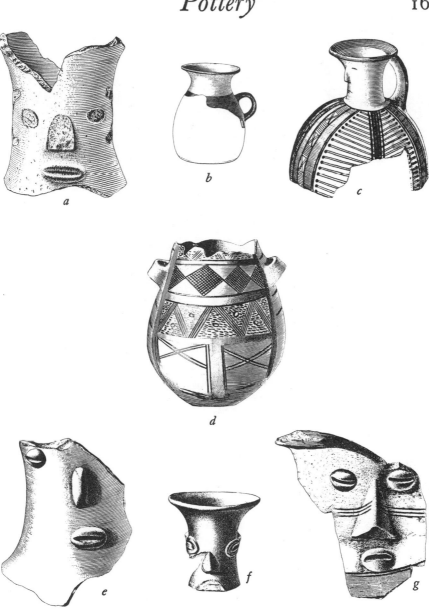

118

Fragments of jugs and jars. *a.* Neck of much-weathered whitish pottery jug. Ears, eyes, nose modeled and chipped off. Mouth modeled. *b.* Three-color ware, much weathered. Handle, red, edged with black; rim, possibly black; neck, red inside, white outside; bowl, red. Diameter of rim, 19 cm. *c.* Three-color ware. Handle, bar and cross pattern. Rim, red; face, painted in black on white background; nose, modeled. Only about one-half of neck was found, and this so weathered that it is not possible to decipher much of the decoration. Bowl, small lines black, vertical bands red edged with small black lines and two white lines. *d.* Coarse yellow ware, decorated on both sides with design in black and red. The only example. Height of fragment, 34 cm.; width, 31 cm. *e.* Much weathered, red pottery neck fragment. *f.* Vertical handle, black ware. Ears, nose, and mouth modeled; eyes modeled and incised. Diameter of neck, 3.2 cm. *g.* Probably three-color ware, but considerably weathered. Face seems to have been painted red, decorated with straight black lines. No evidence of ears. Eyes and mouth modeled and incised; nose modeled. The neck of this jug is so short that the mouth and lower part of the nose are practically on the shoulder of the bowl.

119

a. Pelike-shaped jug restored from fragments found in burial cave. One of a pair; three-color ware. Handles, black lines on red background. Rim, black; neck, inside red, outside white; bowl, red decorated with band in fine black lines on white background edged with two black lines. Height, 15 cm.; diameter of bowl, 11.5 cm. b. Two-color-ware jug; handle restored; rim, red. Design in black lines on yellowish-red background; no evidence of white; three vertical bands red; diamonds of seven or six parallel lines. Crudely made and design coarsely executed. Height, 14 cm.; diameter of bowl, 13 cm. c. Jug with horizontal handle, restored from fragments of about seven-eighths of original. Three-color ware, from burial caves. Handle, black bars and crosses edged with white on red background. Lip, black; neck, white; shoulder, two black lines. Front, conventional necklace, bar and cross design on reddish-yellow background; necklace black, three strings; bars black; crosses very faint but probably white; vertical bands red with black border. Height, 13.5 cm.; diameter of bowl, 12.5 cm. d. Unique two-handled jug restored from fragments found near Snake Rock. Much weathered. Handles triangular in form, fractured above; may have been painted white; one higher than the other. Diameter, 23 cm. e. Small yellow jug, found in burial cave. Handle partially restored. Rim red inside, white outside. Contained three pieces of yellow paint. Height, 6.5 cm.; diameter of bowl, 7.5 cm. f. Three nodules of yellowish earth, probably paint, found in e.

120

Fragments of jugs or jars. *a.* Handle horizontal. Decoration in black and red on yellowish background. Shows use of necklace pattern in two ways: the vertical "fruit-tree" design and the zigzag with disks separated. Probable diameter of bowl, 23 cm. *b.* Much weathered handle, red ware. Nicely modeled head of jaguar or wildcat; seems to have been painted. Eyes incised. Nostrils pierced. Teeth and tongue modeled. Mouth hollow; holes let in at corners, presumably for string to be passed through so that jug could be suspended. Width of head, 3.8 cm. *c.* Much weathered three-color ware. Probably with human features in relief. Framing the face there appears to be a ridge in relief, incised and painted red. *d.* Pelike-shaped jug restored from fragments of nine-tenths of original found in burial cave. Two-color ware; no evidence of black. Handles both red; not exactly opposite to each other, but misplaced by width of one handle. Neck red inside; outside red on one side and white on the other. Bowl painted white on one side, red on the other, alternating with the colors of the neck. Height, 22 cm.; diameter of bowl, 18.5 cm. *e.* Three-color ware of yellowish pottery. Rim painted black on edge, red inside. Face dark red. Eyes modeled and incised, painted black; incising painted white. Nose crossed with two black lines. *f.* Vertical handle, pierced. Black ware. Eyes and mouth modeled and incised; nose modeled. Diameter of neck, 3.8 cm. *g.* Decorated with black or dark red spots on a white background. Diameter of rim, 7 cm.

Cups (Fig. 72, type 15) were also scarce, only twelve having been found, none of which were in the burial caves and only one in the Snake Rock region. They were, instead, all on the west side of the city and ten were in the southwest quarter, the region of the very best houses, the "palaces." Why was this useful and easily constructed article not more used by people who were so fond of things to drink? The ordinary drink was undoubtedly *chicha,* a malt brew. It is drunk today by the country Indians out of gourds, broad rather than deep, but apparently the drinkers of Machu Picchu liked it out of the broad flat drinking ladles, of which we found so many, rather than out of proper cups. Perhaps they liked to have the gas and foam escape as rapidly as possible. Possibly, also, the cups were not used for *chicha* but for some special form of hard liquor. At any rate, it is interesting that none were found in the graves—apparently they did not belong to the women of the last *régime.*

There are perhaps a score of the diota-shaped ollas (Fig. 71, type 7), a kind of cooking pot, fire-blackened and not decorated. Unlike the cups, they are actually more common in the caves than in the city, five occurring in or near dwelling houses, ten in the cemeteries. They seem to have been a late style of cooking pot. They were easy to make, much more so than the beaker-shaped olla, and very serviceable, although harder to lift away from the fire. A modern Indian would be glad to use them today. They are well adapted to a fireplace made of three or four stones.

Amphoras were about as rare as the diota-shaped ollas. They were used for brewing *chicha,* and while easy to dip from, the contents were much more exposed to the air and dust than in the large aryballi. Only two were found in the caves. They could scarcely be regarded as a private vessel.

A few deep plates, either with two handles attached horizontally to the rim or with double nubbins attached to the rim instead of handles, and with the interior decorated with attractive patterns, were also found, but they are not common.

Perhaps the most interesting form of all is a three-legged brazier with a band-shaped handle attached vertically to its top, its mouth formed with a small lip irregular in form and placed on one side. There are three openings or ventholes in the top; the legs are solid and cylindrical. No specimens were seen in any of the burial caves, but pieces of at least twenty-five braziers were found in excavations in the citadel, all much fire-blackened, both within and without. From among these we were able to match up

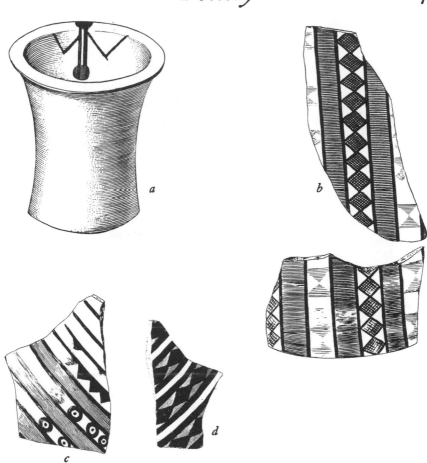

121

a. Yellowish pottery cup, partly restored. Inside decorated with variation of necklace pattern and simple V's. Height, 9 cm.; diameter of rim, 8 cm.; diameter of cup, 5 cm. *b*. Fragments of large, three-color-ware cup. Vertical bands red with black borders; strings of diamonds red or black on white background. *c* and *d*. Decorated three-color-ware potsherds.

122

One of a pair of unusually fine two-handled dishes, found in burial cave. Light brown clay covered with creamy white slip inside and outside, except on the rim, which is colored dark brown. The inside is further decorated with two butterflies, diagrammatically rather than accurately drawn. Of the four antennae, the two central ones are black and the two on the sides red with black tips. The head is red; the eyes, black on a white background; the thorax, red, edged with black; the outer wings, black decorated with white zigzags, circles, and dots, and also with red circles; the inner wings, red decorated with black and white zigzags, white circles with black or red centers, and black circles with white centers. This dish represents the highest degree of artistic skill in decorative design of any pottery found at Machu Picchu. Height, 3 cm.; diameter, 12.5 cm.

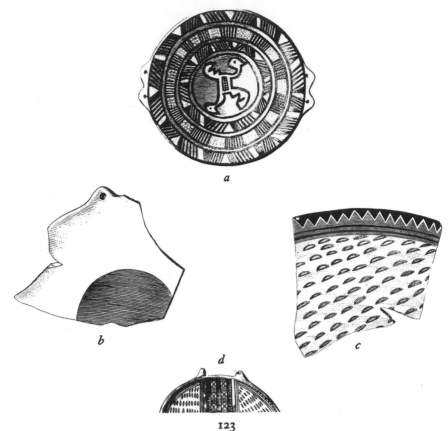

123

Richly decorated three-color-ware plates. *a.* Found in nearly perfect condition in burial cave. Design in black and white on rich red background; three concentric bands surrounding a compound parrot-like figure in black and white. The outer band of black lines divided by irregular white figures; middle band of black bars and white dots; inner band like outer band. Nubbins pierced and painted white. Height, 0.2 cm.; diameter, 13 cm. *b.* Found near Snake Rock. Edge of fragment black; center, red on white background. *c.* Large, heavy dish, 1 cm. thick. Rim, dark red or black; triangles black edged with white on red background bordered by black and red lines. Center, red leaves on yellowish white background. *d.* Large, deep, heavy plate found near Snake Rock. Outside of rim decorated with red band a little more than a centimeter wide, running around the handle; top of rim black. Inside, black triangles bordered by three black lines enclosing mass of leaflike objects painted in black on yellowish background, the whole crossed by conventional bar and cross design, the three heavy lines being red with black borders, the bars, double crosses, and diagonals black, all on a yellowish background.

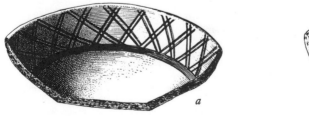

124

Fragments of saucers, much weathered. *a.* Inside, trellis-work, black on yellowish background; outside, reddish. Height, 4.5 cm.; *b.* Rim appears to have been painted with black line edged with black zigzags. Height, 3 cm.

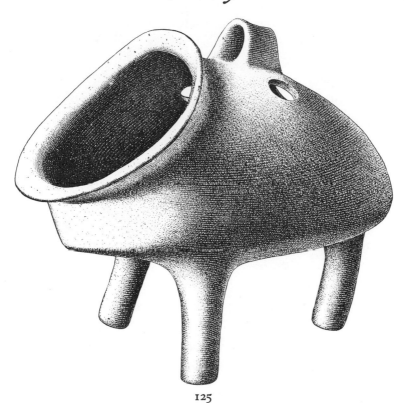

125

Brazier. Restored from fragments of two-thirds of the original. Two of the legs were found, nearly one-half of the mouth, practically the entire body, including three-fourths of the handle. Red ware, no decoration. A single long loop handle and three ventholes on top. Interior and lower portion of the sides and base blackened as by fire. Height to top of handle, about 17 cm.; diameter of holes, 1.5 cm.; width of mouth outside, 13 cm.; rear leg, height outside 7 cm., height inside 5 cm., diameter 1.9 cm.; thickness of brazier, about 0.3 cm.

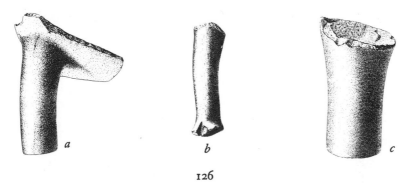

126

a. Fragment and rear leg of red brazier. (The measurement of this leg would seem to indicate a brazier of about the size of Fig. 125.) *b*. Leg of brazier (?). *c*. Front leg of very large brazier. Two other legs of this brazier were found, but not enough fragments to make restoration practicable. Height outside, 8 cm.; height inside, 7 cm.; diameter, 3.4 cm.

enough fragments to restore one of these braziers with reasonable accuracy (see Fig. 125), but prolonged and repeated attempts to restore more than one have proved unsuccessful. An examination of most of the important Peruvian material in Europe and America shows this to be one of the rarest known forms of American pottery. A small model, about two inches in diameter, is in the Museum für Völkerkunde in Berlin, and a slightly larger model, about three inches in diameter, is in the American Museum of Natural History, New York. Neither shows any signs of use. No museum appears to have any other specimens and yet the brazier seems to have been once in fairly common use at Machu Picchu.

Some of the braziers must have been quite large, judging by the leg shown in Figure 126c. So far as we can judge from the fragments, the usual size of the three-legged brazier was about seven inches high, six inches wide, and seven inches long. These braziers appear to have been intended for a charcoal fire in which metals could be kept hot while being worked, the ventholes on top admitting of the insertion of blowpipes. The practice of using blowpipes is referred to in several of the early Spanish chronicles, but there has been some doubt about it as hitherto no practical working brazier with blowpipe holes had been found. The material of the braziers was very thin, apparently in order to enable them to be more readily heated. They were probably used for reheating or annealing bronze knives, axes, and chisels. Professor Mathewson, who made an exhaustive study of the bronzes found at Machu Picchu, feels that there is no question but that small bronze implements could be reheated very conveniently in utensils of this shape. He writes: "If I were going to anneal an article of this kind (small bronze implements) I could easily make use of a utensil of this sort. I could take it to the laboratory now and use it for that purpose. It has an enclosed chamber with provision for blowing, if desired, the openings being properly located for this purpose."

The three-legged braziers were obviously not an ordinary part of the possessions of the last inhabitants of Machu Picchu. Of the thirty-seven braziers represented in the collection, none was found in Cemetery No. 1, only one was found in Cemetery No. 2, and only one in Cemetery No. 3. On the other hand, eight were found in the Snake Rock Cemetery. It does not seem likely that they were used by women. To be sure, one was found in a cave which contained the remains of four women and no men, but this cave had undoubtedly contained other skeletons which had long since disintegrated. My reason for thinking so is that a large pile of sherds

127

Decorated potsherds. *b*, *d*, *e*, *f*, *g*. Three-color ware.

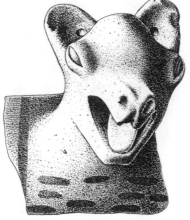

128

129

130

Pot handle of a pattern unusual at Machu Picchu.

Handle of three-color-ware dish; might represent a young llama, or possibly a coyote. Spots black on red; most of head white. Very skilful and highly characteristic bit of modeling. Tongue, throat, and lips carefully modeled, but without teeth; forehead bulges between the eyes, which protrude considerably; ear holes pierced. Width of head, 2.8 cm.; length of head, 3.7 cm.

Fragment of dish handle, much blackened and worn. The ear was broken off long ago and the piece has been much handled since. Length of head, 4.6 cm.

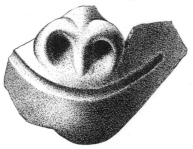

131

132

Portion of pot made in form of monkey's head. Very much weathered. Reddish pottery of fine grain. Width of nostrils, 3.5 cm.

Fragment of coarse, much blackened pottery; probably the mouth of a member of the cat family. Only one other fragment of this or even a similar pot was found. Dimensions, 7 cm. by 8.5 cm.; thickness varies from 0.7 cm. to 1.3 cm.

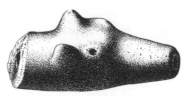

133

Fragment of pot handle or whistle; weathered; hollow. Eyes slightly raised and incised. A rare type, possibly of coastal origin.

134

Trunk and arms of small figurine. Head, neck, back, and legs broken off. Appears to have been an ornament from the neck of a jar or jug.

135

Animal-shaped handle of small dish. From terrace below Temple of the Three Windows. Much weathered. Black and red on white background. Ears and eyes modeled. Length of handle, 6.5 cm.; probable height of dish, 5.5 cm.

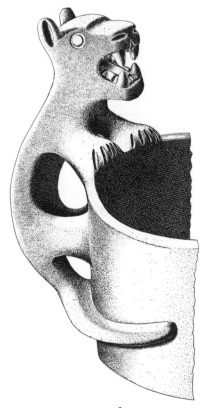

136

Fragment of ceremonial dish restored from pieces of several dishes, most of which were much weathered. The ware is red, but appears to have been decorated in three colors. Tail always turns to right, paws rest on rim; mouth open, expression fierce; teeth and tongue carefully modeled. Upper part of head apparently modeled separately and stuck on to the lower part; ears and nostrils deeply incised; eyes incised and probably painted white. Height, apparently about 11.5 cm.; diameter, probably about 24 cm.

were found at the mouth of the cave, as though they had been thrown out when the later burials were made. From the sherds at this point we can recognize twenty-six different pieces of pottery, or far more than were customarily placed with four bodies. Another brazier, the one which we were able to restore, was brought in by the Indians with the bones of a female skeleton, which led Dr. Eaton to suppose that the brazier belonged to the woman with whose bones it was brought in, and that she may have used it for "parching maize or carrying live coals to rebuild a fire." While there is no serious objection to this theory, I doubt whether it would have been made had Dr. Eaton had an opportunity to visit the enormous rock shelter on the north side of Huayna Picchu, from which came a number of potsherds, including those of this brazier. The cave was by far the largest found anywhere in this region and so extraordinary that the Indians, Richarte and Alvarez, were very anxious that I should visit it and make a flashlight picture of the interior. They had done a lot of digging in and about the great shelter and gathered what they could, finding the bones in a grave at the entrance to the cave. The Indians were very much disappointed at the meager returns, inasmuch as the cave was so large and had been so very difficult to reach, the path to it skirting a sheer rock precipice for some hundreds of feet. Further search, on the occasion of my visit, was rewarded by the discovery of two pairs of bronze tweezers. It is impossible to prove that the braziers belonged to men, but the evidence seems to me to point in that direction.

In conclusion, it is well to remember that remains of nearly four times as much pottery were found in the city (including the Snake Rock region) as in the burial caves outside the city limits. This proportion is maintained in the common two-handled dishes and in the deep plates and ladles, in which food was probably served. The fact that six times as many aryballi were found in the city as in the burial caves is undoubtedly due to the presence of the huge community or family aryballi used for storing water or *chicha,* vessels which were not used in the garniture of the graves and could hardly have been considered as personal possessions. If we deduct these from the totals we find that the smaller or more personal aryballi are also found to exist in similar proportions to the other common dishes. There is, however, a striking discrepancy in the cooking pots or beaker-shaped ollas: instead of the proportion of four to one, we find that it is less than two to one. In other words, only 131 specimens were found in the city, while seventy-three were found in the caves. It is interesting to note that the only other type of pottery found as frequently in the graves is the deep plate or ladle, an individual dish. Pot lids or covers, on the other hand, do not seem to have been common in the graves, the proportion being fourteen to one. Out of the ninety-seven specimens only six were found in the burial caves, while thirty-eight were found in the Snake Rock region. Perhaps they were not used so often with the cooking pots as with the large water and *chicha* jars.

The commonest designs are nearly always geometrical. Many of them, notably the bar-and-double-cross pattern, which occurs so frequently on the handles (see Figs. 89e, 108f, 109c), are clearly imitative of ancient basketry and show the easiest form of binding and making handles. These designs probably originated on handles but took the fancy of the ancient potters, and consequently reappear in various panels and constitute the central portion of a very common pattern. (See, for example, Figs. 81b, 83, 84, 113, 116, 119c.) Another common design we decided to call the necklace pattern, because in several instances, notably the pair of jugs shown in Figure 75, the location of this pattern naturally suggests a necklace, and also because in one of the caves we found a large number of small bronze disks that had evidently been suspended in the form of a necklace, and, if drawn by a native artist, might readily take the form shown in Figures 84, 86c, and 120a, where also the details of the original face (as shown on Fig. 75) are used as separate elements in the decoration. (See Fig. 76.)

With very few exceptions the pottery is purely Inca in design and workmanship. Nevertheless a few types fairly common here are almost unknown elsewhere.

CHAPTER VII

⋯•⟶◆⟵•⋯

METALLURGY AT MACHU PICCHU

METAL articles are easily preserved, yet we only found at Machu Picchu about two hundred little bronzes and a few pieces of silver and tin. The pieces of silver include half a dozen small silver disks perforated near the edge, obviously intended to be used as pendants. There was also a thin silver bracelet, partly engraved with a simple pattern; two silver rings, very simple in design; two small shawl pins; and parts of two pairs of tweezers made of silver, besides two other problematical objects. Nothing of gold was found, our "friends" in Cuzco to the contrary notwithstanding. There are two small chunks of tin, obviously intended for use in the preparation of bronze. The collection of bronzes includes such tools as axes, hatchets, knives, chisels, bars, bodkins, and pointed instruments, such domestic utensils as mirrors, tweezers, small knives, pins, needles, and ear-spoons (?), and such articles of adornment as rings, bracelets, spangles, and bells.

The number of disks or circular pendants found at Machu Picchu was not large. Except for the remains of a necklace composed of some thirty-nine small copper disks, four large bronze disks with handles (probably mirrors), one large silver pendant disk, and five smaller ones constitute the total find.

Of the pins, more than twice as many were found in burial caves as in the city. They belonged to women, most of them apparently being used for fastening the front of the shawl, or shoulder covering. In Bolivia today this custom is still very common, particularly among the Quichuas near Potosí. In that case, however, the head of the pin has of late tended to become more and more like the European spoon. The pins found at Machu Picchu vary in length from three to nine inches and are mostly of the familiar type with flat heads shaped like a half moon. Of these, seven appear to be of silver and twenty of copper or bronze. The larger proportion of the heads were beaten very thin, and have an average thickness of between one and two millimeters; the edges are fairly sharp and appear to have been used for cutting purposes. There is some variety in the shape of

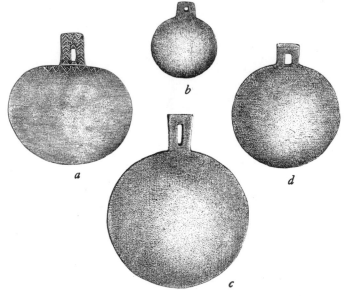

137

Bronze mirrors. *a*. Slightly convex, engraved. From Snake Rock region. Diameter, 7.3 cm.; weight, 30.1 gr.

138

Bronze bracelet from Upper City. Engraved in three places, one end turned back and hammered down. Diameter, 5.1 cm.

139

Silver finger ring from north side of Stairway of the Fountains.

140

Silver finger ring from burial cave. Diameter, 2.1 cm.

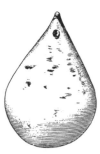

141

Thin bronze pendant, from Snake Rock region. Length, 3.8 cm.

142

Silver armlet from Snake Rock region. Edges turned over and hammered down. Length, 9 cm.

143

Copper or bronze needle, from burial cave. Length, 16.5 cm.; width of head, 1.5 cm.; thickness of head, 0.4 cm.; weight, 13.6 gr. Very heavy corrosion has covered up and preserved the string.

144

Bronze needle, possibly weaver's tool, from Snake Rock region. Length, 45.7 cm.; weight, 60.8 gr. Covered with hard verdigris. The eye of the needle was made by hammering out the shank, bending over the tongue-like extremity, and hammering down the sides to cover the end of the tongue.

145

Bronze pin, from a burial cave. Length, 11.1 cm.; width of head, 1.6 cm.; thickness of head, 0.3 cm.; weight, 8.7 gr. End of the shank is noticeably larger than the rest of the shank. Perhaps when this piece of bronze was cast it was intended to hammer out a larger head.

146

Copper pin from Snake Rock region. Covered with thick coating of verdigris. Length, 10.8 cm.; width of head, 1.9 cm. The head is smaller than the usual type and the hole considerably larger, as though it might have been used as a needle.

147

Very badly corroded copper or bronze pin or needle from a burial cave. Total length, 7.2 cm.; weight, 2.5 gr.

148

Bronze crowbar, from burial cave. Length, 44 cm.

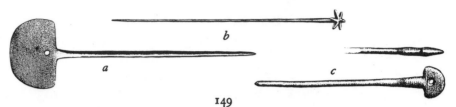

149

Copper pins from Snake Rock region. *a.* Much oxidized. Length, 10.8 cm. *b.* Copper pin with six-pointed star head. Beautifully made. Length, 31.5 cm.; diameter of star, 2.8 cm.; weight, 37.5 gr. *c.* Length, 9 cm.; width of head, 1.45 cm.; thickness of head, 0.3 cm.; weight, 7.7 gr.

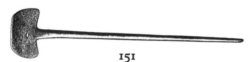

150

Very much corroded copper needle from Snake Rock region. Length, 9.2 cm.

151

Copper or bronze pin from Snake Rock region. Length, 16.15 cm.; diameter of head, 3.45 cm.; thickness of head, 0.2 cm.; weight, 23 gr. Covered with a thick coating of verdigris. The end of the head flattened by use; bears distinct marks of having been sharpened, probably for use as a knife. Irregular, pierced hole.

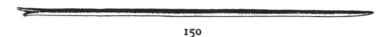

152

Silver pin from burial cave. Length, 7.7 cm.; diameter of head, 1.8 cm.; thickness of shank, 0.15 cm.; thickness of head, 0.05 cm.; weight, 2.3 gr.

153

Silver bolas. Diameter, 3.3 cm.

154

Bronze bolas.

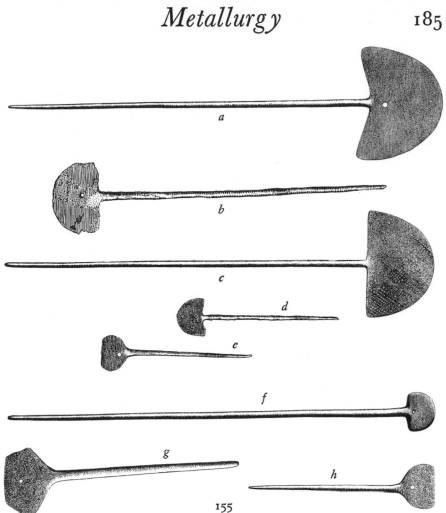

155

Bronze pins from burial caves. *a*. Length 23.5 cm.; width of head, 6 cm.; thickness of head, less than 1 cm.; weight, 19.2 gr. *b*. Very much corroded. Head much flattened. Length, 15.2 cm. *c*. Bears the marks of woolen shawl with which it was probably buried. Considerably corroded. Length, 24 cm.; width of head, 5.8 cm.; thickness of head, 1 mm.; weight, 23 gr. *f*. Corroded; hole drilled. Length, 27.65 cm.; width, 2.45 cm.; thickness of head, 0.46 cm.; weight, 39.9 gr. *g*. Length, 10.8 cm.; diameter of head, 3 cm.; thickness of head, 0.1 cm.; weight, 8.7 gr. Unlike most of the pins, the hole in this one is nearly in the center of the head instead of near the end of the shaft. The shank is unusually heavy. The head of the pin is flattened, and probably was used as a knife. *h*. Length, 8.8 cm.; diameter of head, 2 cm.; thickness of head, 0.05 cm.; weight, 4.4 gr. The head appears to have been flattened and sharpened for use as a knife.

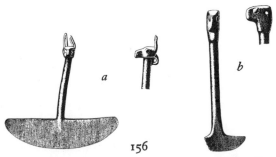

156

Bronze knives. *a*. Length of blade, 4.6 cm.; weight, 6.6 gr. Llama head handle. Snake Rock region. *b*. Total length, 7.6 cm.; weight, 18 gr. Conventionalized animal's head handle. Hole drilled. Blade unusually small. From burial cave.

the head, some being exactly semicircular, others having the points brought down so as to approach a moon three-quarters full, still others somewhat more than a half moon, or somewhat less. All the pins of this shape have holes pierced in the head, generally near the end of the shank, and varying in size from one to three millimeters. In one instance the string still remains in the hole, and has been preserved by being covered over with oxide of copper.

Six of these pins have relatively thicker, heavier heads, which are nevertheless relatively smaller in size in proportion to the length of the shank than in the majority of the pins. Of these, one bears distinctly the evidences of having been used as a cutting implement, but in the others the edge of the head is so well rounded that it could not serve for this purpose. All of the thick-headed pins are of bronze or copper. Besides these flat, half-moon-headed pins, there is one bodkin of unusual length but beautiful manufacture, having a six-pointed star for its head; it is not unlike a large modern hatpin, though the shank is considerably heavier. There are also two pins whose points have been flattened like an ear-spoon, and whose heads are nicely modeled birds—one a humming bird with a very long bill, standing, and the other with outstretched wings and tail, as though floating in the air. In both specimens the body of the bird is pierced with a hole and part of the original string remains in the hole.

There are also three needles, one very long and heavy, and the other two quite small. Most of the bodkins have flattened heads pierced with eyes sufficiently large to permit them to carry a fairly stout cord. In one the eye is very cleverly made by flattening the head of the bodkin to a narrow strip, drawing this strip over, laying it against the shaft of the bodkin and then hammering enough of the sides onto it to secure it, thus making an excellent long needle.

We found half a dozen bronze tweezers, probably intended to take the place of the modern razor. Peruvian Indians seldom had any hair on their faces and were anxious to remove any stray hairs that did appear, and the custom of pulling out undesired facial hairs by primitive tweezers was likewise known among the tribes of Micronesia. The collection of bronzes also includes two or three problematical objects which have defied solution, several little bells like sleigh bells, three or four mirrors of a size and style familiar to the ancient Egyptians, one or two small crowbars, two articles resembling ear-spoons but more probably intended to be used in conveying a small quantity of lime to the mouth when chewing *coca,* and

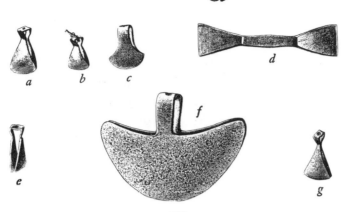

157

Bronze tweezers. *a*. Length, 2.5 cm. *b*. Length, 1.4 cm. *d*. After casting, and before being finished. *f*. Length, 4.7 cm. *g*. Length, 3.2 cm.

158

Silver pendants from the Snake Rock region. Large silver disk pendant found in a folded condition, as though the owner had decided to hide it. Diameter, 9 cm. Hole punched through, and rough edges turned back and hammered down. Thickness of disk, 0.05 cm.; weight, 15.7 gr. In unfolding it some of the creases developed bad cracks. One of them, however, seems to be an old cutting. This injury to the disk may have accounted for its being folded up and put away. Oxidized except where the cracking has caused the oxidization to flake off. Five small silver disk pendants: (1) Diameter, about 1.8 cm.; thickness, 0.03 cm.; weight, 4 gr. Hole punched through and rough edges turned over and hammered down. Slightly oxidized. (2) Hole punched. Diameter, 2.1 cm.; thickness, 0.04 cm.; weight, 1 gr. Very little oxidization. (3) Diameter, 2.15 cm.; thickness, 0.04 cm.; weight, 9 gr. Considerably oxidized. (4) A mate to (2), slightly larger. (5) Diameter, 1.2 cm.; thickness, 0.02 cm.; weight, 2 gr. Slightly oxidized. Hole punched and hammered.

two or three nicely made bolas to which cords were attached by means of a little bar sunk in a small hole.

The throwing of the bolas so as to entangle the legs of birds or animals is an extremely difficult art, taught to *gaucho* boys from their infancy but rarely learned by adult foreigners. In the old days on the ranches of Argentina the *gauchos,* or Indian cowboys, were fond of throwing cattle by means of the bolas, but the practice was usually forbidden by intelligent ranch owners since it frequently resulted in breaking the legs of the victims. Although slings were used by every shepherd in the Andes I have never seen the bolas in use, yet we know that the Incas were familiar with it. Since it does not necessarily cause an animal's legs to be broken but merely tangles them up so that it readily may be captured, we may presume that the first little guanacos to be caught and domesticated, later to become developed by breeding into the useful llamas and alpacas, were caught by means of the bolas. Had the Peruvian Indians not been familiar with this useful device but depended entirely on sling stones or bows and arrows, it is doubtful whether they would have been so successful in domesticating the little South American camels. And had the Indians of our western plains been as familiar with the bolas as they were with bows and arrows they might have domesticated the buffalo.

Of the twenty-three knives, nearly all were found in the city, only four coming from the burial caves. They belonged to men. In shape they were broad and curved like a chopping knife, and in length they vary from three and a half to nine and a half inches. Most of them were in good condition, although nearly all bear marks of use. They are all of bronze or copper. The majority are of the familiar T-shape, with the ends of the handle looped over so that the knife might easily be attached to a string. The handle of one of the T-shaped knives represents the head of a llama, and that of a very stocky little bronze knife ends in the head of an alpaca, or, possibly, dog. The heads of two of the knives appear to end in chisel-shaped points.

The most interesting knife of all those found at Machu Picchu is one of an unusual shape and design, shown in Figure 169. As none of the other knives found at Machu Picchu is of this form, perhaps the knife was not a local product, but had been obtained in trade. The head of the blade is decorated by a small naked boy, clad in breechclout and tasseled cap, lying on his stomach, hauling away in a most lifelike manner on a twisted rope at the end of which is a large fish, almost as long as the boy.

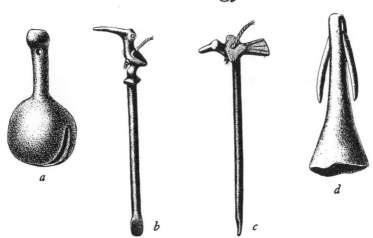

159

a. Bronze bell. From burial cave. Diameter, 2.8 cm. *b*. Bronze spoon. From burial cave. *c*. Bronze spoon. *d*. Bronze earring. From burial cave. Length, 3.7 cm.

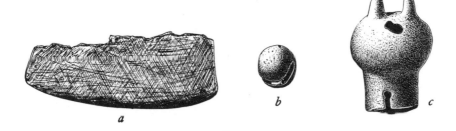

160

a. Fragment of a bronze ax. *b*. Bronze bell. From burial cave. Diameter, 1 cm. *c*. Bronze tip from ceremonial staff (?). From burial cave. Length, 3.75 cm.

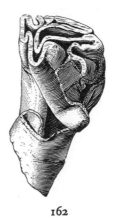

161

Silver handle, possibly from official staff, found near the City Gate. Possibly fragment of bird's head pattern. Length, 4.8 cm.

162

Pure tin for use in casting bronze.

163

Bronze ax.

164

Fragment of bronze chisel.

165

Bronze chisel. Edge turned, possibly by use on
stone. From Eastern Terraces.

166

Bronze ax. From Snake Rock region.

167

Fragment of bronze chisel. From Snake Rock
region.

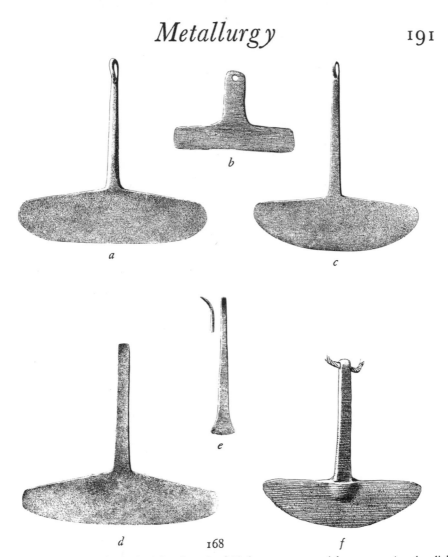

Bronze knives. *a*. From Snake Rock region. Length of blade, 12.55 cm.; weight, 31.7 gr. A rather light blade for its size. Much oxidized. *b*. From Snake Rock region. Total length, 12.4 cm.; weight, 16.7 gr. Very much corroded. An interesting tool; the head bent and sharpened so as to be a scraping chisel. *c*. From Snake Rock region. Length of blade, 11 cm.; weight, 45.9 gr. A strong, well-made knife. The handle shows evidences of having been hammered. *d*. From a burial cave. Length of blade, 6.5 cm.; weight, 26.2 gr. Considerably oxidized. *e*. From burial cave. Length, 4.2 cm.; thickness, 0.1 cm.; weight, 8.7 gr. The handle is wider than that of any other knife. Perhaps this was a scraping rather than a cutting tool. *f*. From a burial cave. Length of blade, 12.9 cm.; weight, 49.6 gr. A strong, serviceable knife. End of handle shaped like a chisel. Covered with thick coating of verdigris.

Bronze knife. From Snake Rock region. Length, 13 cm.; thickness, 0.2 cm.; length of fish, 2.2 cm.; width of man's head, 0.84 cm.; weight, 41.3 gr. The finest example of casting found.

The design and its execution show a high order of artistic sense and good workmanship. The boy has the characteristic beaked nose of the Incas; his cap has the usual ear-flaps; the expression of his face is one of grim determination and, judging by the eye of the fish, he looks as though he were having considerable difficulty in hauling in his prey. The right hand grasps the rope firmly with extended fingers slightly in front of the left hand, and the end of the rope touches the boy's chin. His feet are up in the air, and the general impression is given that he is lying on the bank of a stream, or possibly on the sea beach. A careful examination of several collections of Peruvian antiquities in Munich, Berlin, Paris, London, New York, Cambridge, and Washington has resulted in my being unable to find any knives resembling this in the form of its decoration, although knives of this shape, while rare, are not unknown. It is a charming example of a creative art that delighted in expressing well-known scenes in an artistic manner. Dr. W. H. Holmes, of the United States National Museum, declares it to be one of the finest examples ever found in America of the ancient art of working in bronze.*

It usually has been customary to preserve collections of metal objects from the land of the Incas for exhibition purposes. Sometimes specimens have been submitted for chemical analysis, since this involves merely the drilling of a small hole in the specimen, but no considerable number had ever been thoroughly submitted to metallographic examination, which necessitated mutilation. After consultation with Dr. Holmes, however, it was determined that it would be wise to take advantage of the fact that the exact source of these bronzes was known, and to permit their thorough examination even if it involved mutilation. As a result the looks of many of those bronzes from Machu Picchu which were not of rare or unusual design but which were familiar in collections of Peruvian bronzes have been spoiled, but we have the satisfaction of knowing more in regard to the structure of such objects, the methods of their manufacture, and the reasons for the variation that has been found to exist in the composition of Inca bronzes than has been known before.

The careful study of these bronzes was undertaken by Professor C. H. Mathewson of the Sheffield Scientific School, Yale University.† A rep-

---

* I greatly regret to state that this knife has apparently been stolen from the collection and is not in the Yale University Museum with the other articles found at Machu Picchu.

† For the more technical details of this study, see "A Metallographic Description of Some Ancient Peruvian Bronzes from Machu Picchu," *American Journal of Science,* Fourth Series, XL (1915), 525-616.

resentative group comprising 33 specimens was selected for analysis. This group included 12 knives, 3 axes, 2 pins, 2 chisels, 2 bars, 2 tweezers, a plumb bob, a mirror, a very small spoon—possibly an ear-spoon or lime-spoon—a needle, 2 disks, a rod, 2 irregular masses of metal, and a small fragment of an armlet or bracelet. Of the 33 pieces selected, 30 contained copper, varying in amount from 86 per cent to 99.7 per cent, a practically pure copper knife having a trace of sulphur. The other three pieces include 2 pure silver disks and an irregular mass weighing 160 grams of practically pure tin, 99.79 per cent pure with a trace of antimony. Excluding the 2 silver disks, the mass of pure tin and the pure copper knife, the remaining 29 pieces may be regarded as bronze. Of these 29 pieces of bronze, the tin content varies from 2.1 per cent in the plumb bob to 13.5 per cent in the very small spoons. The average is about 5 per cent. In 3 of the pieces the amount of tin was exactly 5.12 per cent. In copper content the bronzes vary from 86 per cent in the spoon to 96.9 per cent in the plumb bob. Of the 29 pieces of bronze, 16 contained traces of sulphur, none containing more than 0.45 per cent. Ten contained traces of silver and 2 contained traces of zinc, but neither of these two contains more than 0.32 per cent of zinc. Five contain traces of iron, the largest amount being 0.87 per cent. Of the 12 knives in the collection analyzed, one is practically pure copper, the rest are bronze, 11 contain traces of sulphur and 7 contain traces of iron. Of the pins, none have any trace of iron or of silver.

Professor Mathewson found that

the most noteworthy conclusion to be drawn from the analysis from a metallographic standpoint is that which places the whole set of alloys substantially within the range of so-called alpha solutions of tin in copper, viz., from 0 to 13 per cent tin. These alpha solutions are very ductile and malleable and may be easily worked either hot or cold, while beyond this range an embrittling structure-element rapidly appears in quantity, causing the success or failure of mechanical treatment to depend primarily upon the heat treatment employed. It is, moreover, true that the hardness and tensile strength of a given alloy, irrespective of its tin-content may be greatly increased by cold working. Thus, a mechanically hardened alloy containing 4 per cent tin is stiffer and stronger than an annealed alloy containing 13 per cent tin. Many of these implements were left in the hard condition with evident intention. It also seems probable that the tin-content was regulated largely by the adaptability of the metal to casting for a particular purpose.

Professor Mathewson found that some of the bronzes are remarkably pure and that aside from very small quantities of sulphur most of them contain no metallic impurity whatever. Sulphide ores may have been smelted. The elements used were copper and a pure tin of which one or two specimens were found in the ruins. Some archaeologists have taken the position that since the greatest quantity of tin is usually found in those implements that would seem to require the least, the presence of tin in Peruvian bronzes must be regarded as accidental. This hypothesis has been carefully considered by the practiced experts of the largest companies operating in the Andes, members of the Cerro de Pasco Company and the Guggenheim Syndicate. These experts agree that so far as known ores of copper and tin occur in the Andes this is an untenable thesis, for such ores are not found in combination. On the contrary, Professor Mathewson found that while the percentage of tin contained in these bronzes was indeed not governed by the uses for which they were intended, it does appear to have been governed by the requirement of the ancient methods of manufacture. It appears that bronze containing a high percentage of tin yields the best impressions in casting because during the process of solidifying it expands more than bronze having a low tin content. Hence the more delicate or ornamental pieces contain the highest percentages of tin, since the more delicate details of the pattern were thus more readily brought out in the finished product. Had the manufacturers possessed iron or steel graving tools the case would have been different. Furthermore, the manufacturers appear to have known that the operation of casting small delicate objects is facilitated by increasing the tin content, because such alloys retain their initial heat longer and remain longer in a fluid condition. Since small objects would tend to cool rapidly this knowledge was particularly useful and accounts for the higher percentage of tin usually found in small objects of cast bronze.

The metallographic tests further indicate that bronzes were frequently hammered and annealed as the occasion demanded. The early metallurgists were probably unfamiliar with refined methods of heat treatment and so were compelled to sacrifice the extra hardness and strength obtainable in castings by increasing the tin content in objects which required considerable working. Since cold-working was depended upon to produce the final stiffness and hardness of an object and it seems probable that more than one heating was needed in forging the blades of axes and chisels, this process of manufacture necessitated a low tin content in such objects. Had they been familiar with modern refined methods of heat treatment they would not have employed a formula for combining copper and tin which has impressed archaeologists with being that which is unsuited for such objects as axes and large knives.

The knives are found to have been cast generally in one piece and then cold-worked, such reheating as took place being solely for the purpose of softening the metal to facilitate cold-working, which was probably done at less than red heat. Some specimens were found to have been repeatedly hammered and reheated to an annealing temperature. Similar surface conditions have been reproduced in the laboratory by hammering on the anvil with a broad-faced hammer. This hammering might have been done by the ancient metallurgists with several of the stone tools found, notably the highly polished pestles of diorite. Regarding the original size and shape of the castings from which the knives were made, little can be said. Several knives may have been made from one casting. In all cases the blade appears to have been worked and hammered so as to extend the metal more or less uniformly in several directions. In any event the casting structure was thoroughly obliterated, so that the knives in their present condition do not bear much resemblance to the original cast form. Chisels and axes, on the other hand, are not widely different from the castings used in making them.

A number of the cast structures were altered by cold-working with annealing; others by hot-working; and one specimen shows two distinct varieties of bronze in its construction. This is a small knife with a conventionalized llama's head. The head itself has a high content of tin, as would be expected in a small ornamental casting, but the metal of the blade and of the handle which projects up into the ornamental head is of that lower tin content required in blades which had to be cold-worked.

The most unusual bronze specimen is the knife surmounted by the ornamental group comprising a prostrate fisherboy with line and fish. The ornamental handle was cast in a pattern well designed and carefully executed. Attached to it was a body of outlying metal destined to be hammered into the desired shape for the blade but which did not require sufficiently drastic annealing to remove the casting core.

In another knife it appears that the ornamental head was actually cast around a core of lower-tin-content metal which formed the shank and blade of the knife and which may have been hammered out to its desired shape before the head was cast on.

Professor Mathewson goes on to say:

The usual practice in producing the small, more or less ornamental, implements, such as knives and pins with decorated handles, was to cast the ornamental figure with a body of outlying metal which was then wrought into shape by hammering above and below red heat. In some of the objects, the original cast shape was preserved with very little alteration. Thus, one of the finest knives of the collection was tapered mechanically to a blunt edge and constricted a little in the shank but otherwise left in the shape given by casting. On the other hand, a long pointed object, presumably used as a pin of some sort, was cast in the shape of a six-rayed star at the head, while the extension of the piece was attained by prolonged hot working after which no vestige of the cast structure remained. It is noteworthy that where an aperture was desired these metal workers did not undertake to perforate any considerable thickness of metal mechanically. This was invariably secured, as far as our examination was carried, in the practice of casting. We can readily imagine that the task of boring such tough metal as copper or bronze was an extremely difficult one in the absence of steel tools. Considerable perfection was attained in casting practice. Not only were the objects of artistic value but the technique of the process was highly developed. Thus, a ball (bolas) was found with a hemispherical depression bridged by a pin under which a line could be passed, perhaps for fishing purposes. The pin was not set into the ball but was cast in place. We have not been able to ascertain in any case at what point the metal flowed into the mold (pouring gate) or whether anything in the nature of a riser was used to correct shrinkage. Whatever the methods used, the molds were well filled out and only in extreme cases was it necessary to improve the finer detail by mechanical means. A case of the latter sort was observed in which the long attenuated bill of a cast bird was hammered into shape.

Examination of a broken ax blade shows that the implement was probably used upon stone, whereby the edge suffered severely and was appropriately dressed from time to time. The structure near the edge shows severe deformation of a character which could result only from hard usage and not from shaping the edge by hammering along the sides. It is possible that the sharp inner corners of the nice stonecutting were obtained by using bronze axes, since it is difficult to conceive of any stone tools that could have been used successfully for this purpose.

The question naturally arises at this point whether the builders of the citadel did not use bronze implements to a large degree in finishing their best stonework. Even their best bronze, however, was too soft to last long in such work and it is not likely that it was often so employed. Experiments made under the direction of Dr. Holmes in the United States National

Museum have demonstrated that patience, perseverance, "elbow grease," and fine sand will enable stone tools to work miracles in dressing and polishing ashlars, and hammer-stones were doubtless the chief tools used for dressing stone, although it is entirely possible that bronze tools were used in sharp inner corners where hammer-stones could not reach. Furthermore, while the largest ashlars were probably placed in position by means of ropes and long hardwood levers, it was undoubtedly customary to use bronze crowbars in adjusting the smaller ashlars.

The small bronze crowbar was used in a tensile test which gave an ultimate strength of twenty-eight thousand pounds per square inch, although the metal in this particular case is of very poor quality. Worked bronzes of the same composition, when hardened, show still greater strength. Accordingly we know that a fairly large ashlar could have been pried into place without actually breaking such a bronze crowbar.

In summation, the composition of Peruvian bronze was not accidental. Ores yielding accidental bronze of similar analysis to the known manufactured articles are not known to the largest modern miners of copper and tin in Peru. Pure tin, hitherto unknown in archaeological collections, was found at Machu Picchu existing in a form evidently intended for use in casting rather than for any other purpose, though no artifacts of pure tin were found. Highly ornamental objects, requiring very careful casting and a small amount of hammering, and small objects which would otherwise cool too rapidly, are found to contain approximately that percentage of tin best suited to produce a good casting. Those objects whose use required that they have a hammered edge contain a low percentage of tin, which would enable them to be cold-worked. Surely it is very interesting, therefore, to realize from Professor Mathewson's report that the ancient inhabitants of Machu Picchu were extraordinarily acute metallurgists.

CHAPTER VIII

CURIOUS TOKENS AND COUNTERS OF STONE AND CLAY; TOOLS AND UTENSILS OF STONE, BONE, AND WOOD

IN an excavation near the gateway of the citadel, twenty-nine obsidian pebbles, slightly larger than ordinary marbles, were found. One more was dug up a few feet away but none was found anywhere else. They vary in weight from one gram to six grams, and may be described as subangular in character and somewhat faceted in shape. The late Professor Pirsson, of the Sheffield Scientific School, who was kind enough to examine them for me, told me that similar obsidian pebbles are found in all parts of the world, citing especially Honduras, Arizona, and central Europe. The finding of these rounded chunks of volcanic glass in some localities where there has been no recent volcanic action has led to the suggestion that they might be extra-terrestrial, possibly a "meteoric shower." Whatever their origin, their location near the gateway of Machu Picchu would seem to indicate that they might have been used as record stones, possibly to keep tally on those who brought tribute.

Five primitive knives of obsidian flakes were also found within a short radius of the Snake Rock, and two near the Sacred Plaza.

In the excavations on top of the ridge within the citadel we found large quantities of curiously shaped stones of a type not used by the Incas, so far as we know, and of which very few specimens have found their way into any museum. Some of them are in the shape of disks, like poker chips, but varying greatly in size. Others are carved into fantastic shapes. Although their use is problematical I shall refer to them as record stones. Many of them are made of a green micaceous or chloritic slaty schist, a small quantity of which existed at the foot of one of the precipices on Machu Picchu Mountain. In many ways these record stones form one of the most interesting features of the excavations at Machu Picchu. They include 156 stone disks, of which only three were found in caves contain-

170

Problematical stone and clay objects. *a.* Cut from natural flake of green chloritic schist. Length of each side, about 1.3 cm.; average thickness, 0.1 cm. From near City Gate. *b.* Disk or counter. Polished green chloritic schist, found near Snake Rock. A few coarse scratches on it may be intentional or may have been left over from grinding and polishing process. Diameter, 8 cm.; average thickness, 0.7 cm. *c.* Triangular record (?) stone, found in Lower City. Ground and polished green chloritic schist. The largest of twenty found. Approximate lengths of sides, 5 cm., 5.5 cm., 6 cm. *d, e.* Baked clay counters (?), found near Snake Rock. Evidently potsherds rubbed into the shape of an ellipse. Dimensions: *d,* 3.8 cm. by 1.4 cm.; thickness, 1 cm. *e,* 4.4 cm. by 2.4 cm.; thickness, 1.2 cm. *f, g.* Polished green chloritic schist disks or counters. *f,* found in Lower City. An unusually small counter; only eleven have been found as small. Diameter, 1.4 cm.; average thickness, 0.15 cm. *g,* from burial cave. Diameter, 4 cm. *h.* Carefully fashioned of baked clay, possibly for use as counter. Found near Snake Rock. Length, 2 cm.; greatest width, 1.7 cm.; thickness, 1.1 cm. *i.* Chisel-shaped green chloritic schist from burial cave. The smallest of these objects found. Length, 1.4 cm.; average thickness, 0.25 cm. *j.* Found in Upper City. Chisel-shaped, cut from natural flake of green chloritic schist. Length, 2 cm.; width, 0.8 cm.; average thickness, 0.1 cm. *k.* Polished green chloritic schist from Upper City. Representative of large number of similar rectangular problematical objects. Length, 2.9 cm.; average thickness, 0.25 cm.

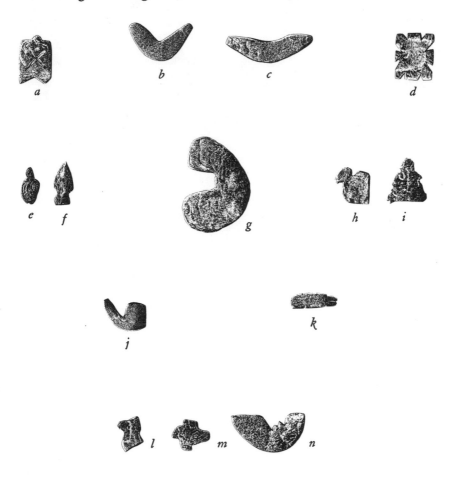

171

Problematical green chloritic schist objects. *a.* Possibly a counter, cut from a natural flake. From center of Upper City. Marked with incised cross on one side. Length, 2.5 cm.; width, 1.7 cm.; average thickness, 0.2 cm. *b.* Polished; boomerang-shaped; from Snake Rock region. Width at points, 3 cm.; thickness, 0.2 cm. *c.* From near City Gate. Polished. Length, 4.3 cm.; width, about 1 cm.; average thickness, 0.2 cm. *d.* Sharply cut and polished, in form resembling a St. Andrew's cross superimposed upon a Greek cross. Comes from burial cave in same vicinity as stone animal objects and may belong to post-Conquest period. Length, 1.1 cm.; average thickness, 0.15 cm. *e.* Tortoise-shaped, cut from natural flake. From near City Gate. Length, 3.2 cm.; average thickness, 0.15 cm. *f.* Model of arrowhead (?) cut from natural flake. From Upper City. Length, 3.9 cm.; width, 1.7 cm.; thickness tapering from 0.3 cm. to 0.1 cm. at the point. *g.* From near Snake Rock; cut from natural flake. The largest of these objects found. Length, 10.5 cm.; greatest width, 7.8 cm.; thickness, 1 cm. *h.* Found near Sacred Plaza; cut from natural flake. Width, about 3 cm.; thickness varying from 0.2 to 0.5 cm. *i.* From Upper City. Polished. Length, 3.7 cm.; thickness, 0.15 cm. *j.* Polished; pipe-shaped; from East City. *k.* From near Snake Rock; polished; may represent fish. Three incised lines at one end on one side, one at other end on both sides. Eye scratched on one side. Length, 3.3 cm.; width, 1 cm. *l.* Possibly bird's head, cut from natural flake. From near City Gate. Eye pierced on one side only. Length, about 1.2 cm.; thickness, about 0.2 cm. *m.* Cross-shaped, cut from natural flake. From near City Gate. Dimensions, 1.8 cm. by 1.4 cm.; average thickness, 0.15 cm. *n.* From Upper City. Partially polished. Length, 3.5 cm.; width, about 1.5 cm.; thickness varying from 0.35 to 0.15 cm.

ing skeletal material, and they may therefore have belonged to an earlier culture than that represented by the age of the majority of the burials.

It is quite possible that this region of rocks and little caves within the citadel was the cemetery of the original citadel and that the reason why so few skeletal remains were found here is due to natural decomposition of the bones in a moist region. The larger bones of any individuals who died in the citadel four or five hundred years ago and were buried in well-sheltered caves on the mountain side might be expected to be found in fairly good condition. On the other hand, if the citadel was inhabited fifteen hundred years ago and burials were made in the exposed caves among the rocks on top of the ridge, it is unlikely that any skeletal remains would exist. This may account for the fact that some of the material found in this part of Machu Picchu seems to represent an earlier culture than the material found in connection with skeletal remains in caves outside the citadel.

The diameter of the largest stone disk found at Machu Picchu is 23.5 cm. (about 9 inches); that of the next largest, which is rather oval in shape, is 23 cm. by 21 cm. The largest one was found in the center of the upper part of the citadel, the other on one of the terraces. Both are unusually large. The next size is slightly under 14 cm. in diameter, but from here down to 1 cm. in diameter there is a complete series. If we divide the 156 disks into classes by centimeters, beginning with the smallest, we find that there are none in the first division—that is, less than 1 cm. in diameter; 24 in the second division, between 1 cm. and 2 cm.; 54 in the third division, between 2 cm. and 3 cm.; 25 in the fourth division, 10 in the fifth, 6 in the seventh, 8 in the eighth, 4 in the ninth, and 7 in the tenth; while of the larger sizes there are from 2 to 4 in each division up to the fourteenth, which includes disks between 13 cm. and 14 cm. in diameter. It will be noticed that there are many more small ones than large ones, half of the disks being 3 cm. or less in diameter. Nevertheless it seems impossible to draw any hard-and-fast dividing line between the sizes, although one might say that the very large proportion of small ones was due to the necessity of providing digits, the lesser number of medium-sized ones to the smaller necessity of providing counters for 10's, and so on up. In the language of the poker table, "they needed more white chips than blue ones"; yet there is nothing to determine where the line could be drawn since all are of the same color and there are no designs on their surfaces. Possibly the largest two disks, which seem out of all proportion to the

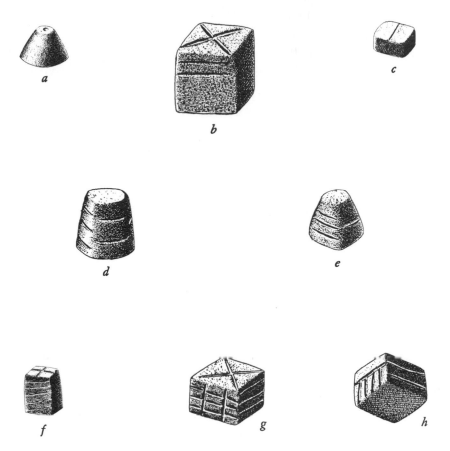

172

Problematical stone and clay objects. *a.* Truncated cone of polished green chloritic schist from Snake Rock region. Pierced at top and bottom but not bored through. Diameter, 2.2 cm.; height, 1.3 cm. *b.* Weathered baked clay, found with *c.* A cross incised on top; nothing on bottom. Only one side appears to be incised and that with two lines. Height, 1.5 cm.; base, 1.4 cm. by 1.4 cm. Similar counters were seen in Cuzco in 1851 by Lieut. Lardner Gibbon and are figured on page 61 of his *Exploration of the Valley of the Amazon.* *c.* Incised baked clay, found in the city; possibly a counter. Length, 1.8 cm.; width, 1.6 cm.; thickness, 1 cm. *d.* Slightly rounded baked clay, found near City Gate. No marks on top or bottom. Four sides incised consecutively with one, two, three, and four lines. Height, 1.2 cm.; width of base, 1.1 cm.; thickness, 1 cm. *e.* Baked clay, found near Snake Rock. Possibly a counter. Incised with lines on four sides but not on top or bottom. Although too much weathered to permit one to speak positively, it appears to have had incisions of one and two lines, respectively, on the sloping sides, and three and four lines on the perpendicular sides. Height, 1 cm.; width at base, 1 cm.; thickness, 0.9 cm. *f.* Baked clay, from near Snake Rock. Top, an incised cross; nothing on bottom. One side incised, other three sides not marked. Height, 1.8 cm.; base, 1.4 cm. by 1 cm. *g, h.* Two views of possible counter of baked clay found near City Gate. No marks on bottom; top, an incised cross. One pair of opposite sides incised with two and three lines, respectively; the other pair with five crossed lines and four lines incised to a fifth, respectively. Height, 0.9 cm.; width, 1.2 cm.; thickness, 1.2 cm.

others, may have been intended as covers for water jars. Indeed, eight or ten of the larger disks could easily have been so used. It seems to me probable, however, that the relative infrequency of large disks was due to their having been used as counters, and that we may suppose the large counters signified a large number.

The two largest disks are rough hewn, partially ground and polished; most of the large disks, in fact, are roughly made, but a few are nicely rounded, ground, and polished to a fairly consistent thickness. Only one was incised, the largest of the regular series measuring nearly 14 cm. in diameter. It has a single cross incised on one side in the center of the disk, the bars being respectively 4.5 cm. and 5 cm. in length. Four of the disks were perforated and the edges of one disk were notched with four small incisions. A careful examination of the smaller disks or counters shows that practically all were carefully ground and polished, a large number being nicely rounded. Nearly all still show the scratches made in the grinding and polishing. A few were ground so thin as to be translucent. Although in a few specimens the scratches seem a bit puzzling, as though they had been done intentionally, I have not been able to come to the conclusion that any of them were graphic or other than accidental. While there are suspicious scratches on perhaps a dozen of the disks and occasional markings that resemble tallying, there seems to be no regular rule about the scratches. Since the stone—green micaceous schist—is soft and easily scratched, it was quite suitable for being marked with tallies if it were so desired, and the tally could easily have been erased later by a slight amount of grinding and polishing. If that had taken place, however, I believe that we should be in no doubt about the marking, and that more of them would have been found to contain clear tally marks such as actually do exist on the baked-clay cubes to be referred to later.

A group of exceedingly well-made smaller disks, sixteen in all, besides a discoidal stone pendant of similar size, was found in one hole near the Snake Rock. All of them are carefully ground and polished and all bear, in addition to the marks of grinding and polishing, suspicious scratches, yet even here there is no certainty that they bore tally marks. Fourteen of these are 3 cm. in diameter. In addition to the disks of green micaceous schist there are one or two of sandstone or other rock. While nearly all the disks were clearly ground and polished, two or three flat discoidal pebbles of similar material were found in connection with the artificial disks.

Forty-two oblong stone counters or "chips" were found, all of green

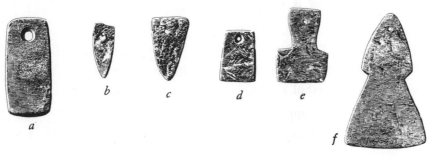

173

Green chloritic schist pendants. *a.* From near Snake Rock. Polished; lower edge sharpened like a chisel. Hole rather large; pierced with blunt instrument; reamed on both sides. *b.* From center of Upper City. Tooth-shaped. In another excavation in the Upper City, not far from this locality, a similar object of about same size, but not pierced, was found. Length, 2.2 cm.; width, 0.8 cm.; thickness, 0.2 cm. *c.* From Upper City. Length, 2.7 cm.; greatest width, 1.6 cm.; thickness, 0.15 cm. *d.* From terraces between Upper and Lower City. Carefully made and polished; some polishing scratches still show. Hole drilled with a fairly blunt instrument; reamed on one side. Length, 2.1 cm.; width, 1.5 cm.; thickness, 0.3 cm. *e.* From burial cave. Cut from a natural flake; not polished. Marks of cutting would seem to indicate a dull, metallic instrument, or possibly a hard stone scraper. Very fine hole pierced by sharp instrument; not reamed. Length, 3.1 cm.; width, 2.2 cm.; thickness, 0.1 cm. *f.* From near Snake Rock. Polished; lower edge sharpened. It is possible that this object was intended to represent an ax or hoe bound to, or sunk into, a wooden handle. Hole reamed on both sides. Length, 5.8 cm.; width, 3.3 cm.; thickness, 0.3 cm.

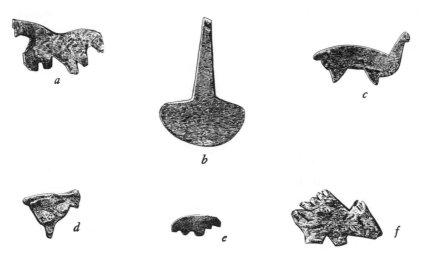

174

Problematical green chloritic schist objects. *a.* Cut to represent anteater. Slightly polished; eye lightly pierced. Length, 4.2 cm.; height about 2 cm.; thickness, 0.25 cm. *b.* Good model of bronze knife from burial cave, cut from natural flake. Edge partly ground. Length, 2.8 cm.; greatest thickness, 0.15 cm. *c.* Polished and cut to represent otter or ferret-like animal. Dark flake of schist serves as eye on one side, but apparently there is no eye on the other. Length of body, 5.5 cm.; height, 2 cm. *d.* Cut to represent parrot on perch. Partially polished. Eye pierced. Length, 3 cm.; thickness, 0.3 cm. *e.* Possibly represents a guinea pig. From terraces between Upper and Lower City. Polished. Length, 2.7 cm.; height, 1 cm.; thickness, 0.25 cm. *f.* Represents peccary or possibly hedgehog. Found in burial cave. Cut from natural flake, unpolished. Eye pierced. Length, 4.1 cm.; thickness, 0.25 cm.

schist. Most of them are about 0.3 cm. in thickness although two or three are thicker and rougher than the others. The longest is 5.8 cm. in length and about 2 cm. in width. The widest is 3.2 cm. in length and 2.5 cm. in width. The smallest is 1.4 cm. in length and about 0.3 cm. in width. Nearly all bear marks of having been ground and polished but none appears to have been engraved, although a number have irregular scratches of a suspicious character which might, however, have been made accidentally in the course of manufacture. Most of them came from the Snake Rock region and the upper part of the citadel.

The collection also includes nineteen triangular, or roughly triangular, unpierced problematical chips, found generally in places where other types of record stones occurred. None came from the burial caves. Besides those problematical chips which may be classified under the heading of disks, oblongs, or triangles, there are a number of very irregular ones, some of which are incised, others carved into highly problematical shapes impossible of classification. Some of the triangles and oblongs are pierced with holes as though for use as pendants or amulets.

In one grave four little thin green stone chips were found, each one carved to represent a denizen of the jungle. Possibly they were buried with their owner and designer, who, in carving them as silhouettes of a peccary, an anteater, an otter, and a parrot, may have wished to record a visit to the forests of the lower Urubamba. Two or three chips were found representing in miniature an Australian boomerang. One has the outline of a pipe, another of the head and shoulders of an animal, still another of a small flat reel or spool on which thread could be wound. Several are carved in the shape common to bronze knives and axes but in miniature. These might well have been used as offerings to the god of metallurgy, in the hope that the castings would come out successfully.

Most of these little green chips, however, appear to be record stones and probably belonged to an earlier culture than that of the Incas. They have been found in Ecuador, although they are almost wholly unknown in such European and American collections of Peruvian antiquities as I have seen. Very few were discovered at Machu Picchu in connection with burial caves; they came mainly from excavations in the citadel, and occurred in greatest profusion in the vicinity of Snake Rock, which was possibly the most ancient cemetery.

Similar record stones were found by Professor Saville and by Dr. Dorsey on the Island of La Plata, off the coast of Ecuador. An eminent

Peruvian archaeologist, Señor Gonzales de la Rosa, believes that the predecessors of the Incas kept their accounts by means of record stones. The Incas themselves used *quipus,* knotted strings of different colors arranged in decimal series. In discussing his Ecuadorian record stones Professor Saville quotes from Velasco, the author of a history of the Kingdom of Quito, who, quoting in turn from an ancient Spanish missionary chronicle, the work of Friar Marcos de Niza—a work that is not known to exist at the present time—says that the Caras, or ancient rulers of Ecuador, "used a kind of writing more imperfect than that of the Peruvian *quipos*." They kept their records by means of "little stones of distinct sizes, colors and angular form" arranged in containers of wood, stone, or clay. "With the different combination of these they perpetuated their doings and formed their count of all." By means of these crude archives they kept a record of their kings. That the system seems to have been unsatisfactory and imperfect is shown in Velasco's statement that some interpreted the deposits to mean that eighteen rulers covered a period of seven hundred years while others interpreted the succession of the eighteen as covering only five hundred years.

In treating of the burial customs of the ancient pre-Inca rulers of Quito, Velasco says that above the mummy of each ruler was a little niche, inside of which "were the small stones of various shapes and colors which denoted his age, the years and the month of his reign." Professor Saville notes that little stones of distinct sizes, colors, and angular shapes used for the purpose of keeping historical and other records are to be found in various places on the western coast of Ecuador not far from the southern frontier of Colombia. The Caras were eventually conquered by the Incas and forced to adopt their customs, including the use of *quipus,* or record strings.

The finding at Machu Picchu of similar record stones made of the local green micaceous or chloritic schist would seem to indicate that at some time in its history Machu Picchu was inhabited by people who had not yet learned to use string records. No record stones have been found elsewhere in this region, and were it not for Professor Saville's discoveries we would have been at a loss as to how to regard the little green chips of Machu Picchu. Under the circumstances it seems proper to suggest that the high niches in the Principal Temple were intended to receive collections of record stones and were purposely placed out of reach so as to obviate the likelihood of their being disturbed. That none were found in

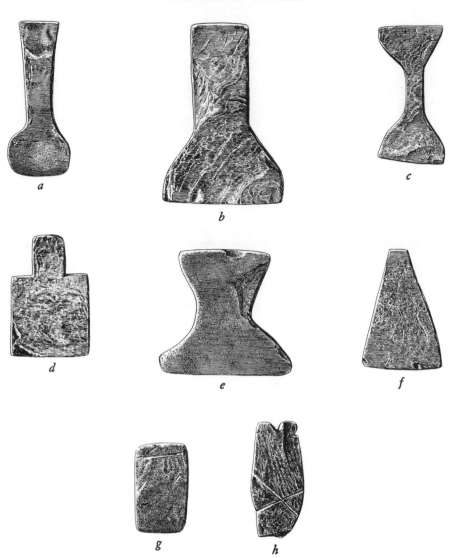

175

Problematical green chloritic schist objects. *a.* Knife-shaped; from burial cave. Polished. Length, 5.3 cm.; thickness tapering from 0.5 cm. to 0.2 cm. *b.* Cut from natural flake, partly talcose. Ax-shaped; from burial cave. Edge thin but not sharpened. Length, 6.3 cm.; thickness tapering from 0.5 to 0.2 cm. *c.* Polished; from burial cave. Resembles pair of bronze tweezers in embryo. Length, about 4.7 cm.; thickness tapering from 0.4 cm. in center to 0.15 cm. on ends. *d.* Polished; spade-shaped; from Snake Rock region. Very carefully made. Length, 3.1 cm.; average thickness, 0.25 cm. *e.* Ax-shaped, from burial cave. Polished. Length, 4.2 cm.; average thickness, 0.5 cm. *f.* From Snake Rock region. Like a chisel or celt, but without sharpened edge. Polished. Length, 3.6 cm.; average thickness, 0.25 cm. *g.* Possibly a counter; polished, from Snake Rock. Marked with incised line on one side. Length, 3.6 cm.; width, 2.2 cm.; average thickness, 0.13 cm. *h.* Possibly a counter; from near center of Upper City. Roughly polished; two incised crossed lines on one side; two nicks in one end. Length, about 4.5 cm.; thickness varying from 0.5 cm. to 0.1 cm.

these niches need not necessarily destroy this hypothesis. In the first place, when the time came for the use of record stones to be abandoned in favor of *quipus* they all might have been removed by order of the high priest and buried near the Sacred Plaza. In the second place, when the Principal Temple was no longer used for worship the priests may have carried away or hidden the record stones which were in its high niches. In the third place, it must be remembered that the Principal Temple was stripped of any ornaments or objects of interest which it contained long before my first visit in 1911. It would have been one of the first things to be found by treasure seekers or prospectors working their way along the top of the ridge and it is to be presumed that they long since would have carried away anything of interest which it contained. Finally, it is interesting to note that our careful searches and excavations in other groups of Inca ruins in this region, including Choqquequirau, Rosaspata, and Patallacta, have not yielded any similar stones, tokens, or counters.

In *Inca Land* I had occasion to refer to the story in Montesinos that before the invention of *quipus,* or knotted mnemonic strings, there was another method of keeping accounts. Since the tradition in Montesinos relates to an event centuries old at the time of his investigations, it is barely possible that the old method of writing which is referred to in the tradition means the use of record stones and incised terra-cotta cubes such as have been found at Machu Picchu. Stone counters, "poker chips," "dice," and other tokens probably represent an ancient method of reckoning which was superseded by the invention of the knotted string. The presence of these stone chips at Machu Picchu may be accounted for partly by the occurrence of green micaceous schist in one of the neighboring cliffs and the ease with which it could be worked. Conversely, the absence of these tokens in other parts of the Peruvian highlands may be due to the rarity of the material out of which they were made. It is thus possible that the use of stone counters was carried to a greater degree at Machu Picchu than elsewhere in Peru but that the invention of the *quipu* and the ease with which it could be adapted to a decimal system prevented the spread of the use of stone counters. Whether one prefers to regard the story in Montesinos as a somewhat embroidered account of an actual event or as a reference to the abandonment of the use of record stones and the commencement of the use of the *quipu* is not important. The interesting fact remains that at Machu Picchu we have evidence of a different system of notation from that employed by the Incas at the time of the Spanish Conquest.

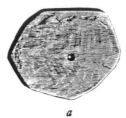

a
b

176

Polished green chloritic schist pendants (?). *a*. Possibly whetstone. An unusually thick, solid piece; flat edges of circumference much scratched. Evidently a handy tool, to be carried attached to neck, belt, or wrist, so as not to be lost easily. Diameter, 4 cm.; thickness, 0.65 cm. *b*. From near Snake Rock. Hole pierced without reaming. Diameter, 2.8 cm.; thickness, about 0.2 cm.

177

Two of twenty stone beads, possibly malachite, found in burial cave. In another cave were found a few others of same size and shape, but better preserved. Two dozen were found embedded in hard mud around base of skull taken from another cave. They vary in diameter from 0.4 cm. to 0.25 cm.

a
b

178

179

Tooth-shaped slate or soapstone pendants. With incised collars and elbow-shaped holes. From burial caves. *a*. Hole bored from top and one side. Length, 2.5 cm.; diameter about 0.9 cm. *b*. Hole pierced from top and one side. Length, 1.9 cm.; width, 0.7 cm.; thickness, 0.6 cm.

Stone bead or necklace spreader, pierced with seven holes; from cave which appears to have contained a fairly recent burial, as we found there a fragment of cloth and a small green bead of fused glass. Carefully polished; possibly talc; incised. Length, 2.6 cm.; width, 0.5 cm.; thickness, 0.4 cm.

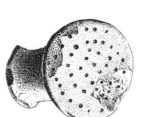

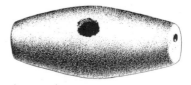

180

181

Problematical object of baked clay, probably an ear plug, with holes pierced for small feathers. Length, 3 cm.; diameter of widest end, 2.8 cm.

Whistle of baked clay from house nearest Main City Gate; possibly used by sentry in giving alarm. When blown like flute it gives very shrill whistle. Ends indented. Length, 6.8 cm.; greatest diameter, 3 cm.

We also found a few tokens or counters of baked clay, shown on page 203. They are extremely rare in collections of Peruvian antiquities. There were likewise a few clay disks made of rounded potsherds, marked on five sides so as to be used as counters up to five.

Also of potter's clay were ear-plugs, flutelike whistles, paint dishes, and dicelike counters. Very little is known about these last, and although they are fairly common at Machu Picchu, few, if any, have found their way into the larger museums of the world.* Like the stone disks, they do not seem to have been used by the Incas but probably by an earlier people previous to the invention of the *quipu*. They are incised with straight lines and crosses clearly intended to represent a numerical tally. One terra-cotta ear-plug was found, its outer surface covered with small holes in which possibly little colored feathers had once been placed. We know that the Inca nobles were distinguished by the large size of their ear ornaments, to receive which the lobe of the ear had to be punctured and stretched. This was such a conspicuous feature of the nobles that the *conquistadores* called them *orejones*, "big ears." Spindle-whorls of baked clay were also found.

Besides the record stones, artifacts found at Machu Picchu include beads in the shape of disks, perforated bars—possibly used as spreaders, pendants, points for needles or shuttles, whorl bobs for spinning, polishing stones, scrapers, knives, pestles, and mortars. There are two pestles made in the shape of cylinders, seven or eight inches long and two or three inches in diameter, very beautifully cut and polished. Some of the mortars are merely circular or oblong depressions in roughly squared rectangular blocks. Two or three mortars, possibly intended for ceremonial purposes, were cut out of broad, thin slabs looking strikingly like old-fashioned gravestones, over two feet long and nearly a foot and a half wide. Near them were found equally long thin slabs with a curved edge—the ceremonial rocking-stone pestle or muller.

Scattered over the ridge near the Snake Rock and the Temple of the Three Windows, Mr. Erdis found pieces of a beautifully decorated rectangular dish, originally carved out of a single piece of schist. By assiduously going over a fairly large area with a fine-tooth comb and examining every single pebble, he finally was successful in finding nearly all the pieces of this beautiful dish, which is probably pre-Inca and of very great age.

* Two were seen in Cuzco in 1851 by Lieut. Lardner Gibbon and are figured on page 61 of his *Exploration of the Valley of the Amazon*, Washington, 1854.

182

Spindle whorls of baked clay, found in Snake Rock region. *a.* Diameter, 4 cm.; thickness, 0.6 cm.; diameter of hole, 0.9 cm. *b.* Fashioned from a potsherd. Diameter, 3 cm.; thickness, 0.7 cm.; diameter of hole, 0.6 cm. *c.* Modeled for this purpose. Hole punctured before baking. Decoration an incised triple cross. Diameter, 3.6 cm.; thickness, about 1 cm.; diameter of hole, 0.4 cm.

183

Spindle whorls; *a-c* of baked clay. *a.* Found in Snake Rock region. Modeled for this purpose. Hole punctured before baking. Decoration on top, six incised radii and four incised circles; on bottom, seven incised radii. Diameter, 1.9 cm.; thickness, 0.9 cm.; diameter of hole, 0.4 cm. *b.* From same cave as *c.* Modeled for purpose; hole punctured before baking. Of unusual form; deeply incised with two concentric rings. Diameter of base, 2.8 cm.; thickness, 1.2 cm.; diameter of hole, 0.9 cm. *c.* From burial cave. Modeled for this purpose, hole punctured before baking. Conical in form. Incised on top with double cross and on bottom with circle. Height, 1.6 cm.; diameter of base, 2 cm.; diameter of hole, 0.4 cm. *d.* Stone, from center of Upper City. Diameter, 1.8 cm.; thickness, 0.6 cm.

184

Bone spindle whorl, from Snake Rock region. Diameter, 2.7 cm.

185

Bone weaver's tool, from burial cave. Length, 25.4 cm.

186

Coarse-grained gray granite dish or mortar, with two nubbin handles, from near Snake Rock. Rough workmanship. Flat on bottom and polished by use. Diameter about 30 cm.; height, about 14 cm.; interior, diameter, 21 cm.; depth, 7.8 cm.

187

Circular dish or mortar of bluish gray, coarse-grained granite, from north side of Stairway of the Fountains. Interior of dish, instead of being finished smooth, has a ledge running completely around it at depth of 5.5 cm., with width of about 1.5 cm., the sides down to the ledge being nearly perpendicular. Below ledge the dish is rounded and cup-shaped. Possibly it was unfinished. Diameter, about 30 cm.; height, 13.5 cm.; interior, diameter about 25.5 cm.; depth, 10.2 cm.

188

Dense gray granite mortar with cuplike depression found on terrace near expedition camp. Flattened and polished on bottom, rough hewn on sides. Edges of cup slightly raised, indicating that grinding had taken place on part of other surface of stone as well as in the cup-shaped depression. With this was found a round stone pestle. Length, 36 cm.; width, 35 cm.; height, 7 cm.; cup nearly round; diameter, 13 cm.; depth, 2.5 cm.

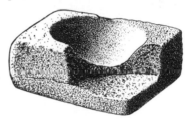

189

Roughly squared gray granite mortar found in Snake Rock region. Might have been used with pestle like one figured in 194 or those figured in 192b and 196. Length, 30 cm.; width, 25 cm.; height, 11 cm. Cup round; diameter, 18 cm.; depth, 3.5 cm.

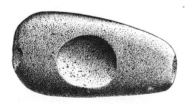

190

Three-in-one stone; combination hammer-stone, mortar, and pestle. From Snake Rock region. Specialized from small bowlder of trap rock. A similar stone found in the same vicinity. Length, 21 cm.; width, 11 cm.; thickness, 4.5 cm.

191

Rough granite bowlder with rectangular depression. Length, 39 cm.; width, 26 cm.; dimensions of depression, 18.5 cm. by 13 cm.; depth, about 4 cm.

192

Stone pestles from near Snake Rock. *a*. Made from solid piece of chloritic schist. Ground and polished. Length, 18 cm. *b*. 5.5 cm. by 4.5 cm. *c*. Polished. These pestles were probably used in mortars like those in Figs. 186 and 189. 4.4 cm. by 4.7 cm.

193

Rocking mullers. *a*. Fine-grained gray granite. In this case effort has been made to hew stone roughly so as to secure convenient size and shape. It may be noted that only in connection with an irregular pair of metates were two bowlder rocking mullers or grinding stones found. Length, 38 cm.; width, 21.5 cm.; thickness, 7 cm. *b*. Found near Snake Rock in same excavation with a metate of similar material (mica andesite). Roughly hewn on both sides and on three edges. Polished by use on curved edge. Length, 69 cm.; greatest width, 30 cm.; average thickness, 3.5 cm.

194

195

Cylindrical muller or pestle, from Snake Rock region. Coarse-grained gray granite. Length, 28.5 cm.

Andesite pestle from near Snake Rock. Ground and polished. Length, 20 cm.

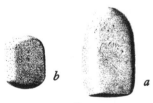

196

Mullers or pestles. *a*. From Snake Rock. An extremely compact dark gray stone of the nature of flint or very fine quartzite. It would make a good polishing stone because it is so dense and hard, but could not have been used so well for hammering, as it might give off flakes. As this stone grinder has on one side a flat surface and on the other is so shaped that it might be held under the hand, while on one end it has a rounded surface and on the other is so shaped that it can be held in the hand in an upright position, it may be classed as being both a muller and a pestle. A muller of similar material and of about the same size was found in an adjoining excavation. Length, 15 cm.; width, 9 cm.; thickness, 6.5 cm.; weight, 1,800 gr. *b*. From upper end of Main Stairway. Granite. Five similar mullers or pestles were found not far away in the Snake Rock region. Another one was found near the City Gate; another at the upper end of the Main Stairway; and another on the edge of the East City. Length, 9 cm.; width, 7 cm.; thickness, 5 cm.

It is about eight inches long by five inches wide and two and a half inches high. He also found another smaller dish of similar design. A number of crude stone dishes and bowls were found, one nearly circular and about twelve inches in diameter and five inches in depth. Pieces of two or three handsomely made circular stone dishes showing evidence of having been carefully cut and polished were found. Such dishes are eagerly sought by Peruvian collectors of antiquities, so it is not surprising that we found no good examples. Relatively few objects of stone occurred in any of the burial caves.

Hundreds of hammer-stones were found in and about the citadel, indicating the great importance and frequent use of this primitive paleolithic implement which enabled the old stone masons to accomplish such incredible feats. They consist usually of hard, compact pebbles or cobblestones of diorite or other firmly consolidated rock material. Sometimes slight depressions permitted the thumb and finger to hold them securely, but in most instances there is only the chipped point of the pebble to show that it was used as a hammer-stone. One cobblestone, eight inches long and four inches wide, bears evidence of having been used by its ingenious owner for three different purposes. This original three-in-one tool has a small depression carved in its side which could serve as a mortar for grinding pigments; its ends are both abraded by its having been used as a hammer-stone; and one side is smoothly rounded so that it could be used as a rocking-stone pestle or muller.

Here and there among the ruins were found stone-pegs or roof-pegs that had become detached from adjacent structures; also pieces of eye-bonders.

Among articles of wood I may mention a charred fragment of a dish which possibly was an inch and a half deep and six inches in diameter; a nicely made crochet needle over five inches long, the handle slightly flattened, incised on the edges and decorated with a feather pattern; a needle five inches long made from a large stout thorn, its base flattened and perforated; another needle about four inches long with a small metallic ring fastened to the base. No examples were found of that painted woodenware frequently seen in collections of Cuzco antiquities which seems to represent an art practiced during the early days of the Spanish Conquest under the influence of European design.

Four bone articles were found: a whorl bob made possibly from the end of a femur, and three pointed tools, possibly a kind of weaver's batten

197

Rectangular stone dish. Restored from twenty-four pieces, or nearly all, found in the careful excavations around Snake Rock. The dish had been broken and the pieces widely scattered at a very remote period. One can only surmise that it was used for ceremonial purposes. Made of soapstone, a rare material at Machu Picchu. The form of decoration is also not one commonly found here; in fact, with the exception of the similar smaller dish (Fig. 198), nothing resembling this has been found in the vicinity. The border is engraved in relief, and runs all the way around the dish. It consists of a very interesting and original grouping of fretwork, scrolls, and spirals. Outside length, 21 cm.; width, 15.5 cm.; height, 7 cm.; inside length, 18.7 cm.; width, 13.4 cm.; depth, 5.2 cm.

198

Small rectangular stone dish. Restored from six fragments constituting about three-fourths of the original. The pieces were widely scattered in the Snake Rock region, some of them being a hundred feet apart and several inches below the surface. Made of soapstone, the same material as the one shown in Fig. 197. It has à somewhat similar design, engraved but not raised. This pattern is similar to that on one of the stone chairs found by Professor Saville in Ecuador. Length, 9.5 cm.; width, 5.5 cm.; height, 3.5 cm.; inside length, 8.2 cm.; width, 4.2 cm.; depth, 2.6 cm.

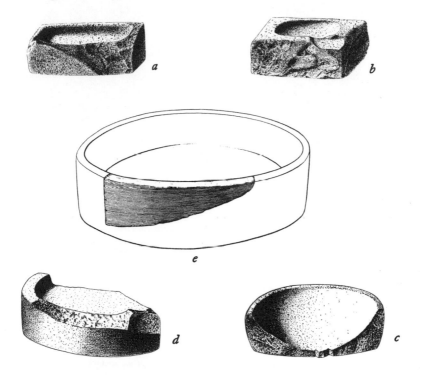

199

a. Rectangular andesite dish or mortar, partially broken, found near upper end of Stairway of the Fountains. Length, 18 cm.; width, 12.5 cm.; height, 8 cm. *b.* Granite mortar found in Snake Rock region. Finished smooth on three sides, rough on the fourth. Length, 19.5 cm.; width, 17 cm.; height, 8 cm. Cup, round; diameter, 13 cm.; depth, 4.2 cm. *c.* Circular soft light granite dish or mortar from Snake Rock region. On account of softness of material it was easy to make the dish deep. Diameter about 24 cm.; height, 9 cm.; inside diameter, 19.5 cm.; depth, 7 cm. *d.* Shallow, fine-grained gray granite dish or mortar, from north side of Stairway of the Fountains, nicely finished and polished. Diameter probably about 30 cm.; height, 9 cm.; depth, 3 cm. *e.* Very large stone dish, possibly of diorite, probably 70 cm. in diameter. Restored from single fragment found below Upper City.

200

Small clay dishes restored from fragments found near Snake Rock; roughly molded, hardly more than sun baked. *a.* Possibly paint dish. Length, 7 cm.; width, 4 cm.; height, 2.5 cm. *b.* Seems to have some white paint on inside and one of the sides. Some of the fragments show a certain amount of firing. Length, 6.5 cm.; width, 3.5 cm.; height, 1.5 cm. Fragments of five or six of these little dishes were found.

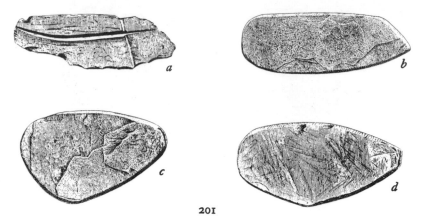

201

Stone polishers or grinding stones. *a.* From East City. Deep groove on one side. Length, 8.6 cm.; width, 2.8 cm.; average thickness, 0.6 cm. We found four other stones with deep cuts in them as though they had been used for grinding a sharp point, one in Snake Rock region, one each in Upper and Lower City, and one on Main Stairway. *b.* From Snake Rock region. Green chloritic schist, ground and polished. Length, 9.5 cm.; width, 3.5 cm.; average thickness, 0.6 cm. *c.* From near Snake Rock. Green chloritic schist, ground and polished. In same vicinity stone token of similar shape, but only about one-fifth the size, was found. Length, 7.4 cm.; width, 4.6 cm.; average thickness, 0.9 cm. *d.* Green chloritic schist from between Upper and Lower City, ground and polished more on one side than the other. Has many scratches of suspicious character, but probably accidental. Length, 8.2 cm.; width, 4.2 cm.; average thickness, 0.5 cm.

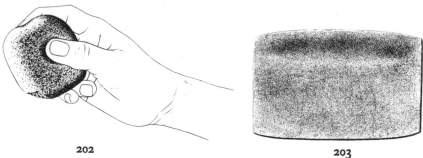

202

Very dense quartzite hammer-stone found at foot of Main Stairway. Drawing indicates how this specialized pecking stone might have been used for finishing off stone surfaces. It has several indentations on the sides enabling it to be held firmly and at same time gently. Quantities of hammer-stones were found, some of them highly specialized, and others only roughly adapted to use. Although this particular stone is only 7 cm. in diameter, it weighs 675 gr.

203

Large, fine-grained lava metate, found near Main City Gate. Probably mica andesite, the surface lava type; not like any rock in vicinity; must have been brought from great distance. Would have been useful in polishing the small flat disks of chloritic schist. Edges are roughly hewn and so is back. One side is polished. There is a slight depression near one edge as though this had been used more than rest of polished surface. Length, 69 cm.; width, 44 cm.; thickness, 4 cm.

204

Andesite (?) knife from Upper City. Length, 8.5 cm.; width, 3 cm.

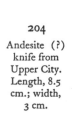

206

Flint or lava knife found near Snake Rock. So dense that it gives musical tone when struck smartly. Length, 11.7 cm.

205

Slate knife or scraper from Lower City. The notch may have been to permit wooden handle to be attached firmly. Length, 11 cm.; width, 4 cm.; average thickness, 0.5 cm.

207

Stone peg used inside a house as clothes-peg; outside as point to which roof could be tied. From Intihuatana Hill. Reddish granite. The rough-hewn part was intended to be bonded into a wall. Total length, 52 cm.; length of cylindrical portion, 22 cm.; diameter, 12 cm. Scores of similar stones are still in position in the buildings all over the city; sometimes they are larger and squarer, sometimes smaller and roughly rounded or triangular.

208

Fragments of schist eye-bonders. *a*. From north side of Main Stairway. Intended to be bonded into wall of gable at right angles to its slope and flush with its surface as fastening for roof purlins. On each slope of gables of story and a half house, four of these eye-bonders are usually found embedded, as shown in Fig. 50*a*. Width, 18 cm.; thickness, 3.5 cm.; hole, biconical, smallest diameter, 2 cm. *b*. From near Round Tower. Width, 21 cm.; thickness, about 8 cm.; hole, biconical, smallest diameter, 4 cm. May have been intended to project over lintel of gateway as means of securing vertical bar behind gate. See Fig. 50*b*.

209

Weathered flake of andesite, resembling a spearhead, found in Upper City. Length, 6.1 cm.

210

Flat, green chloritic schist, ground and polished, found in Lower City. Judging by marks on the edges, it seems to have been a tool for polishing or scraping. Length, 8 cm.; thickness, about 0.8 cm.

211

Obsidian knife, from near Sacred Plaza. Length, 12.1 cm.

212

Bone awl or weaver's tool from burial cave. Length, 10.9 cm.

213

Bone awl from burial cave, engraved and pierced with small hole. A similar one from the coast of Chile is in the Field Museum. Length, 8.6 cm.

214

Fragment of wooden dish, charred.
Length, 8.2 cm.

a *b* *c*

215

Disks or counters, *a* and *c* fashioned of baked clay potsherds, *b* of stone. *a*. Design in black on red background. Diameter about 4 cm. *b*. From near Snake Rock. Beautifully ground and polished. Unique in the following respects: Material is lava instead of common green chloritic schist of which practically all of the other stone disks are made; it is ground with extraordinary accuracy, and is almost a perfect circle and of practically uniform thickness. Diameter, 8.1 cm.; thickness, 0.75 cm. *c*. Diameter, about 6 cm.; thickness, 0.8 cm.

or reed, still used in the hand looms of Peru to force the thread of the woof or filling, as passed between the warp threads by the shuttle, as near as desirable to that part of the woof thread which just previously has been embraced by the warp threads. Two of them are perforated; one has a nicely decorated handle, consisting of two conventionalized birds facing each other.

In this moist climate—for we had frequent showers even in the dry season—it is not to be supposed that articles of wood or cloth would last very long. A few very small fragments of nicely woven woolen ponchos or woolen textiles were found in some of the burial caves where they were most thoroughly protected against the weather. They were so decayed, however, as to make it impossible to determine the size or nature of the original garments.

CHAPTER IX

THE BUILDERS OF MACHU PICCHU

THE more one studies the beautiful masonry of the citadel of Machu Picchu, the more one marvels that a people so skilful should have been willing to spend so much time and labor in such a remote inhospitable corner of the Andes; and the more one wishes that the builders had practiced the art of writing and had left behind them decipherable inscriptions which in the course of time might have been translated to tell us something of their history. The story of Mesopotamia, Egypt, and the classic lands of the Mediterranean was fortunately confided to clay tablets, stone inscriptions, and manuscripts of papyrus and vellum, but except for the remarkable hieroglyphic date stones of the Mayas the story of the prehistoric America has no such kindly aids for those who would investigate it. Its historians must piece together contradictory traditions, fragments of cloth and pottery, ruins of houses, temples, and terraces, and such artifacts as can be obtained, and from these put together what must be at best a very fragmentary story on the details of which no two experts probably ever will agree. The best that one can do is patiently to study all the evidence which can be collected, and put together a story which at least is not capable of being destroyed by any known incontrovertible evidence. Since the stories which have come down to us from the early *conquistadores* and their descendants, like Garcilasso Inca de la Vega, are so contradictory and conflicting, their evidence can hardly ever be said to be incontrovertible. Where it runs clearly counter to the known habits of the highlanders and the evidence gained by excavation and observation it may be accepted as less likely to be true than statements not so substantiated.

The popular picture of the civilization of the Incas is based on Prescott's charming account, which in turn was based largely on the writings of Garcilasso, himself the son of an Inca princess. Unfortunately for the accuracy of Garcilasso, however, he left Peru when a boy in his teens, never returned, lived most of his life in Spain, and did not write his celebrated chronicles of the Incas until he was an old man. In the intervening years he had presumably repeated frequently the stories of the land of his birth and his mother's people. He knew what pleased and astonished his European auditors, he knew what shocked them, he knew what seemed to them reasonable and admirable, altogether worthy of praise. It was natural, therefore, that in the course of the thirty or forty years of his life in Spain before he began to write his book he should have come to believe that his mother's people were quite different from what they really were. He wanted Europeans to admire his maternal ancestors and he wrote his book accordingly, his boyish recollections being colored, perhaps consciously, perhaps to a large degree unconsciously, by the requirements of his audience.

A writer who has recently begun to come into his own, Fernando Montesinos, an ecclesiastical lawyer of the seventeenth century, wrote a different sort of book. He appears to have gone to Peru in 1629 as the follower of that well-known viceroy, the Count of Chinchon, whose wife was cured of malaria by the use of Peruvian bark or quinine and was instrumental in the introduction of this medicine into Europe—a fact that has been commemorated in the botanical name of the genus *Cinchona*. Montesinos was well educated and appears to have given himself over entirely to historical research. He traveled extensively in Peru and wrote several books. His history of the Incas was spoiled by the introduction, in which, as might have been expected of an orthodox ecclesiastical lawyer, he contended that Peru was peopled under the leadership of Ophir, the great grandson of Noah. Pushing aside his clerical prejudices, however, one finds his work to be of great value, and the late Sir Clements Markham, foremost of English students of Peruvian archaeology, was inclined to place considerable credence in the statements of Montesinos.

In Montesinos there are a number of references to a place called Tampu-tocco, from which the Spaniards were apparently told that the Incas came. "Tampu" means "a place of temporary abode or a tavern"; "tocco" means "window." "Tampu" may also mean "an improved piece of ground or farm far from the town."

As has already been told in the account of the battle of La Raya,* Montesinos states that after the death in battle of Pachacuti VI, last of the great Amautas or kings who ruled Peru for more than sixty generations, the remains of his faithful followers retired to the mountains, going to Tampu-tocco, which was a healthy place where they hid the body of

---

* Vide *Inca Land*, pp. 119-120.

216a. DEFENSES OF MACHU PICCHU.
SUMMIT OF INNER WALL, SHOWING CITY GATE AND FORTIFICATIONS

216b. A GENERAL VIEW OF ABOUT
ONE-HALF OF THE CITY OF MACHU PICCHU

On the left, the western agricultural terraces. Above, the Sacred Plaza, connected by a fine stairway with Intihuatana Hill. Slightly to the left of the center foreground is the region of rough bowlders from which came most of the bronze pins and artifacts. In the center above the long stairway is Private Garden Group, and below it, on the extreme right, Ingenuity Group.

their king in a cave and where they were found by refugees fleeing from
the general chaos and disorder which followed the invasion of the southern barbarians. Montesinos says they made their capital at Tampu-tocco
and elected a king, Titi Truaman Quicho. Under him and his successors
the people of Tampu-tocco lived for over five hundred years, all record of
which is lost.

Clearly Tampu-tocco must have been a place remote, well defended
by nature from the rest of the Peruvian plateau, or it would not have been
possible for the disorganized remnant of Pachacuti VI's army to have
taken refuge there and set up an independent kingdom with only five
hundred armed followers. The Spaniards who asked about Tampu-tocco
got the impression that it was at or near Paccari-tampu, a small town eight
or ten miles south of Cuzco, in the vicinity of which there are the ruins
of a small Inca town and near it a little hill consisting of several large
rocks the surface of which is carved into platforms and in one place into
two sleeping pumas, and beneath which are caves said to have been used
recently by political refugees. There is enough about the characteristics of
the remains near Paccari-tampu to lend color to the story frequently told
to the early Spaniards that this was Tampu-tocco. Yet the surrounding region is not difficult. There are no precipices. There are no natural defenses
against the invading force which captured the neighboring valley of
Cuzco. A few men might have hid in the caves of Paccari-tampu but it
was no place where an independent kingdom might readily have been
established by a disorganized handful of the followers and chief priests
of Pachacuti VI. Furthermore, there are no windows in the architecture
which would justify the name of Tampu-tocco—a place of temporary
abode or farm far from a town, and characterized by windows.

The citadel of Machu Picchu, on the other hand, is such a place.

We know that Cuzco was practically deserted. Apparently it was
sacked by the invaders. The chief remnants of the members of the old
régime enjoyed living at Tampu-tocco, says Montesinos, because there is
the very famous cave where the Incas, as the historians say, first originated
and where, they firmly assert, there never have existed such things as
earthquakes, plagues, or tremblings; and because, if fortune should turn
against their new young king and he should be killed, they could bury him
and hide him in this cave as in a very sacred place. Apparently, then, this
was the place where they hid the body of Pachacuti VI, probably in the
cave under the Semicircular Temple at Machu Picchu. At any rate, fortune

was kind to the founders of Tampu-tocco. They had chosen an excellent place of refuge where they were not disturbed and their ruler became known as the king of Tampu-tocco, but to him and his successors nothing worth recording happened for many centuries until the establishment of the kingdom in Cuzco. During a period roughly estimated at five hundred years, but which may have been longer or shorter, several of the kings of Tampu-tocco wished to establish themselves in Cuzco, where the great Amautas had reigned for so many centuries, but they were obliged to give up the plan for one reason or another until a king called Tupac Cauri, who had chosen also to call himself Pachacuti VII, began to regain the power of his ancestors and reconquer some of the cities and provinces adjacent to Tampu-tocco. Montesinos says he attempted to abolish idolatry and other evil practices which had become widespread since the overthrow of the old *régime*. He sent messengers to various parts of the highlands asking the people to stop worshiping idols and animals, to cease practicing evil customs which had grown up since the fall of the Amautas, and to return to the ways of their ancestors, but he met with little encouragement. His ambassadors were killed and very little reform took place.

Tupac Cauri, discouraged by the failure of his attempts at reformation and desirous of learning its cause, was told by his soothsayers that the matter which most displeased the gods was the use of letters. Thereupon he ordered that under penalty of death nobody should use the kind of letters with which they had begun to write upon parchment and the leaves of certain trees. This mandate was observed with such strictness that the Peruvians never again used letters until the coming of the Spaniards. Instead, they used threads, strings, and knots, the simple mnemonic device called the *quipu*.

The above is a very curious and interesting tradition relating to an event supposed to have occurred many centuries before the Spanish Conquest. We have no ocular evidence to support it. The skeptic may brush it aside as a story intended to appeal to the vanity of persons with Inca blood in their veins, yet it is not told by the half-caste Garcilasso, but by that careful investigator, Montesinos, a pure-blooded Spaniard. As a matter of fact, to students of Professor Sumner's "mores" and "folkways" the story rings true. Some young fellow, brighter than the rest, had developed a system of ideographs which he scratched on broad smooth leaves. It worked. People were beginning to adopt it. The conservative priests, however, did not like it: there was danger lest some of the precious secrets heretofore handed down orally from priest to neophyte might become public property. Nevertheless, the invention was so useful that it began to spread rapidly. There followed some extremely unlucky event—perhaps an epidemic, or at all events something regarded as extremely unfortunate from the point of view of the ruler. What more natural than that the newly discovered ideograph should be blamed for it? As a result the king, aided and abetted by the priests, determined to abolish this new thing. Its usefulness had not yet been firmly established; in fact, it was inconvenient. The leaves blew away or withered, dried, and cracked, and the writings were lost. Had the idea been permitted to exist a little longer someone would have found how easy it was to scratch ideographs on rocks, and then it would have persisted. The rulers and priests, however, found that the records of tribute to be paid, for instance, could perfectly well be kept by means of the *quipus,* with the additional advantage that the importance of those whose duty it was to remember what each string stood for was assured. The plague passed away, everyone breathed easier, and no one realized at the time how near the Peruvians had come to developing a written language. After all, there is nothing strange or unlikely about such a supposition. One has only to look at the history of Spain itself to realize that royal bigotry and priestly intolerance crushed any new ideas that were arising in that country during the reign of Philip II, and the banishment of hardworking, artistic Moors and clever, businesslike Jews made it impossible for Spain to take that place in modern European history to which the discoveries of her navigators and the courage of her soldiers entitled her.

Since the account in Montesinos relates to an event centuries old at the time of his investigations, it is barely possible that the old method of writing which is referred to in the tradition is the use of record stones and incised terra-cotta cubes, such as have been found in large numbers in the oldest part of Machu Picchu. Stone counters, "poker chips," "dice," and other tokens of a sort not used by the Incas undoubtedly represent an ancient method of counting. In the more recently built parts of Machu Picchu practically none of the record stones were found, nor were there any in the graves which contained the more recent skeletal material together with the typical Inca pottery of "Cuzco style." Obviously, the last inhabitants of the citadel did not use the record stone when they were there. The invention of the far more convenient *quipu* had caused the use of uncertain, easily displaced stone counters to disappear.

Montesinos, continuing his description of the kingdom of Tampu-tocco, takes it for granted that Tampu-tocco was at Paccari-tampu, as all the other chroniclers have done even though there is so little there which fits into the requirements of the case. He says that Tupac Cauri established in Tampu-tocco a kind of university where boys were taught the use of *quipus,* the method of counting, and the significance of the different colored strings, while their fathers and older brothers were trained in military exercises—in other words, practiced with the sling, the bolas, and the war-club, perhaps also with bows and arrows. Thus around the name of Tupac Cauri, Pachacuti VII, the story of various things which took place during the Dark Ages in Tampu-tocco is gathered. Finally, there came the end of this epoch when the royalty and the military efficiency of the little kingdom were on a high plane. The ruler and his counselors, ever bearing in mind the tradition of their ancestors who centuries before had dwelt in Cuzco, determined to make the attempt to reëstablish themselves there. Their effort failed. An earthquake which ruined many buildings in Cuzco, caused rivers to change their courses, destroyed many towns, and was followed by the outbreak of a disastrous epidemic, determined them to give up their plans. In Tampu-tocco there was no pestilence; apparently the earthquake did not affect that point. It is worth recalling to mind in this connection that a severe earthquake in Cuzco would do great damage at Paccari-tampu, less than ten miles away. It might, however, do none at Machu Picchu, located, as it is, in the heart of an intrusive granite formation where, so far as one can judge from the condition of the ancient buildings, there have been no very severe earthquakes.

In the following years the inhabitants of Tampu-tocco became more and more crowded. Every available square yard of arable land had been terraced and cultivated. The men were intelligent, well organized, and accustomed to discipline, but they could not raise enough food for their families; so at length they set out to find arable land, under the leadership of the active, energetic ruler of the day, whose name was Manco Ccapac.

There are many stories of the rise of Manco Ccapac, who, when he had grown to man's estate, assembled his people to see how he could secure new lands for them. After consultation with his brothers, he determined to set out with them "toward the hill over which the sun rose," as we are informed by Pachacutiyamqui Salcamayhua, an Indian who was a descendant of a long line of Incas, whose great-grandparents lived in the time of the Spanish Conquest, and who wrote an account of the antiquities of Peru in 1620. He gives the history of the Incas as it was handed down

217a. OUTSIDE WALL OF ONE OF THE CLAN GROUPS, SHOWING TWO TYPES OF CONSTRUCTION

Below, the retaining wall for the terrace on which the group stands; above, a defensive w: of smaller rocks; note, in left center, end of conduit for drainage.

217b. MACHU PICCHU, WEST CITY

This photograph gives the best general view of the west side of Machu Picchu, and shows the agricultural terraces at the extreme left just above the Semicircular Temple. Next, to the right, is the beautiful outer wall of the King's Group and above it the five terraced

groups of the Upper City. Next, right, is the Four-Door Group and the Main Stairway. Still farther to the right are the terrace gardens within the City and above them the Sacred Plaza and the Temple of the Three Windows, with Intihuatana Hill on the extreme right.

to the descendants of the former rulers of Peru. In it we read that Manco Ccapac and his brothers succeeded in reaching Cuzco and settled there. Manco married one of his own sisters in order that he might not lose caste and that no other family be elevated by this marriage to an equality with his. He made good laws, conquered many provinces, and is regarded as the founder of the Inca dynasty properly so-called. The Ttahuantin-suyus, ancient name for the highlanders of Peru, soon came under his sway with good grace and brought him rich presents. The Inca, as Manco Ccapac now came to be called, was recognized as the most powerful chief, the most valiant fighter, and the most lucky warrior in the Andes. His captains and soldiers were brave, well disciplined, and well armed. All his affairs prospered greatly. "Afterward he ordered works to be executed at the place of his birth, consisting of a masonry wall with three windows, which were emblems of the house of his fathers whence he descended." The windows were named for his paternal and maternal grandparents and his uncles.

So far as is known at present, there is no place in Peru, except at Machu Picchu, where the ruins consist of anything like a "masonry wall with three windows" of such a ceremonial character as is here referred to. There is no question in my mind, therefore, that the Temple of the Three Windows, which has been described as the most interesting structure within the citadel, is the building mentioned in the chronicle written by Pachacutiyamqui Salcamayhua in 1620.

Although none of the other ancient chronicles give the story of the first Inca ordering a memorial wall to be built at the place of his birth, they nearly all tell of his having come from a place called Tampu-tocco, or a country place remarkable for its windows. To be sure, the only place assigned by them as the location of Tampu-tocco is Paccari-tampu, which, as has been said, is about eight or ten miles southwest of Cuzco and has some interesting ruins; but careful examination shows that there were no windows in the buildings of Paccari-tampu and nothing to justify its having such a name as Tampu-tocco. The climate of Paccari-tampu, like that of most places in the highlands, is too severe to invite or encourage the use of windows, while to highlanders accustomed to the climatic conditions of Cuzco and vicinity the climate of Machu Picchu must have seemed mild and consequently the use of windows was agreeable. As a result, the buildings of Machu Picchu have far more windows than any other important ruin in Peru.

Nevertheless we should have more difficulty in abandoning the testimony of a majority of the chroniclers in favor of Tampu-tocco and Paccari-tampu were it not for the existing contemporary records of a legal inquiry made by the viceroy Francisco de Toledo in 1572 at the time when he put to death Tupac Amaru, the last Inca. On the twenty-first of January, 1572, fifteen Indians who were descended from those who used to live near the important salt terraces around Cuzco, on being questioned, agreed that they had heard their fathers and grandfathers repeat the tradition that the first Inca, Manco Ccapac, came from Tampu-tocco when he arrived to take their lands away from their ancestors. They did not say that the first Inca came from Paccari-tampu, which, it seems to me, would have been a most natural thing for them to have said if it were true. In addition to this testimony, there is the still older testimony of some Indians born before the arrival of Pizarro, who, two years before, in 1570, were examined at a legal investigation made in Xauxa. The oldest witness, ninety-five years of age, on being sworn, said that Manco Ccapac was lord of the town where he was born and had conquered Cuzco but that he had never heard what town it was that Manco came from. The Indian chief who followed him was ninety-four years old and also denied that he knew where Manco Ccapac was born. Another chief, aged ninety-two, testified that Manco Ccapac came out of a cave called Tocco and that he was lord of the town near that cave. Not one of the witnesses stated that Manco Ccapac came from Paccari-tampu, although it is difficult to imagine why they should not have done so if, as the Spaniards believe, this was the original Tampu-tocco. At all events, there is an interesting cave at Paccari-tampu and the chroniclers, not one of whom knew of the important ruins at Machu Picchu, were willing enough to assume that this was the place where the first Inca was born and from which he came to conquer Cuzco. Yet it seems hardly possible that the old Indians should have forgotten entirely where Tampu-tocco was. Their reticence in regard to it must be laid, it seems to me, to the fact of its having been so successfully kept secret by reason of its location in a remote place whither the followers of Pachacuti VI fled with his body after the overthrow of the old *régime,* and in the same remote fastness of the Andes to which the young Inca Manco fled from Cuzco in the days of Pizarro.

Certainly the requirements of Tampu-tocco described in Montesinos are met at Machu Picchu. The splendid natural defenses of the Grand Canyon of the Urubamba made it an ideal refuge for the descendants of the Amautas during the five or six hundred years of lawlessness and confusion which succeeded the barbarian invasions from the plains to the east and south. The scarcity of violent earthquakes, and also the healthfulness, both marked characteristics of Tampu-tocco, are met at Machu Picchu. The evidence of both pottery and record stones points to an era preceding Inca times. The story of Pachacutiyamqui Salcamayhua of the construction of a memorial wall with three windows at the place of Manco Ccapac's birth points clearly to Machu Picchu. Machu Picchu also meets the requirements of a place whose existence might easily have been concealed by those who were in the secret, and whose location might have been unknown to a large part of the population at the time of the Spanish Conquest.

Accordingly, I am convinced that the name of the older part of Machu Picchu was Tampu-tocco, that here Pachacuti VI was buried, and that here was the capital of the little kingdom where, during the centuries —possibly eight or ten—between the Amautas and the Incas, there were kept alive the wisdom, skill, and best traditions of the ancient folk who had developed the civilization of Peru, using agricultural terraces as its base. It seems to me quite probable that Manco Ccapac, after he had established himself as Inca in Cuzco, should have built a fine temple to the honor of his ancestors. Ancestor worship was common among the Incas and nothing would have been more reasonable than the construction of the Temple of the Three Windows in their honor.

Furthermore, there is so little arable land capable of being developed within a radius of ten or fifteen miles of Machu Picchu that it would have been perfectly natural for the chiefs of this region to have sought to conquer the great stretches of arable land near Cuzco. When they once got control of Cuzco and the rich valleys in this vicinity, convenience, superstition, and regard for the great Amautas from whom they traced their descent would have led them to establish themselves once more at Cuzco. There was no longer any necessity for them to maintain the citadel of Tampu-tocco. Consequently Machu Picchu may have been practically deserted for three hundred years while the Inca Empire flourished and grew until it covered a large part of South America. In the meantime Tampu-tocco—"out of sight, out of mind," a sacred place whose whereabouts was undoubtedly known to the priests and those who preserved the most sacred secrets of the Incas—was forgotten by the common people.

Then came Pizarro and the *conquistadores,* and with their conquest the necessity of saving whatever was possible of the ancient religion. The Spaniards craved gold and silver, but the most precious possessions of the Incas were not images and utensils but the personal attendants in the House of the Sun, the sacred Virgins of the Sun, who, like the vestal virgins of Rome, were from their earliest childhood trained to the service of the temple and to ministering to the wants of the Inca. Professor Sumner has pointed out how the growth of such an institution supplanted human sacrifice. Accordingly it is interesting to note that human sacrifice had long since been given up in Peru and its place taken by the consecration of beautiful damsels to the service of the chief divinity. Some of the Virgins of the Sun were captured but others escaped and accompanied the young Inca, Manco, who had been set up by Pizarro as a dummy ruler but who rebelled and fled into the inaccessible gorges and canyons of Uillcapampa.

We have seen in *Inca Land* how Manco established himself at Uiticos, where, near an ancient shrine—a great white rock over a spring of water— he restored in some degree the fortunes of his house. Not too far removed from the great highway which the Spaniards were obliged to use in passing from Lima to Cuzco, he could readily attack them. Furthermore, he was surrounded by fertile valleys and friendly tribes. Had he established himself at Machu Picchu he would not have been so conveniently located for attacking the Spanish caravans nor for supplying his followers with arable lands. It is possible, however, that he placed most of the Virgins of the Sun in the ancient citadel of his ancestors, at Machu Picchu. It will be remembered that Father Calancha relates the trials of the first two missionaries in this region, who, at the peril of their lives, entered the sequestered valley of Uiticos and later urged the Inca to let them visit the largest city in the region, where was the "university of idolatry."

While it is possible that this place which Calancha refers to as Vilcabamba the Old, the outskirts of which were reached by the monks in a three days' journey over a rough road from Pucyara, may have been the "pampa of ghosts," it seems to me more likely that it was Machu Picchu.

In the excavations in the older part of the citadel the evidence points to an earlier culture than that represented by Inca or "Cuzco style" pottery and artifacts. Furthermore, in no other Peruvian ruin is there so clear evidence of a modern Inca town having been superimposed on a distinctly earlier masonry. The older part is far finer than the newer, and the recent could have been built rapidly to meet the needs of the refugee Virgins of the Sun. In fact, an examination of the walls of the houses shows that the citadel had been rapidly enlarged as if to accommodate an increasing population.

Examination of the ruins of what are known to be fairly recent Inca buildings on the islands of Lake Titicaca, where few of the structures are dated earlier than 1300 A.D., and of the ruins of Manco's palace at Uiticos, probably built about 1540, shows that the Incas in their later construction used a considerable amount of clay and adobe in bonding their masonry, thus obviating the necessity of spending an enormous amount of time and labor shaping the ashlars with the precision used in earlier times.

It seems probable, therefore, that at Machu Picchu we have not only the ruins of Tampu-tocco, the cradle of the Incas, the birthplace of Manco Ccapac, the first Cuzco Inca, but also the ruins of Uillcapampa, the sacred city of the last Cuzco Inca, the "university of idolatry," and the home of a considerable number of the Virgins of the Sun and attendant priests. In the buildings and walls we have two distinct styles, probably separated several centuries in development—an early period when the citadel was small, a second period when the structures of late Inca design had to be built on top of ancient terraces and ancient walls. Second, in the more recent burial caves we have pottery of "Cuzco style," while in the more ancient part of the citadel we have different and earlier types, besides the problematical stone objects or record stones whose use does not appear to have been known to the Incas. Finally, there is the skeletal evidence. The bones of the original builders probably had long since disappeared and the remains found in the burial caves must be those of the more recent inhabitants of the citadel. It appears that these are chiefly the skeletons of women and effeminate men. In the burial caves of the surrounding region a considerable proportion of skulls are those of males who had submitted to the surgical operation of trepanning, doubtless as a result of wounds received in battle.* None such were found at Machu Picchu; doubtless because this was not a place where in its latest epoch soldiers lived and died. Undoubtedly in its last state the citadel was the carefully guarded treasure house where that precious worship of the sun, so violently overthrown in Cuzco, was restored and where there found refuge those consecrated women whose lives had from earliest infancy been devoted to sun worship and who had been sufficiently fortunate to escape the animosity of the bigoted *conquistadores* who turned the ancient Temple of the Sun into a European monastery.

* These may, however, be the skulls of persons who died of disease.

Surely this granite citadel which has made such a strong appeal to us on account of its striking beauty and the indescribable grandeur of its surroundings appears to have had a most interesting history. Selected as the safest place of refuge for the last remnants of the old *régime,* becoming the site of the capital of a new kingdom, giving birth to the most remarkable family which South America has ever seen, abandoned when Cuzco once more flashed into glory as the capital of the Peruvian Empire, it was again sought out in time of trouble when the foreign invader arrived—this time from the north—with his burning desire to extinguish all vestiges of the ancient religion, and so finally became the home and refuge of those consecrated women whose institution formed one of the most interesting features of the most humane religion of aboriginal America. Here, concealed in a canyon of remarkable grandeur, protected by nature and by the hand of man, the Virgins of the Sun gradually passed away on this beautiful mountain top and left no descendants willing to reveal the importance or explain the significance of the ruins which crown the beetling precipices of Machu Picchu.

If the theory of Machu Picchu as Tampu-tocco is correct, it may be that the principal temple in Cuzco, now the Dominican Monastery but known to the *conquistadores* as the Temple of the Sun, was built during the reign of the Incas as an echo, on a large scale, of the Semicircular Temple at Machu Picchu. If this latter temple was constructed above the cave where tradition says Pachacuti VI, last of the Amautas, was buried, it would naturally have been the most revered spot at Machu Picchu.* Certainly the stonework of its surroundings has rarely been equaled and never surpassed in beauty and strength. When the Incas left Tampu-tocco, therefore, and took up their residence in Cuzco, nothing would have been more likely than for them to have built their first temple in a manner resembling the finest temple at Tampu-tocco. Probably the semicircular character of the Machu Picchu temple was caused by accident rather than by design, and was due to the natural curve of the great rock beneath which lay the mausoleum of Pachacuti VI and his immediate family. This particular architectural feature in the Temple of the Sun in Cuzco was not required by the nature of the gravel bank on which it rests in common with all the rest of the city. Moreover, a wall with a flattened curve is not characteristic of ancient Peruvian structures but occurs very rarely. What more likely, then, than that the builders of the Cuzco temple had the Semicircular

* Vide *Inca Land,* Chapter XVIII.

Temple of Machu Picchu in mind? The occurrence of "snake holes" in both structures and their absence elsewhere would also seem to lend color to this theory and helps to strengthen our belief that Machu Picchu was Tampu-tocco, and that the Inca rulers of Cuzco not only constructed at Machu Picchu a ceremonial wall with three windows to commemorate and honor the home of their ancestors but built in Cuzco a semicircular temple for a similar purpose.

We may be reasonably sure that the people of Tampu-tocco believed in ancestral worship, had ideas of modesty, decency, and chastity closely resembling those of England and America. Of course, certain things did not shock their sense of propriety because they did not live in an age when modern conveniences have made things seem improper which were formerly so common as not to be noticed. Undoubtedly they did have a strong sense of the family tie and kinship. To live at all they had to work hard. Nature was not as kind to them as she was to the Polynesians whose easily obtained fish, cocoanuts, sweet potatoes, and breadfruit gave them abundant time for indulging in sports and pastimes without the necessity of having to develop a system of intensive agriculture. Festivals they did have. Days after the harvest was gathered or after planting was finished might be devoted to ceremonials which included a considerable amount of drunkenness, but the normal daily life of the people involved regular and hard work. It was lightened by being done in common, but the incentive of individual achievement was lacking. There was also no want of faith in a central government which provided against want and saw to it that the lazy were forced to work and the ambitious were given interesting problems in the intricacies of masonry and metallurgy.

An elaborate system of highways, three or four feet in width, connected the citadel with the valleys and towns of Uillcapampa and permitted the free passage of burden bearers, whether men or llamas.

In the art of war they exhibited skill in defense rather than in developing weapons of offense. Fortifications constructed so as to admit of lateral fire were not uncommon and high walls, even dry moats, were not unknown. Sightly eminences are frequently found to have been fortified. Properly selected signal stations marked by ruined walls testify to the ancient system of communication.

They had no machinery except the lever and the inclined plane. They did not understand the use of iron nor had they conceived of the importance of a wheel or even of an arch. They did, however, make huge fiber ropes which they used in the construction of suspension bridges over impassable rapids. Such were also used probably in the handling of Cyclopean ashlars weighing from five to twenty tons, which were brought from their quarries and fitted together with a skill that has amazed all beholders.

Sculpture existed in a rude form, as is evident from the decorations on their pottery, which show some skill in copying the heads of birds and animals. They also had knowledge of the use of color.

Their music, if they had such, was, so far as one may judge from the present-day music of the highlanders, a very simple affair, limited to a few notes repeated continually in a minor key.

Judging from the large number of trepanned skulls which we found in caves within a radius of twenty-five miles of Machu Picchu, brain surgery appears to have been practiced to a considerable degree, their surgical tools being probably of bronze or obsidian. So far as we can tell, the cause of the operation in some instances appears to have been disease; in others, the evidence points to the conclusion that the operation was intended to relieve pain caused by wounds received in battle. Since their favorite weapon was the sling and clubs were not unknown, it is not surprising that the skulls of many soldiers should have needed the relief that came from skilful trepanning. Some of the operations were so "successful" that the incision in the skull appears fresh enough to point to the fact that the patient died before the wound healed. In others, notably in the remarkable case of a trepanned skull having five holes, the edges show evidence of healing and we may be sure that the patients actually survived the painful operation.*

Although the use of modern anesthetics was unknown, it seems quite probable that the patients could have chewed a large amount of *coca* leaves, sufficient to have considerably deadened their sensibilities.

From a study of the ancient chronicles we learn that the Incas were fond of worshiping high places, fine views, waterfalls, springs, and huge, irregular bowlders. They also worshiped the wonders of the air and sky—rain, thunder, the starry firmament, the moon, and, above all, the sun.

The Quichua language furnishes side lights on some of the ancient customs. An abundance of expressions for all stages of drunkenness shows that prohibition was not common. The absence of words meaning "to buy" or "to sell" indicates that their commercial life was probably limited to barter. The word which means "work" is the same word as that for

* As has been said, these holes may have been caused by disease and not by surgery.

"cultivate the soil," which was, in truth, the principal work of the Peruvian highlanders. The extent to which agriculture dominated the people and their dislike of military ideas may be inferred from the fact that the word for "soldier" also means "an enemy."

The family tie is still very strong in the Peruvians of today, as shown in the extent to which members of a family will go in alleviating suffering and distress among distant relatives. Perhaps this is their most striking and delightful trait.

The people of the citadel were familiar with a large number of birds, for the Grand Canyon of the Urubamba is one of the principal highways for birds migrating between the highlands and the lowlands. Flycatchers are numerous and include such familiar forms as our gray kingbird and black phoebe, besides unfamiliar species marked with rich colors and a large pugnacious species living in cliffs and having a remarkably loud call. Robins, swallows, and swifts are common, as are tanagers and humming birds. Parrots occur in large numbers and must have furnished food for the ancient builders, for the flesh of parrots is rich and sweet.

The small Andean spectacled bear is common in the vicinity of Machu Picchu and so is a vile-smelling skunk called by the Indians *amjas*. Vampire bats also infest the valley just below Machu Picchu and are described by Mr. Heller as representing one of the most highly specialized of existing species. Owing to its having abandoned an insect diet, this bat has lost its leaf nose, and its gullet is so restricted that only blood can be passed through it. Its legs are well developed and enable it to move fairly rapidly on the ground. If molested and thrown to the ground it will turn and bite savagely. The teeth are admirably adapted for making incisions in the skins of other animals. With its undershot jaw, short-cropped ears, and broad muzzle it has a strikingly bulldog appearance. In size it is somewhat larger than our common brown bat and much heavier built; the spread between the tips of the outstretched wings is eight or ten inches and the length of the body is three and a half inches. These bats are commonly found living in colonies in caves, suspended from the ceiling in clusters of great size. The animals which they attack are cattle, horses, mules, and donkeys. Possibly their presence here is accountable for the absence of llamas in this vicinity, since llamas are frequently seen in the streets of Arequipa, which is over a thousand feet lower in elevation than Machu Picchu.

About the terraces of Machu Picchu itself, the commonest birds seen today are the crested sparrow, the black-headed grosbeak, the goldfinch, the gray dove, and the brown robin. The mammals known to occur on the ridge within the limits of the fortress are the black forest opossum, the spectacled bear, the white-tailed deer, the proboscis-nosed skunk, the brown weasel, a large rodent the size of a woodchuck, and several smaller rodents.

The food of the people of Machu Picchu probably included some of these mammals, an occasional deer or opossum, but more likely the greatly desired guinea pig. There are also a few fish to be found in the river. We may presume, however, that the diet of the builders was largely a vegetable one, including potatoes of more varieties than are common in the United States, several varieties of maize, and a number of root crops with which we are not familiar.

For a further account of these matters, and others pertaining to Machu Picchu, the reader is referred to a forthcoming book by Mr. Philip A. Means, who has given a great deal of time and study to the subject. It will be based on the very authentic information furnished by its author's researches in Peru and by his study of various original works that have not been previously known.

It has been my design in the present volume to show the results of our explorations and excavations, and to give some indication of the possible significance of the finds without attempting dogmatic or positive interpretations.

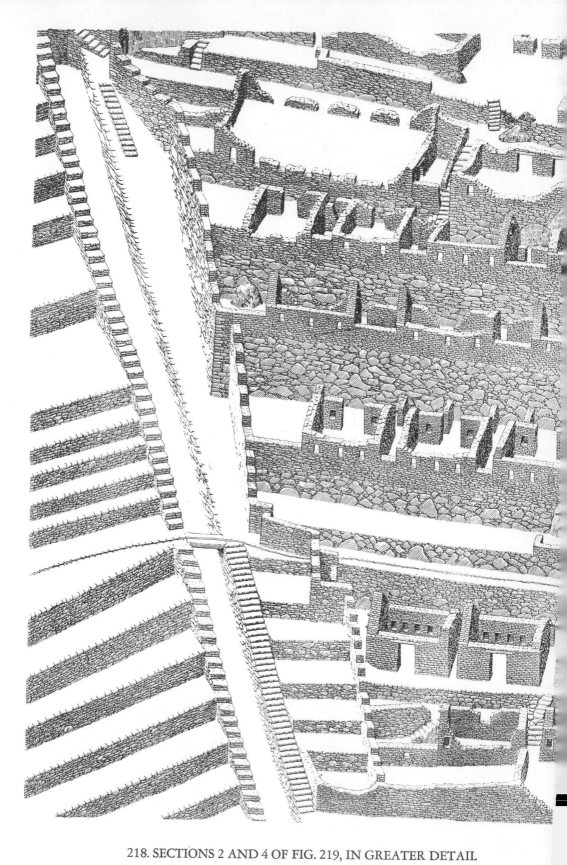

218. SECTIONS 2 AND 4 OF FIG. 219, IN GREATER DETAIL

Right foreground, Principal Stairway, with Semicircular Temple on left,
King's Group on right. Right center, Snake Rock.

INDEX

ACCLAHUASICUNA, at Machu Picchu, 107–108
Adobe, 67, 97
Agouti, 110, 112
Agriculture, 8, 48, 71, 228, 237
Alpacas, as design on pottery, 142, 144; developed from guanacos, 188
Altar, in Principal Temple, 59, 62; in Semicircular Temple, 93
Alvarez, 3, 14, 15, 106, 178
Amautas, or kings, 224, 226, 231, 234
Amaybamba, 23
American Museum of Natural History, New York, 156, 174
Amphitheater, 50, 52
Amphoras, 112, 170
Ancestor worship, 59, 79, 95, 235, 236
Anesthetics, 234
Animal heads, on drinking ladles, 132, 135, 146; on jugs, 162; on knives, 188
Animals, as handles, 156; carved on stone chips, 206
Annealing, 174, 194–196
Anteater, stone-chip, 206
Antimony, 193
Aobamba Valley, 26
Arab culture, suggested in Inca pottery, 122
Arch, unknown to Incas, 89, 235
Architecture, 46, 50–97; "Egyptian style," 93
Arequipa, 237
Arteaga, Melchor, 3, 7–10, 104
Aryballi, 73, 110, 111, 113, 122–132, 178
Ashlars, Cyclopean, 61, 65, 67, 236
Atahualpa, 111
Awls, bone, 112
Axes, bronze, 181; annealing of, 174; as stone chip, 206; chemical analysis of, 193, 195; used on stone, 196
Azequia (conduit), 48, 87

BALBOA, account of Inca conquests by, 23
Bar and cross design, 158, 179
Barbotine technique, 95
Barbour, Dr. Thomas, 15
Bar-holds, 44, 62, 76, 81, 82, 95
Barracks, 41
Bars, bronze, 181; chemical analysis of, 193; stone, perforated, 211
Basketry binding design, 140, 158, 160, 179
Bastion, semicircular, 63
Bats, vampire, 237

Beads, bone, 114; disk-shaped, 211; glass, 114, 116; wampum, 135
Beaker-shaped ollas, 109, 110, 111, 112, 113, 148–156, 178
Bear, Andean, 25, 27, 29, 237, 238
Beautiful Wall, 90–93, 231
Beer, see Chicha
Bells, bronze, 135, 181, 186
Binding design, on pottery, 160
Birds, of citadel, 237; on cooking pots, 152; on pins, 186; parrot design, 148
Birds' heads, on drinking ladles, 132, 135, 140, 142, 144, 146
Bloch, Dr. Iwan, 108
Bodkins, bronze, 181, 186
Bolas, 188, 196
Bone articles, 215; awls, 112; beads, 114; beef, found in burial cave, 115, 116; pendants, 135
Boomerang, Australian, stone-chip, 206
Bottle-shaped graves, 102, 107
Bottle, stirrup-shaped, 115, 164
Bowlders, artifacts beneath, 16; "bivalve," 56; graves beneath, 16; in stairways, 46; in walls, 44, 56; mortars in, 82; sacred, 79
Bowls, two-handled, 112, 164
Bracelets, bronze, 181; chemical analysis, 193; silver, 181
Braziers, three-legged, 105, 170–178
Bridge, Heald's, 4–6; San Miguel, 1, 3, 35, 52
Bronze, annealing of, 174; articles found in burial caves, 101, 102, 108, 115, 135; axes, 181; bars, 181; bells, 135, 181, 186; bodkins, 181, 186; boring of, 196; bracelets, 181; chemical analysis of, 193–194, 197; crowbars, 39, 112, 113, 197; disks, 179, 193; ear-spoons, 181, 186, 193; hatchets, 181; ingots, 112; knives, 111, 181, 188, 192, 193, 195, 211; method of working, 194–196; mirrors, 110, 181, 193; needles, 181, 193; pins, 110, 111, 113, 181, 186, 193, 196; rings, 181; rods, 193; spoons, 110, 193; strength of, 197; surgical tools, 236; tools, 181, 196–197; tweezers, 110, 178, 181, 186, 193
Bronzes, number found, 181
Buckles, European, found at Uiticos, 114
Bumstead, A. H., 23, 78
Burial caves, amphoras in, 170; aryballi in, 127, 178; cups in, 170; drinking ladles in, 135, 178; near City Gate, 106; ollas in,